External Shocks and Stabilization Mechanisms

Eduardo Engel and Patricio Meller
Editors
CIEPLAN, Chile

Published by the Inter-American Development Bank
Distributed by The Johns Hopkins University Press

Washington, D.C.
1993

1372

The views and opinions expressed in this publication are those of the authors and do not necessarily reflect the official position of the Inter-American Development Bank.

External Shocks and Stabilization Mechanisms

© Copyright 1993 by the Inter-American Development Bank

Inter-American Development Bank
1300 New York Avenue, N.W.
Washington, D.C. 20577

Distributed by
The Johns Hopkins University Press
701 West 40th Street
Baltimore, Maryland 21211

Library of Congress Catalog Card Number: 93-077818
ISBN: 0-940602-58-X

AUTHORS

Basch, Miguel
Economist, CIEPLAN Researcher.
Chávez, Gonzalo
Economist, Catholic University of Bolivia
Engel, Eduardo
Economist, formerly of CIEPLAN, and now Associate Professor, University of Chile, and Assistant Professor of Public Policy, Kennedy School, Harvard University.
Espejo, Justo
Economist, Catholic University of Bolivia.
Hausmann, Ricardo
Economist, Researcher for the Institute of Advanced Studies in Management (IESA), Venezuela.
Meller, Patricio
Economist, CIEPLAN Researcher.
Morales, Juan Antonio
Economist, Catholic University of Bolivia.
Powell, Andrew
Economist, Associate Researcher for the Institute of Advanced Studies in Management (IESA), Venezuela.
Rigobón, Roberto
Economist, Associate Researcher for the Institute of Advanced Studies in Management (IESA), Venezuela.
Valdés, Rodrigo
Economist, CIEPLAN Researcher.

FOREWORD

This book is the first of a series from the Centers for Research in Applied Economics, a project managed by the Economic and Social Development Department that aims to promote Latin American research of mutual interest to the countries of the region. By bringing together the research endeavors of institutions in different countries, the program seeks to disseminate applied economic and social research findings to support policy recommendations that address diverse regional problems.

This book examines the financial mechanisms necessary to reduce adverse effects on countries whose major exports are subject to large, unforeseeable fluctuations in world market prices. For the Latin American countries, which have a comparative advantage in the production and export of natural resource-based products, the subject is particularly timely since the lowering of instability reduces risk and increases investment incentives.

The three country studies in this book address some practical alternative financial mechanisms for responding to external shocks. These mechanisms range from the establishment of a domestic stabilization fund to the use of futures markets and to the issuance of bonds tied to commodities. The studies on Chile, Bolivia, and Venezuela were produced by CIEPLAN (Corporación de Investigaciones Económicas para Latinoamérica), IISEC (Instituto de Investigaciones Socioeconómicas), and IESA (Instituto de Estudios Superiores de Administración).

The Chilean study by CIEPLAN examines the usefulness of financial mechanisms for the country's copper exports. It provides specific policy recommendations that combine three types of instruments and explains some of the important reasons why, to this date, these instruments have not had more widespread application in the Latin American countries. The study by IESA on Venezuelan petroleum focuses on a stabilization fund since the size of the futures market is small compared to the magnitude of Venezuela's trade in petroleum. The authors present an analysis of the stochastic process followed

v

by oil price and export data. Using the results, they determine the dynamic properties of the proposed spending rule with its goal of reduction of uncertainty. The study by IISEC for Bolivia examines the use of both commodity exchanges and a domestic stabilization fund for major Bolivian products.

Each study provides an analysis of new Latin American policy tools. In addition, each makes an important contribution to the practical work required to implement risk management instruments in distinct Latin American countries.

Nohra Rey de Marulanda, Manager
Economic and Social Development Department

CONTENTS

CHAPTER ONE

REVIEW OF STABILIZATION MECHANISMS FOR PRIMARY COMMODITY EXPORTERS*

Eduardo Engel
Patricio Meller

Relevance of the Topic

The international price movements of primary commodities is an age-old topic in Latin America's economic debate. In the past, the mono-exporting nature of natural resources was associated with the slow development of the region's economies; it was held that there had been a persistent deterioration in the Latin American countries' terms of trade, which justified industrialization as a long-term strategy to stimulate high economic growth.

The essays in this volume once more highlight the importance of the prices of primary commodities for Latin American economies, but instead of considering their long-term impact, focus on their short-run effects. There is a bit of irony to the fact that the impact of a positive commodity price shock was called the "Dutch disease" rather than the "Latin American disease," since this phenomenon has affected Latin America's economies for over a century. A possible explanation for why Latin American economists "overlooked" this phenomenon is their exaggerated emphasis on long-term considerations, to the detriment of relevant short-run issues such as those analyzed in this volume.

The question explored in this volume is how to neutralize the short-term effects of major international commodity price fluctuations. The analysis centers on two potential stabilization mechanisms: stabilization funds and financial instruments.

In the early 1980s, Latin America was confronted with a triple shock that

* The authors are grateful for the comments of Miguel Basch, José de Gregorio, Montague Lord, and Juan Antonio Morales.

would later be linked to the problem of the external debt: a drastic reduction in foreign credit, a fall in the international prices of its main exports, and a rise in international interest rates. These latter two phenomena implied that while the external debt service (expressed mainly in dollars) rose significantly, the foreign exchange income generated by exports fell. Thus, to avert this simultaneous double negative shock, arose the question of how Latin American countries could incur debt in their own currencies, that is, in a currency related to their current income. This volume examines the use of various financial instruments, such as commodity bond issues by Latin American countries, that can be used to achieve this objective; furthermore, it suggests an important role for multilateral organizations, such as the Inter-American Development Bank and the World Bank, acting as financial intermediaries.

A second mechanism to offset the impact of primary commodity price fluctuations analyzed in this volume is the design of stabilization funds. Such a fund stabilizes expenditures of those resources generated by selling the primary commodity. After a critical review of the simple rules currently suggested by the World Bank for creating stabilization funds (SFs), the basic principles for the design of SFs are derived. These include choosing the target variable that requires stabilization, considering the level of resources held in an SF when deciding how much to spend or accumulate, incorporating the anticipated evolution of the commodity price in the near future, and being aware of the asymmetry that exists between the benefits associated with an expansion in public spending and the costs associated with a contraction. The studies in this volume analyze different alternatives for the design of an SF.

Next a brief review is presented of the specific characteristics of the export basket and the international prices of the main primary commodities exported by Bolivia, Chile, and Venezuela, the three countries examined in this volume. The different macroeconomic effects generated by the high variability of international commodity prices also are discussed.

Although the export basket of the Latin American countries was significantly diversified during the 1980s, in most cases a single product (generally a primary commodity) has maintained a relative share of over 40 percent. In Venezuela, for example, oil accounted for nearly 95 percent of exports in the 1970s; this percentage fell to 80 percent in the 1990s. In Chile, thanks to the export boom that led to the diversification of export products in the 1980s, the relative importance of copper in total exports fell from 80 percent in the 1960s to 45 percent in the 1990s. In Bolivia, a slightly different phenomenon can be observed: before 1965, tin constituted nearly 70 percent of exports; in the 1980s, a combination of three primary commodities—tin, zinc, and natural gas—accounted for 70 percent of exports.

Empirical evidence shows that international commodity prices are highly volatile; that is, they are subject to large unanticipated fluctuations. For example, in a 30-year period (1960-89) the price of a pound of copper (in 1980 US dollars) oscillated between $0.54 and $1.87; furthermore, in some years, the annual variation was nearly 50 percent. In the case of Venezuela, the large oil price swings have resulted in a decline in the value of per capita oil exports (in 1990 US dollars) from $1,800 in the 1970s to $600 in the 1990s.

Unstable export income gives rise to a series of phenomena, both micro- and macroeconomic, that affect the welfare of a country's population. At the microeconomic level, individuals prefer constant flows of consumption to highly volatile flows and are thus willing to forgo part of their income to stabilize consumption. The fraction of income that individuals are willing to pay toward this end will depend on the uncertainty of their income and their degree of risk aversion. Using classic microeconomic results (see Newbery and Stiglitz, 1981), the works in this volume conclude that the annual microeconomic costs of risk are on the order of 0.7 percent of GDP for Bolivia, 1 percent for Chile, and 3 percent of non-oil GDP for Venezuela.[1]

While more difficult to quantify, the macroeconomic costs of commodity price fluctuations are possibly higher than the microeconomic costs just described. Among macroeconomic costs, the most salient are, first, those associated with variability in the level of the country's foreign exchange reserves. When international prices fall, this can provoke a balance of payments crisis; when international prices rise, it can lead to an appreciation of the exchange rate (with the well known dangers of "Dutch disease" or a "construction boom"), as well as inflationary pressures through an expansion in domestic spending. It is also interesting to note that exchange rate uncertainty may have an adverse effect on investment, since the relative profitability of investments in tradeable and nontradeable sectors will depend on exchange rate variations. Therefore, the larger the uncertainty with respect to the evolution of the exchange rate, the lower the level of total investment.

When a large fraction of the primary commodity being exported is produced by state-owned enterprises, international price variability gives rise to a second important macroeconomic phenomenon: fluctuations in public sector revenues.[2] For example, oil exports generate on average 70 percent of fiscal revenues in Venezuela, copper exports by Chile's state-owned CODELCO account for 20 percent of fiscal revenues in Chile. Primary commodity exports typically generate less fiscal revenue than foreign exchange, since the former are usually equal to state owned enterprises' profits and therefore subtract production costs from revenues. Yet, the percentage fluctuations in fiscal

---

[1] These estimates assume that all income uncertainty translates into spending uncertainty; in practice, the actual cost will be less than that estimated.

[2] This phenomenon occurs, albeit to a lesser degree, in the case where the primary commodity is in private sector hands; in this case, it manifests itself through tax revenue levels.

revenues may be considerably higher than that in foreign reserves, for precisely the same reason. It follows that fluctuations in fiscal revenue may be more important than fluctuations in foreign reserves. For example, in the case of Chile as a result of fluctuations in the international price of copper, the fiscal contributions of CODELCO increased fivefold (in 1988 US$) between 1986 (US$350 million) and 1989 (US$1.728 billion). Sudden contractions in fiscal revenues generate a series of phenomena whose social impact goes beyond the contraction itself ("multiplier effects")—for example, inflationary processes, investments in infrastructure that remain unfinished (e.g. hospitals, schools, and roads), etc.

In sum, both positive and negative international commodity price shocks can have serious macroeconomic effects on Latin America's economies, creating internal and external disequilibria, variations in public and private sector income and expenditures, inflationary pressures, appreciation or depreciation of the exchange rate, and sharp variations in production, investment, and employment. The costs of adjustment associated with negative international price shocks of a country's main export product can be considerable. Venezuela is a case in point; here, the annual costs of adjustment in the 1980s were over 6 percent of non-oil GDP.

Since commodity price fluctuations have various negative effects on the welfare of a country's population, the question arises of whether the economic authority can actually counteract these negative effects more efficiently than private agents. To answer this question, it is important to note that the macroeconomic effects described above may be viewed conceptually as negative externalities, thus the free-market solution produces more of these ills than is socially desirable. Hausmann *et al.* (in this volume) discuss a similar phenomenon when examining the problems of the incentives produced in the wake of a commodity-price windfall: it may be socially optimal to save the additional income during the boom, but coordination failures lead each player (particularly interest groups) to seek to benefit herself as much as possible in the short run, for if she does not, it will be others that will reap the benefits.[3]

Given the large number of variables affected by commodity price instability, there is a question as to which variable a Latin American economy should stabilize. The most natural option would appear to be to stabilize the price of the primary commodity itself. However, from a macroeconomic perspective, it is more relevant to reduce instability in earnings and consumption than in prices; indeed, in welfare terms, what is crucial is to smooth out consumption as much as possible, without affecting its average level. Thus, for example, stabilization mechanisms can be designed that, taking price uncertainties as

---

[3]   Readers will recognize a situation analogous to the well known prisoner's dilemma, in which coordination failure leads to a noncooperative equilibrium, with its consequent social costs.

given, aim at minimizing their macroeconomic effects. In fact, the essays in this volume present stabilization mechanisms for each of the countries analyzed, in which the variable to be stabilized is public expenditures, with uncertainty in the corresponding revenues as given.

Consequently, it is possible to distinguish between stabilization mechanisms centered on the origins of these fluctuations, stabilizing the commodity price or the corresponding earnings directly, and those that, taking income fluctuations as a given, focus on reducing their impact on the economy. International price stabilization agreements, export diversification, and financial instruments belong to the first group, while stabilization funds are to be found in the second.

In this volume, two of the stabilization mechanisms mentioned above are studied in detail: stabilization funds and financial instruments. Before doing so, let us briefly examine some aspects related to the two remaining mechanisms.

An international primary commodity price stabilization agreement[4]—generally for a period of about five years—may require the creation of a reserve stock of the commodity or an assignment of export quotas for the exporting countries. These agreements lead to a variety of problems. On the one hand, they require the elimination of short-term price fluctuations in a market in which both short- and long-run pressures may exist to bring about major price reductions; operating at disequilibrium prices eventually generates rising costs that end up imposing the market clearing price. Anticipating this, exporting countries increase their supply thereby widening the initial disequilibrium. On the other hand, the reserve stocks necessary to sustain the equilibrium price represent a considerable volume of resources, which have proven difficult to assign among participating countries. With the specific exception of OPEC, the success of an international pricing agreement depends fundamentally on the approval and backing of the industrialized nations. Recent experience provides numerous examples of failure in the attempts to regulate international commodity prices (see Gilbert, 1987).

Industrialized countries prefer to neutralize the effects of transitory primary commodity price fluctuations by using compensatory funds instead of intervening in international commodity markets; this is the purpose of the IMF's CFF (Compensatory Financing Facility) and the European Community's STABEX (Stabilization System for Export Earnings, which may be used only

---

[4]   The price specified by an agreement of this type has generally been defined as an equitable price for both producers and consumers; from the operational standpoint, it is assumed to correspond to the long-term equilibrium price, with a 15 percent band on either side (MacBean and Nguyen, 1987). However, in the case of primary commodities, the existence of a long-term equilibrium price has been called into question; this is an aspect analyzed in this project.

by members of the Lomé Convention). During the 1970s and 1980s, the total financial resources provided annually by the CFF were, on average, five times those of STABEX; in a peak year (1983), the resources provided to all the developing countries by the CFF were US$2.57 billion. Moreover, while access to STABEX resources is linked automatically to fluctuations in the countries' income generated by variations in international commodity prices, access to the CFF, since 1983, has required the affected country to discuss policy changes with the IMF. Before 1983, countries automatically and immediately could receive up to 50 percent of the IMF quota to offset an adverse international price shock, their only obligation being to repay the loan (Hewitt, 1987). In line with their inherent nature, these compensatory funds provide financial resources that are available only after a negative shock occurs. A novel modality, employed by the IMF in a program with Mexico (1987), links the level of financial resources provided through the CFF inversely to the evolution of the international price of one commodity (in this case, oil)—that is, lower international prices would involve larger financial credits. The level of resources traditionally provided through the CFF is usually linked to the performance of the country's total exports.

The object of export diversification is to cushion the impact of income volatility associated with exports of a primary commodity that has a relatively high share of the total export basket; the basic principle is equivalent to that of an economic agent who diversifies risk by including assets in her portfolio that yield different rates of return with different means, variances, and correlations. A country that wishes to promote an export diversification strategy, however, should bear in mind the following: (1) Export diversification should not be carried out in a manner that conflicts with the principle of comparative advantage and the channeling of investments toward sectors with the highest marginal profit rate; ignoring this may generate income stability in the exporting sector, but at the cost of a major decline in the average level of earnings (Petzel, 1989). In the extreme case, the domestic impact of income instability from commodity exports could be reduced to zero by totally eliminating such exports; in addition, it is unlikely that the remaining productive sectors would be able to generate in the short and medium run the level of earnings produced by the commodity exporting sector; (2) natural commodities are a specific factor of production—stock of underground reserves—that cannot be reallocated or used in other productive activities (Hausmann et al.). Moreover, in several Latin American countries, these commodities enjoy Ricardian rents; thus their rate of return in the short and medium run is greater than that deriving from the production of other tradeable goods; (3) As the Chilean case illustrates, export diversification does not eliminate the problem of unstable fiscal revenues caused by the volatility of the international commodity prices (in this case, copper).

Stabilization Funds

A stabilization fund (SF), in the most general sense, is a mechanism that saves or spends resources with the object of stabilizing a specific aggregate variable. Theoretically, expenditures and consumption are a function of permanent income; it follows that short-term fluctuations should have very little impact on spending levels, thereby leading to the idea of saving for precautionary motives in "good" times (where commodity prices are higher than the long-run equilibrium level) and incurring debt in bad times. However, recent experience in Latin America (during the 1970s and 1980s) has shown that external credit is procyclical; thus the incentives to save in times of bonanza are even greater, for there will be constraints on access to credit in "bad" times. This motivates considering self-insurance mechanisms like stabilization funds.

The variable that a stabilization fund should target is current and future private consumption, for this variable is closely linked to social welfare. Indeed, it is the macroeconomic instability associated with commodity price fluctuations that justifies establishing a stabilization fund; the corresponding microeconomic effects can be offset most efficiently by household savings. The essays in this volume present SFs that stabilize fiscal expenditures. This variable is a good proxy for social welfare only if the feedback effect of public spending fluctuations on private consumption can be ignored. Since fluctuations in public expenditure affect social welfare because they have a negative impact on variables like infrastructure projects, public-sector salaries, and social expenditures—activities in which the private sector has little incentive to assume the role of the public sector—the feedback effect described above can be ignored insofar as the objective described above is concerned. Furthermore, if the analyses in this volume are compared with those made in the 1970s, it will be noted that earlier works are often not specific with respect to the variable being stabilized. The studies in this volume, in contrast, highlight a very important variable in any stabilization policy, whose relevance was understated in the earlier literature. It should also be noted that, by focusing on stabilizing fiscal expenditures, the SFs proposed in this volume assume that the relative size of the public sector in the economy is not varying systematically over time; if this were not the case, it would be a matter of stabilizing the deviation in public spending from a desired trajectory; the SFs proposed here can easily be adapted to this scenario.

Once the variable to be stabilized has been determined, it is necessary to formulate a rule for saving and spending that will govern the SF. By manner of illustration, we present the operational method of the Copper Stabilization Fund (FEC), created by Chile in 1987 as part of the Structural Adjustment Loan (SAL) agreement with the World Bank. The fund estimates the long-term price of copper as a simple average of the spot price (London Metal Exchange) of the last six years. The first four-cent difference between the current price and the long-term estimated price does not produce changes in the level accumulated in the fund. The marginal propensity to save or spend the next six-cents' difference is 0.5. Finally, any difference over 10 cents is saved or spent, depending on whether the current price is above or below the long-term estimated price. The only additional consideration is that, since this is a self-insurance instrument, the resources accumulated in the FEC can be spent only if the available balance is positive.

Basch and Engel (in this volume) point out several shortcomings of this type of SF. In the first place, this saving-spending rule does not take into account the amount held in the fund. A well-designed fund should be such that the higher the level in the fund, the lower the incentive to save. The FEC does not satisfy this principle: no matter how much is in the fund, the amount to be saved or spent depends only on the difference between the current price and the estimated long-run price. A second shortcoming of the FEC is that it does not incorporate expectations concerning the short-term price of copper. A saving-spending rule should lead to greater savings if the price of copper is expected to fall in the next period than if it is expected to rise; the FEC does not meet this requirement.

The saving-spending rule of the FEC is similar to that of SFs implemented in other countries. These rules are "appropriate" (in the sense that they are close to being socially optimal) if government revenues in different periods are independent and the utility function is quadratic. Both assumptions are inadequate: it is well known both that a quadratic utility function does not adequately capture behavior under conditions of uncertainty[5] and that commodity prices (and therefore generally the corresponding revenues) are highly persistent.[6] This motivates discussing how a SF should be designed that is optimal for more realistic utility functions or more realistic assumptions on the evolution of international prices.

Below we present the most important elements for a savings-spending rule of the revenues arising from primary commodity exports with fixed production. In this case, revenues are proportional to the commodity's price, and it therefore suffices to consider this price when designing the SFs operational rule. This rule will depend on the relative importance of the transitory and permanent components of the commodity price shocks and how easy it is to distinguish between them. A mistake in identifying the nature of the shock can prove very costly: during the last two decades Latin American countries

---

[5]   It implies that risk aversion increases with income.

[6]   If the current price is relatively "high", it is much more likely that the price of the subsequent period will also be "high", rather than fall; see, for example, Deaton and Laroque (1992).

identified positive shocks as permanent and negative shocks as transitory; when the true nature of shocks was exactly the opposite (Corden, cited by Basch and Engel).

When constructing a time-series model to predict a future commodity price based exclusively on historical prices, it is often concluded that the best forecast of future prices does not differ substantially from the current price, duly discounted. A price series with this property is called a "random walk." It is well known that if commodity prices follow a random walk and the welfare function to be maximized is one of those customarily used in economics (quadratic or with constant elasticity of substitution), then an SF is useless for improving social welfare. Since in this case all commodity price shocks have no transitory component, the best course of action is to adjust expenditures fully and immediately to the new level of revenues.

It is interesting to note that it is not enough to depart from the random walk assumption somewhat to justify the use of an SF; if the price series is near a random walk, the optimum SF accumulates virtually nothing (Arrau and Claessens, 1991).

The price series of most primary commodities analyzed in this volume do not differ substantially from a random walk. This is true for copper, tin, oil, and zinc; in all these cases it is impossible to forecast future prices, based exclusively on current and historical prices, with an (absolute) prediction error significantly below that obtained by using the current price as a predictor. The sole exception among the primary commodities considered in this study is that of Bolivian natural gas between 1988 and 1991, whose price evolved in a manner that made it possible to forecast future prices better than by using the current price. In fact, as a result of the bilateral negotiations of 1987 between Bolivia (the seller) and Argentina (the buyer), it was determined that if P_t denotes the unit price that Bolivia receives for the sale of natural gas in quarter t, then:

$$P_t = 0,30 P_{t-1} + 0,70 P^*_{t-1},$$

where P^*_t denotes the average price of a basket of fuels placed in Buenos Aires (Morales et al., this volume)[7]. It follows from this equation that Bolivia knew with absolute certainty three months ahead of time the income it would receive from the sale of natural gas. Furthermore, the best forecast of the price in quarter t, based on the information available two quarters before, was equal to $0.09 P_{t-2} + 0.91 P^*_{t-2}$,[8] which is still better than taking the latest available price as a forecast.

---

[7]   This rule was discarded in 1992.

[8]   This assumes that P^*_t follows a random walk.

The above discussion leads to the conclusion that to establish an SF for copper (the Chilean case) or oil (the Venezuelan case), some of the assumptions of the conceptual framework just described have to be abandoned.[9] This can be accomplished in two ways.

First, other variables in addition to the commodity price can be used to obtain future price forecasts that are significantly better than the current price. One way of achieving this is by using an econometric model.

Based on the econometric model developed by Vial (1987), Basch and Engel construct an SF of this type, combining these predictions with the saving-spending rules derived by Deaton (1991). The Vial model is roughly 30 percent more precise in its forecasts than a random walk; moreover, it is quite reliable in determining whether the current price is in the ascending or descending phase of the cycle. This makes it possible to predict whether the price of the next period will be higher (and thus the incentives to save, less) or lower (in which case it is more desirable to accumulate resources in the SF). This SF considers the fact that, since it is a self-insurance instrument, the relevant variable when deciding how much to save or spend is the disposable funds— that is, the sum of the amount accumulated in the fund and the current income. The rule employed by this fund is simple: if disposable funds are below a certain threshold, the entire fund is spent; the marginal propensity to spend when the disposable funds are above this threshold value is larger (1) the brighter the outlook for the future (based on predictions by the Vial model), (2) the higher the time discount rate, and (3) the lower risk aversion. The resulting fund exhibits a more reasonable behavior than that of the FEC, avoiding the overaccumulation of resources that appears to have occurred in the FEC during the ascending phase of the copper price cycle. In contrast to the FEC, the saving-spending rule of this fund takes into account both the level held in the fund and short-term forecasts concerning the price of copper.

A second way to obtain relevant stabilization funds when a price series follows a random walk and no alternative predictive model exists is to undertake a more detailed study of the costs and benefits associated with fluctuations in the chosen economic aggregate. Since the funds proposed in this volume seek to stabilize public spending, the costs associated with fluctuations in this aggregate variable are discussed below.

For the purposes of this analysis, public expenditures are disaggregated into three components (public investment, social expenditures, and public sector salaries). It is argued that, whether for purely economic or political reasons, the benefits derived from increases in any of these components are less than the costs associated with decreases of equal magnitude.

---

[9] Owing to the peculiar properties of the price series for natural gas (just described), this is not true for the Bolivian case.

In the case of public investment, a sudden drop in fiscal revenues can cause projects to be left unfinished: this occurred in Latin America in the early 1980s, when roads, hospitals, and schools were abandoned half way through the project. Since a large fraction of the capital employed is specific to the project in question (irreversible investment), drops in spending can translate into welfare losses that are greater than the drop itself, for some capital goods will be left idle (for example, an uncompleted dam, half a bridge, the shell of a hospital).

Decreases in social expenditures (health, education, housing, social security) and reductions in the public sector payroll (layoffs of public employees or a drop in remunerations) have a political cost greater than the benefits generated by equivalent increases; this is due to the fact that the decreases come at the same time as adjustment processes in which welfare losses take on a greater weight than the benefits obtained in expansionary periods.

The asymmetries just described should lead economic authorities to be cautious in raising the level of public expenditures, especially if the increase is to be prolonged beyond the current period.[10] For example, when deciding to raise the pensions of retirees or begin the construction of a new port, it should be born in mind that future revenues may be less than budgeted and, consequently, pensions may have to be cut (with the corresponding political and welfare costs) or an infrastructure project left unfinished (with the consequent loss of specific capital).

This leads Basch and Engel to consider a policy maker that annually solves the following optimization problem:

$$\max \sum_{t \geq 1} \beta^t E_0 \left[G_t + \left(\sum_{j \geq 1} \gamma^j G_{t-j} \right) - \left(G_{t-1} - G_t \right)_+ \right] \qquad (1)$$

subject to:

$$A_t + Y_t - G_t \geq 0, \qquad t = 1,2,3,\dots \qquad (2)$$

where:

E_0 : expected value based on the available information at $t = 0$
G_t : public expenditures during year t
Y_t : fiscal revenues during year t

---

[10] If all temporary earnings are spent exclusively on projects of short duration, this problem does not arise. The cost of a policy of this type would be that more short-term projects would be undertaken than is socially desirable.

A_{t+1} : amount accumulated in the SF at the start of year $t + 1$
(hence $A_{t+1} = A_t + Y_t - G_t$)

ß : discount rate

γ : rate at which the benefits of public spending are depreciated

$\bar{x}_+$: is equal to $\bar{x}$ if $\bar{x} \geq 0$ and equal to 0 otherwise

α : parameter that measures the magnitude of the asymmetry between the benefits associated with increases in public spending and the costs associated with decreases.

The first two terms of the welfare function in (1) indicate that the larger current expenditures and the larger the spending in previous periods, the greater is welfare in the current period. If there were no additional term, there would be no incentive to save, and the optimal response would be to spend all current income in each period. However, the last term in the utility function justifies the establishment of an SF. This term subtracts from the previous terms a quantity proportional to the drop in public spending (should there be a drop)[11] and is equal to zero otherwise. Constraint (2) establishes that the amount accumulated in the SF cannot be negative.

To illustrate the reasoning behind the maximization problem just described, it is interesting to discuss what happens when current earnings are above expenditures of the previous period. If the last term of (1) were not present, the best course of action would be to spend all the income. However, the presence of this term means that the current welfare derived from spending all earnings should be weighed against the possibility of having to reduce public spending in future periods. The more spending is increased in the current period, the more likely it will be necessary to cut it in the future, incurring the corresponding cost. It is this effect that summarizes the asymmetries discussed earlier.

Solving the problem of dynamic programming set forth in (1) and (2) is particularly difficult; in addition to the difficulty inherent in this type of problem, constraint (2) is stochastic: future earnings are not known at the time the problem is solved. Basch and Engel present a methodology that evaluates an approximate solution based upon a series of linear programming problems. Applying this methodology, they construct a stabilization fund for (total) fiscal expenditures for Chile during the 1975-1990 period. The evolution of this fund depends on the degree of uncertainty regarding future fiscal revenues in each period. In a scenario characterized by great uncertainty with respect to future revenues, the optimal fund does not significantly improve welfare. However, if the levels of uncertainty are moderate, the resulting SF successfully smooths out fiscal expenditures, as shown in Figure 1.1.

---

[11] Alternatively, this term could be proportional to the drop in income per capita, were there a drop in this variable, and equal to zero otherwise.

**Figure 1.1   Fiscal Expenditure with Stabilization Fund and Low Uncertainty
Chile, 1975-1986**

Billions of 1988 US$

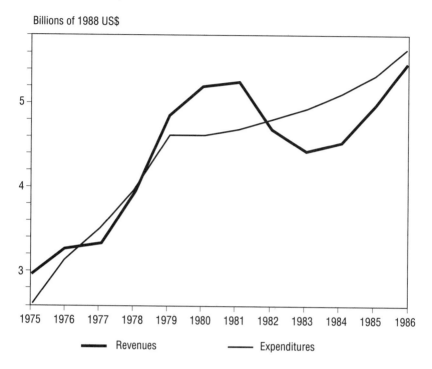

The major limitation of the SF just described is that solving the corresponding optimization problem does not lead to an explicit rule for saving or
spending. Hausmann *et al.* construct a stabilization fund for Venezuela's fiscal
expenditures, employing a similar theoretical base. This SF does not take into
account part of the dynamic complexity inherent in these problems, yet derives
an explicit saving-spending rule. Instead of considering the present discounted value maximized in (1), these authors maximize the term correspond-
ing to the current period, substituting $(G_{t-1} - G_t)_+$ with αA_{t+1}. Thus, they capture
the effect of present decisions on future welfare through a term proportional
to the amount held in the SF: the larger this amount, the smaller the probability
of having to reduce public spending in the future. The parameter α now
measures the relative importance given to present expenditures and present
savings aimed at smoothing spending fluctuations in the future. These authors
consider an additional cost associated with fluctuations in public spending,
which is that of reallocating resources among various sectors of the economy.
To this end, they add a term proportional to the square of the variation in public
spending. Combining this conceptual framework with the assumption that

**Figure 1.2   Fiscal Expenditure with Stabilization Fund
Venezuela, 1972-1990**

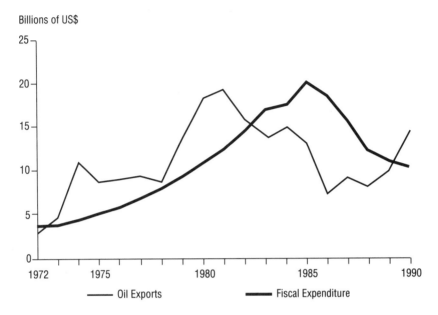

Billions of US$

—— Oil Exports   ——— Fiscal Expenditure

income follows a trinomial process (three possible values in the growth rate for each period), Hausmann *et al.* obtain the following saving-spending rule:[12]

$$G_t = 0.34_{t-1} + 0.20Y_{t-1} + 0.17A_{t-1} + \tag{3}$$

$$+0.17\sqrt{7.75G_{t-1}^2 + 2.4Y_{t-1}G_{t-1} + 0.7A_tG_{t-1} - 0.42Y_{t-1}A_{t-1} - 0.44Y_{t-1}^2 - 0.12A_t^2}.$$

Figure 1.2 shows what the evolution of public spending in Venezuela would have been for the 1972-1990 period had the SF proposed by Hausmann *et al.* been in place. This graph shows that the fund successfully dampens the fluctuations in public expenditures.

Both the stabilization fund for public spending proposed by Basch and Engel for Chile and the one proposed by Hausmann *et al.* for Venezuela, on average, accumulate large levels of resources. In the Chilean case, the maximum amount saved is 30 percent of annual public expenditures; in the Venezuelan

---

[12] The values of the parameters are obtained through simulations, assuming that the behavior of the SF conforms to a series of desirable properties. Moreover, a limit to the velocity with which the SF may be spent is imposed exogenously.

case, the SF would have accumulated three times the annual level of public expenditures during the peak year (1983). Since both funds are approximations of optimal saving rules, it is the case that the high levels accumulated are socially desirable; even though they possibly reflect the large fluctuations in revenues during the time period considered.

In the Bolivian case, the private sector has the main responsibility for the commodity exports under consideration, zinc and tin. Here, the objective of an SF also is to stabilize the earnings of private exporters; consequently, this group should be among those most interested in establishing the SF.

Morales *et al.* recommend for Bolivia a combination of two SFs (SF1 and SF2) for primary commodity exports by state-owned enterprises. The first fund's objective is to stabilize state revenues in the face of international price fluctuations; the second fund's objective is to stabilize public spending. These authors reject the idea of establishing one SF for every major commodity being exported (three in Bolivia's case). Instead, they suggest that a single fund (SF1 described above) be used, because this leads to a reduction in the variance of the multicommodity fund; however, the saving-spending rules should be defined separately for each commodity. The basic premise is that SF1 "filters out" all the instabilities generated by the various commodities; when the resulting earnings are transferred to SF2, this fund's role is to eliminate the instability that still prevails in order to bring about a smoother evolution in public spending.

Financial Instruments

Primary commodity-exporting countries can reduce the instability of income flows generated by their exports by issuing various financial instruments, transferring part of the risk associated with international price fluctuations to domestic and foreign agents.[13]

The most well-known financial instrument is possibly the futures contract. The seller agrees to deliver a certain quantity of the commodity to the buyer on a given date. These contracts are realized through authorized commodity exchanges and are highly standardized, making them particularly liquid: 95 percent of the time, the seller of a futures contract settles the contractual obligation before its expiration date, purchasing a futures contract for the same amount and date as the original commitment.

One problem with futures contracts is that the volume traded on these markets is relatively small. Thus, countries that are among the largest exporters

---

[13] Among domestic agents, privately owned Pension Funds may be interested in acquiring this type of instrument.

of a commodity cannot expect to sell a significant portion of their output on these markets without dramatically affecting the price. For example, monthly oil production in Venezuela is three times the amount traded in three-month futures contracts; in the Chilean case, quarterly production of copper is equivalent to 70 percent of the transactions carried out on the futures market. In contrast, Bolivia produces less than 1 percent of the world's zinc output, and less than 8 percent of the world's tin production; thus, futures markets offer an attractive way to eliminate part of the uncertainty in the corresponding revenues.

A second problem with futures markets is that the liquidity of these contracts decreases rapidly as the length of their term increases. In general, these markets vanish almost entirely when considering periods of more than a year. This problem can be partially overcome by employing the "rollover" strategy (sequential contracts). For example, the equivalent of a two-year futures contract can be generated by a series of six-month futures contracts, as follows:

- In the first period, four six-month futures contracts are sold. To simplify matters, we assume that each contract is equal to the semiannual production of the country in question.
- In the second half of the year, one of the four open contracts from the previous period is settled with the current production, and the three remaining contracts are settled by purchasing the primary commodity on the spot market. During this period, three six-month futures contracts are sold.
- In the third period, one of the open contracts is settled with the current production and the two remaining contracts by purchasing the commodity on the spot market. During this period, two six-month futures contracts are sold.
- In the fourth period, one of the contracts is settled with the current production, and the other contract, by purchasing the commodity on the spot market. During this period, one six-month futures contract is sold.
- In the fifth period, the pending contract is settled with the current production.

If we assume that commodity prices follow a random walk (with a nil real rate of growth) and that future prices are equal to their best prediction at the close of the contract, the total earnings during the two production years just described will be equal to the real price of this production before the biennium considered. That is, under the above assumptions the strategy of sequential contracts just described will resolve all income uncertainty two years in advance.

Basch and Engel show that if Chile had employed a strategy of sequential contracts from 1976 to 1988 similar to the one just described, its income variability (measured by the corresponding variance) would have been 64 percent less, while the corresponding average earnings would have been 5 percent less. However, as previously mentioned, this strategy does not solve the problem of the small volume of the futures markets; on the contrary, it makes it more evident, for in some periods Chile might sell four times its current output on the futures market. If we add to this the fact that before closing a series of sequential contracts, the selling country may go through times when it must cover significant temporary gaps, it can be concluded that, except in the case where the country is not a major world producer, futures contracts (even when combined with rollovers) are not an attractive mechanism for stabilizing earnings.

A second series of financial instruments that can serve to stabilize commodity export earnings are bonds whose principal and dividends are expressed in terms of the commodity price: commodity-linked bonds. Thus, for example, in the simplest case of a bond that pays no dividends, Bolivia today can sell a zinc bond that commits it to paying within three years the equivalent of the world price of 1,000 tons of zinc at that time. What makes this type of instrument appealing from the country's perspective is that the periods in which its debt obligations are high coincide with boom periods in export earnings and vice versa; that is, the correlation between income and expenditures generated by instruments of this type is highly attractive to commodity-exporting countries.[14]

A transaction that involves a financial instrument is based fundamentally on the confidence that the debtor inspires in the creditor regarding whether she will meet her contractual obligations; in the case of transactions between individual agents (for example, an individual and a bank), the debtor provides solid guarantees to ensure that the contract is met. In the case of transactions between countries, however, it is generally not possible for the debtor country to provide real guarantees. This creates problems of sovereign risk and country risk. Because of Latin America's recent external debt problem, there exists an additional surcharge that the countries of the region must pay to gain access to the international credit market or place financial instruments on that market.

It is easy to see that neither the stabilization funds nor the sale of futures presents the problem of sovereign risk—in the first case, because they are self-insurance instruments, and in the second, because the differences that arise between the two positions are settled day to day. Sovereign risk, however, is especially important for commodity-linked bonds; the greatest risk of non-compliance is associated with the case in which there is a sharp increase in the commodity's price. Thus, for example, in the simplest case of a bond without

---

[14] Note that something similar occurs for producers who use the commodity in their production process.

dividends, whose principal is denominated in units of the commodity, when the effective commodity price at the close of the contract is very high, the temptation of the debtor country to renege on its commitment will be large. Failure to meet contractual obligations generates the cost of default: the country will not be able to place new commodity bonds on the market in the future. A more realistic situation related with the problem of sovereign risk is the temptation of the country to "force" the creditor agent to accept new bond issues in place of the cash originally agreed upon.

To reduce income fluctuations due to changes in commodity prices, Basch and Engel consider different combinations of financial instruments known as options. Options are divided into two groups: "puts" and "calls." A put (call) option gives the buyer the right to sell (buy) a certain amount of a commodity on a given date in the future (expiration or maturity date) at a given price (strike price).[15]

Basch and Engel run a series of simulation exercises for Chilean copper, both *ex ante* and *ex post* with various types of puts and calls and combinations thereof. The results obtained show that this type of instrument significantly reduces fluctuations in earnings, with a relatively small drop in average earnings, as long as the country risk is not very high.

To summarize, it would be advisable for Latin American primary commodity exporters to begin operating slowly with a variety of financial instruments so as to acquire the corresponding know-how and prevent sharp increases in the risk premium or coverage costs. Later, they should gradually attempt to expand the size of operations in these markets; commodity bonds are particularly promising in this respect.

The Special Case of Natural Gas

The Bolivian study illustrates the special characteristics of natural gas exports among primary commodities. Natural gas is a product with limited geographical mobility. This creates a specific regional market in which a bilateral monopolistic relationship is a likely outcome. Negotiation within this bilateral monopoly may include extraeconomic considerations.

Because of the magnitude of the investment involved and because it creates a natural monopoly, sales contracts for natural gas tend to be long-term; these contracts stipulate the volumes to be traded, as well as the pricing rules to be applied.

---

[15] This describes European options. In the case of an American option, the buyer of the option can exercise her right to buy or sell during the entire period preceding the expiration date of the option.

The 1968 agreement to sell Bolivian natural gas to Argentina provides a good reference point. This contract employed the "take-or-pay" clause, which obligates the buyer to acquire the volume initially specified in the contract, whether or not that volume is used. In addition, the contract set the price in fixed nominal terms for a 13-year period. This agreement contained no specific clauses to rescind the contract or alter the prices stipulated.

After the contract was signed in 1968, going into effect in 1972, the oil price shocks of the 1970s occurred. Argentina, furthermore, discovered natural gas reserves in its own territory. These two events generated tensions and pressures to revise the prices of the initial contract.

In view of this experience, Morales *et al.* suggest that to minimize conflicts over future natural gas contracts, agreements of this type should ensure that (1) the rule governing the acquisition of a volume of natural gas in the "take-or-pay" modality be more flexible, although a minimum threshold should be maintained; (2) the price of natural gas be tied to the price of a basket of international prices (spot or futures) for petroleum derivatives. The price level of natural gas would fluctuate within a band whose lower boundary corresponds to the fixed and operational costs of natural gas production, while the upper boundary would be determined by the value of substitute fuels. This method of price setting, similar to the one applied in the gas contract between Bolivia and Argentina from 1988 to 1991, has the dual advantage of not straying from the international reference variables and of stabilizing fluctuations.

Final Considerations and Conclusions

This volume examines two specific mechanisms to cushion the impact of international commodity price fluctuations: stabilization funds and financial instruments. These are not necessarily alternative instruments; Basch and Engel even suggest that combining both mechanisms may be appropriate. However, for purposes of discussion we shall examine separately the suggestions for establishing an SF and using financial instruments.

When state enterprises are the main exporters of a commodity, it is suggested that the central purpose of the SF be to stabilize public spending. In this volume, alternative designs for SFs are suggested. One fund, designed for Chile, employs an econometric model (Vial, 1987) to predict future copper price trends. The marginal propensity to spend from the fund is larger if the price is expected to rise during the next period and smaller if it is expected to fall. The corresponding saving-spending rule is simple and does not have the shortcomings of the Copper Stabilization Fund currently in use in Chile. Two additional stabilization funds for fiscal expenditures, for Chile and Venezuela, are derived, based on a careful analysis of the costs and benefits associated with fluctuations in fiscal expenditures. Employing utility functions that are different from those customarily used in economics, these SFs capture the asymmetries between the benefits associated with increases in public spending and the costs associated with decreases in this aggregate variable.

An important aspect is the average (and peak) level of resources that an SF should accumulate. The political viability of these funds is low if the amounts saved are too high, for these are countries with severe resource constraints and urgent problems that require rapid solutions, making it difficult to hold large quantities of "idle" resources in an SF. Assuming that, faced with a negative external shock, a government wished to prevent an annual reduction in public spending of 5 percent in real terms during three consecutive years, and since public expenditures constitute between 20 percent and 25 percent of GDP, the SF should accumulate at most between 3 percent and 4 percent of GDP; these magnitudes are lower than those resulting from the optimization rules in the studies of Chile and Venezuela. However, this is possibly due to the fact that the periods for which these rules were applied (the 1970s and 1980s) corresponded to periods with extremely large fluctuations. If future fluctuations in fiscal revenues are smaller than those of recent decades, the level of resources in these funds can be expected to be within the above threshold. The above-mentioned coefficients can be adapted gradually to any decrease in optimal public spending resulting from a decision to reduce the size of the state's participation in the economy.

From this discussion it follows that the key role of the SF consists in stabilizing public expenditures in countries where state enterprises are the main exporters of the commodity; the monetary impact of the resources held in the SF can easily be neutralized by establishing a special account in foreign exchange, whether in the central bank or the treasury. Thus, the SF should not be used as a mechanism to stabilize the real exchange rate. The central bank's international reserves, the exchange rate policy regime, and monetary policy are more adequate mechanisms to accomplish this. Moreover, no direct relationship exists between the objective of stabilizing public expenditures and that of stabilizing the real exchange rate. The SF, furthermore, should not be included in the regular accounting of the Central Bank's international reserves.

In principle, an SF can be used to stabilize public expenditures in any country whose fiscal revenues fluctuate considerably, no matter what the origin of these fluctuations. However, as the paragraph above implies, the specific manner of operating the fund and avoiding the monetary impact of the accumulated resources will depend on the sources of the fiscal revenues that give rise to the fluctuations. For example, the SF of a country whose fluctuations in fiscal revenues derive from variations in the income of state enterprises that export a commodity should operate differently from that of a country where these fluctuations can be attributed to variations in tax collection, as may be the case in Bolivia.

This volume presents a series of financial instruments that can help reduce the uncertainties associated with primary commodity export earnings. It is not necessary to opt for any one of these instruments; given the relatively small size of the operations linked to primary commodities, it is suggested that the countries begin to participate gradually in the futures markets and undertake options operations, avoiding sharp variations in the transaction levels. Acquisition of the necessary know-how and credibility in the international financial markets is important. As a priority, it is recommended that countries employ commodity-linked bonds (i.e., oil bonds, copper bonds, gas bonds), which are not only hedging instruments but credit instruments as well; moreover, the bond market may acquire a far greater dimension than markets for other financial instruments, thus permitting access to a major source of external credit in which contractual commitments are linked to the evolution of the debtor country's earnings.

How should political and social pressures to use the resources held in an SF be avoided? In the Chilean case the creation of the FEC, with the saving-spending rules described above, has led to an easing of pressures on the Ministry of Finance to raise public spending during periods where the international price of copper was high. The existence of the FEC has allowed external pressures on the government to be neutralized. However, further and explicit legal measures are required to prevent the government itself from succumbing to the temptation to spend these resources, especially on the eve of election campaigns—this is something that also occurred in Chile in 1988 and 1989. The National Budget Law should specify at the beginning of the year the level of SF resources that may be used during that year in order to cushion the impact of potential negative shocks.

There is a phenomenon analogous to the temptation to spend the SF for electoral ends for the case of financial instruments: the government may increase the issue of commodity linked bonds in preelectoral periods. Yet using financial instruments has an advantage over an SF: it avoids the problem of the visibility of the SF's accumulated resources. Another problem to consider in the case of financial instruments is that the managers of state enterprises exporting the commodity should have incentives to stabilize the flow of earnings; precisely the opposite frequently occurs. For example, if the ex-post spot price is higher than the price for which the corresponding futures contract was sold, public opinion (and the comptroller authority in several countries) may interpret the corresponding difference as a loss resulting from speculative activities.

The above considerations aside, possibly the greatest constraint on using financial instruments is the problem of sovereign risk described earlier. Here, multilateral agencies like the Inter-American Development Bank and the World Bank can play a crucial role, taking advantage of their independence and the information they possess about the issuing countries, to help develop markets for commodity bonds. The role of the multilateral agencies may range from acquiring part of the bonds to set an example to other eventual buyers, to issuing instruments that combine the bonds of several countries (lowering the average risk of these instruments), to providing support or collateral backing for commodity bond issues.

It is also advisable to combine an SF with financial instruments, in order to cushion the impact of external shocks. The relative importance of the SF will be larger in times of macroeconomic instability (in the commodity-exporting country), since the sovereign risk premium to be paid on the issue of the commodity bonds will be very high at those times. As commodity bond markets develop, these bonds will offer a particularly attractive alternative in periods of macroeconomic stability (low sovereign risk).

Finally, it is interesting to note that Basch and Engel propose to reduce sovereign risk by using the SF as a collateral for the commodity bonds; this may require commodity bond issues to be linked to the level of resources in the SF. What makes this alternative especially attractive is that in periods of high sovereign risk (if the SF did not exist)—that is, when the international commodity price is high—the incentives to spend the SF are low; thus, these resources will be available to back up the commodity bonds. Conversely, when the international commodity price falls, a good part of the SF will be spent, but the sovereign risk will also be considerably lower.

BIBLIOGRAPHY

Arrau. P., and S. Claessens. 1991. Commodity stabilization funds. World Bank, Washington D.C. October. Mimeo.

Basch, M., and E. Engel. 1991. Shocks transitorios y mecanismos de estabilización: el caso chileno. CIEPLAN, Santiago. July. Mimeo.

Deaton, A. 1991. Saving and liquidity constraints. *Econometrica 59* (no. 5):1221-1248.

Deaton, A., and G. Laroque. 1992. On the behavior of commodity prices. *Review of Economic Studies* 59 (no.1):1-24.

Gilbert, C. 1987. International commodity agreements: Design and performance. *World Development 15* (no. 5):591-616.

Hausmann, R., A. Powell, and R. Rigobón. 1991. Facing oil income uncertainty in Venezuela: An optimal spending rule with liquidity constraints and adjustment costs. IESA, Caracas. Mimeo.

Hewitt, A. 1987. Stabex and commodity export compensation schemes: Prospects for globalization. *World Development 15* (no. 5):617-632.

MacBean, A., and D. Nguyen. 1987. International commodity agreements: Shadow and substance. *World Development 15* (no. 5):575-590.

Morales, J.A., J. Espejo, and G. Chavez. 1991. Shocks externos transitorios y políticas de estabilización para Bolivia. IISEC, Universidad Católica Boliviana, La Paz. Mimeo.

Newbery, D., and J. Stiglitz. 1981. *The theory of commodity price stabilization.* Oxford: Clarendon Press.

Petzel, T. 1989. Financial risk management needs of developing countries: Discussion. *American Journal of Agricultural Economics* 71 (no.2):531-533.

Vial, J. 1987. An econometric study of the world copper market. Ph.D. diss., University of Pennsylvania.

CHAPTER TWO

TEMPORARY SHOCKS AND STABILIZATION MECHANISMS: THE CHILEAN CASE*

Miguel Basch
Eduardo Engel

Introduction

For most Latin American countries, a single primary commodity accounts for a large fraction of total exports. For example, copper represented about 70 percent of Chile's exports in the early 1970s, and even though its relative importance has decreased, it still accounts for 45 percent of total export earnings.

It is well known that primary commodity prices are highly volatile. For example, in the 30-year period from 1960 to 1989, the price of a pound of copper fluctuated between 54 cents and 187 cents (in 1980 U.S. dollars), with annual variations sometimes as high as 50 percent. As a result of the high volatility in the prices of Latin American countries' main exports, revenues from selling these goods often undergo great fluctuations.

Furthermore, since for many of these countries—e.g., Chile, Mexico, and Venezuela—the main commodity exported is produced by state-owned enterprises, price changes have a major impact on fiscal revenues. This generates a series of negative effects on the performance of macroeconomic variables such as foreign exchange reserves, public expenditures, inflation, and investment. For example, in the case of Chile, fiscal revenues coming from the profits

* The authors are grateful for the comments and the suggestions of Héctor López M., Daniel Kaufmann, Montague Lord, José Luis Mardones, Patricio Meller, Susana Mondschein, Pilar Romaguera, Rodrigo Valdés, and Joaquín Vial. Rodrigo Valdés provided outstanding research assistance. Any error or omission is entirely our responsibility.

of CODELCO[1] increased fivefold between 1986 and 1989, soaring from US$350 million to US$1.728 billion (in 1988 U.S. dollars).[2] It is therefore desirable to design instruments that protect these economies from the negative effects of transitory commodity price shocks and help smooth out the effects of permanent shocks.

The degree of protection from exogenous shocks enjoyed by the Chilean economy has improved in recent decades, as has also been the case for other Latin American countries. Thus, for example, a substantial effort has been made to increase the flexibility in resource allocation. Chile has also diversified its basket of export goods, as well as its sources of external credit. However, reallocating domestic resources remains—by the very nature of these reallocations—a slow process that sometimes leads to social distortions. By the same token, there has not been enough diversification, since copper exports still account for 45 percent of total export revenues. Furthermore, Petzel (1989) appropriately argues that comparative advantages should not be abandoned in favor of diversification when, in addition to the desired stabilization of income, it is accompanied by a pronounced drop in the average level of these earnings. Thus, in Chile's case, it is interesting to consider the possibility of using a variety of stabilization mechanisms to counteract the effects of shocks such as fluctuations in the price of copper.

A variety of stabilization mechanisms are available to countries facing highly unstable export earnings. These mechanisms can be divided into three major groups, according to the degree to which the country in question controls their implementation and operation:

- Mechanisms whose establishment and operation depend exclusively on the country.
- Mechanisms whose establishment depends exclusively on the country but whose operation depends on both the country and third parties.
- Mechanisms whose establishment and operation depend on both the country and third parties.

In the first group, we find instruments such as stabilization funds, buffer stocks, and export diversification. The second group includes financial instruments like futures and forward contracts, options, swaps, and commodity-linked debt instruments. Finally, in the third group there are mechanisms like international primary commodity agreements and financial compensation schemes, such as the European Community's STABEX and the International Monetary Fund's CCFF (Compensatory and Contingency Financing Facility).

---

[1] CODELCO is the Spanish acronym for Chile's state-owned copper corporation.
[2] This change is of the order of 5 percent of GDP.

This essay explores the feasibility of employing some of the instruments from the first two categories mentioned above to counteract the effects of transitory shocks on the Chilean economy and smooth out the effects of permanent shocks. The study considers these instruments because, to a large extent, the decision of using them is not subject to the will of third parties.

The first section presents a simplified conceptual framework that analyzes the main characteristics of the three stabilization mechanisms studied in this essay: stabilization funds, selling copper futures contracts, and floating copper bonds. This simple framework is valuable for understanding the main problems faced when using these instruments. It is also useful for obtaining an approximation of the value to Chile of stabilizing copper earnings.

A mechanism that has traditionally been suggested for countering the effects of fluctuations is a stabilization fund. This was the key component of the World Bank adjustment programs implemented in Chile around 1985. After describing the Copper Stabilization Fund (FEC) currently in place in Chile, the second section discusses a number of shortcomings present in the FEC's design and then presents a series of alternative criteria useful for designing stabilization funds. If the FEC had been designed following these guidelines, it would have performed significantly better than it has so far.

International financial markets have responded to high commodity price volatility with a variety of new financial instruments, such as futures contracts, forwards, options, commodity-linked bonds, etc. For example, Chile purchased a price cap option just before the expiration of the Allies' ultimatum to Iraq to withdraw from Kuwait (January 15, 1991).[3] This option guaranteed that Chile would not pay more than US$35 a barrel for oil from January 15, 1991, to April 15, 1991.[4] The third section explores how well particular financial instruments such as futures and copper bonds stabilize export earnings.

Section four presents the main conclusions and policy recommendations of this study. The main conclusion asserts that an appropriate combination of a stabilization fund with sales of futures contracts and copper bonds can significantly dampen the negative effects of copper price fluctuations and other shocks to the Chilean economy, thereby improving general welfare. However, this essay also shows that whether these instruments achieve their objective or not critically depends on their proper implementation. The remainder of this paper provides a detailed set of guidelines that should be considered when designing these stabilization instruments.

---

[3] As this example shows, the stabilization mechanisms considered in this essay are useful for dealing with a wider set of external shocks, beyond price fluctuations of major commodity exports.

[4] See Valdés (1991) for a detailed analysis of this transaction.

A Simplified Conceptual Framework

This section begins by discussing what variables should be targeted when designing policies that offset the effects of transitory shocks on a country's economy. Although the answer seems obvious, this issue is far more complex than it appears. This discussion is followed by an evaluation of the potential benefits that can accrue from stabilization policies. Finally, simple versions of the three instruments examined in this essay—stabilization funds, futures, and copper bonds—are presented. This allows for the possibility of illustrating the main issues that have to be considered when designing these instruments in a simple setting.

Objectives of Stabilization Mechanisms

The literature on stabilization mechanisms from the 1970s is not always precise as to what should be the objective of these mechanisms for a mono-exporting country.[5] Some authors target the exported good's price fluctuations; others, the fluctuations in earnings generated by these exports; a third group, the variations in the real exchange rate, etc. Furthermore, it is frequently forgotten that the problem is not one of smoothing fluctuations "at any price," because a policy that manages to dampen fluctuations often has a negative effect on the average value of the target variable (export earnings, for example). It follows that the design of stabilization policies should begin by carefully considering which variables these policies should target, and then proceed to select the mechanisms that best achieve its objectives.

The goals of stabilization policies will depend on what are the negative effects of transitory shocks on a particular country's economy, at both the macro- and microeconomic levels. We discuss each of these effects separately below.

Macroeconomic Impact

Several works explore the macroeconomic impact of price fluctuations on mono-exporting economies.[6] The macroeconomic impact of price fluctuations will be evident in their effect on one or more aggregate variables, such as

---

[5] See, *inter alia,* Newbery and Stiglitz (1981) and Behrman (1987) for an excellent discussion of this topic. Although considerably more technical, Gelb (1979) is also relevant.

[6] See, for example, Adams, Behrman, and Levy (1989); Bevan, Collier, and Gunning (1987); and Hausmann (1990). Segments of this part are based on Adams *et al.* (1989) and Bevan et al. (1987).

employment, inflation, income, and the real exchange rate. Among the potential effects, the following stand out:

- A balance of payments crisis caused by negative shocks to export earnings.
- "Dutch disease"-type effects. These occur when a transitory increase in the price of the country's main export over a relatively long period of time produces an increase in the relative prices of nontradeable goods. The manufacturing industry deteriorates substantially, and the external sector of the economy is in a particularly vulnerable position when the primary commodity's price eventually drops.
- The impact of instability on growth rates.[7]
- Direct impacts on the earnings of producers of the export good, which will depend on whether the good is produced by the state or the private sector and, in the latter case, the degree of concentration in the respective industry.[8]
- Effect on fiscal revenues. This will also depend on whether the export good is in private hands (in which case it shows up in tax revenues) or in the hands of the state (in which case the effect is direct). To the degree that the government cannot or will not adjust fiscal spending in the wake of negative shocks, these shocks may give rise to inflationary processes.
- The impact on employment. This also depends on the specific characteristics of the good exported. If it is an agricultural commodity (and therefore labor-intensive), the impact of a negative shock on employment is considerably larger than if it is a mineral commodity.
- Effects on the exchange rate and on export-sector investments. This will depend largely on the country's exchange rate regime.

Three types of approaches have been applied in the literature to attempt to quantify the magnitude of the above effects on a given economy. One of them is based on computable general equilibrium models, another estimates a system of structural equations, and a third is based on national accounts.[9] The main limitation of these studies is that their conclusions are particularly sensitive to the specifications utilized and that it is difficult to check the validity of these specifications.

---

[7] Even though the empirical evidence validating this effect has been questioned in several works, Kaufmann (1991) provides strong evidence in favor of this relation. He studies the relation between the profitability of investment projects and a variety of macroeconomic variables.

[8] The primary commodity that generates the export earnings may be in the hands of both the state and the private sector, as is the case with copper in Chile.

[9] See Adams, *et al.* (1991) for citations of several works based on the first two types of models, and Bevan *et al.* (1987) for an application of the third type of approach.

Microeconomic Impact

An alternative method of describing the effects of transitory shocks is to consider their direct impact on the welfare of a country's population. This approach suggests a study of the effects of these shocks on consumption levels (both present and future). This is germane since our interest in the macroeconomic effects of transitory shocks is ultimately justified because they lead to a fall in (current or future) consumption and thereby affect social welfare. Moreover, it is well known that most individuals are risk averse—that is, they are willing to forgo part of their income to smooth fluctuations in their consumption levels. Hence, we should consider not only consumption levels, but variations in these levels over time, as well.

The above considerations justify exploring the possibility of stabilizing consumption directly—especially that of the lower-income sectors—instead of ameliorating the effects of transitory shocks on aggregate variables that affect welfare. One example of a stabilization mechanism of this type is a stabilization fund that finances unemployment insurance for layoffs occurring after a transitory negative shock. In this case, the stabilization policy has an important redistributive component, in contrast to policies designed to offset the macroeconomic effects, where the redistributive effect is less clear. It goes without saying that there is no conflict between the two strategies and that it is possible to combine instruments that offset the effects of transitory shocks on macroeconomic variables and target the poor's consumption levels.

In the final analysis, the objective of stabilization policies is to enable the population to attain higher and more stable levels of consumption. Consequently, it is pertinent to compare various stabilization policies by estimating the present discounted value of the expected utility of the "representative consumer:"

$$E_0 \left[\sum_{t \geq 0} (1 + \delta)^{-t} \ U(c_t) \right], \tag{1}$$

where E_0 denotes the expected value (based on information available in period $t = 0$), c_t consumption (of the representative individual) in period t, $U(c)$ the instantaneous (sub)utility function (with $U' > 0$ and $U'' < 0$), and δ the intertemporal discount rate.

The "value" placed by the representative consumer on fully avoiding fluctuations in consumption can be calculated from equation (1).[10] This is equivalent to determining the representative consumer's cost of uncertainty.

---

[10] What follows is based on Wright and Newbery (1989); Kletzer, Newbery, and Wright (1990); and Wright and Newbery (1989).

For this purpose, we consider the extreme case where in each period, consumption is equal to income.[11] We assume that per capita income in a given period, y_t, is equal to the sum of the historical mean[12] and a transitory shock. Transitory shocks are independent from one period to another, have a zero mean, and are identically distributed.

We define the annual cost of risk (or risk premium) as that fraction of average income that the representative consumer is willing to forgo in order to maintain a fixed stream of consumption. A simple calculation shows that this cost is approximately equal to:[13]

$$\text{Annual cost of risk } \approx \frac{1}{2} R V^2, \qquad (2)$$

where R denotes the representative consumer's relative risk-aversion coefficient, and V, the coefficient of variation of her income—that is, the quotient of the standard deviation and the mean of y_t. Thus, the present value to the consumer of ensuring a constant consumption flow, beginning in the following year, is expressed by:

$$\text{Present value of the annual cost of risk } \approx \frac{RV^2}{2\delta}, \qquad (3)$$

where δ denotes the time preference rate.

Next we use (2) and (3) to evaluate the cost of risk in two "typical" scenarios.

- First, we assume that the only stochastic component of income is export earnings (from a given primary commodity such as oil, copper, or tin). We also assume that, on average, this component represents a fraction of total earnings and that the quantity exported remains constant over time with prices across different periods being independent and identically distributed. A simple calculation shows that V^2 is equal to $\eta^2 V_p^2$, where V_p denotes the coefficient of variation of prices. In what follows, we take $\eta = 0.2$ and $V_p = 0.4$, which constitute typical values for Latin America.[14]
- In the second scenario, we assume that GDP per capita for different years

---

[11] This means that there are no mechanisms to smooth consumption: it is impossible to save (in particular, it is impossible to store goods), the labor supply is totally inelastic, the country has no access to credit, etc.

[12] The existence of this mean supposes zero average growth in per capita income.

[13] This result is obtained by noting that the risk premium, $\rho/\bar{y}$, is implicitly defined by $u(\bar{y}_t - \rho) = Eu(y_t)$. The expression for ρ can be obtained by approximating both sides of the latter identity by their first and second order Taylor expansions respectively and solving for ρ.

[14] See Deaton and Laroque (1990) for estimates of V_p for several primary commodities, based on data from this century.

is independent and identically distributed, with a standard deviation equal to 8 percent of its mean value.

If in both scenarios described above we take $R = 3$ and $\delta = 0.10$,[15] equations (2) and (3) imply an annual cost of risk of (approximately) 1 percent of GDP, and the corresponding present value is (approximately) equal to 10 percent of GDP.[16]

We conclude that the "value" that a country's population places on avoiding fluctuations in consumption caused by changes in the prices of exports is on the order of 1 percent of GDP per annum. These calculations should be interpreted with caution, since they may be biased in either direction. First, they may overestimate the cost of uncertainty because they do not take into account a variety of instruments available to consumers for smoothing consumption. Second, they may underestimate the cost of risk because they do not incorporate the effects that price fluctuations have on aggregate variables affecting the population's level of consumption. A third limitation of this framework is that it is based on the maximization of a rather arbitrary objective function, an issue we return to in the second section.

The Optimal Stabilization Fund in a Simple Case

In this section, we determine the optimal stabilization fund for a simple scenario and quantify the extent to which it reduces the risk. The main modification to the analytical framework considered at the end of the last section is that the country can now invest or save that fraction of its income that it deems appropriate at an annual interest rate equal to r.

A country that is able to save and has access to credit, saves part of its income in periods in which revenues are above their average value and spends these savings in years with negative shocks. A stabilization fund is a mechanism that makes it possible to implement this policy of dampening consumption variations. We shall denote the amount accumulated in the fund at the start of period

---

[15] Estimates of R in industrialized countries vary between 1 and 3. We chose $R = 3$ because we believe that the level of welfare in less developed countries is more sensitive to income fluctuations.

[16] In a scenario analogous to the first one considered here, Adams, Behrman, and Levy (1989) conclude that the annual cost of risk will take values that vary between 5 percent and 25 percent of export earnings; these quantities are greater than those calculated here. The difference is due to the fact that these authors assume that consumption is equal to export earnings or, alternatively, that all income that does not derive from exports is subject to the same degree of uncertainty as the latter.

t by A_t.[17] Since there is the possibility of incurring debt, A_t may take both positive and negative values.[18]

To derive an explicit savings rule, we assume that the instantaneous utility function is quadratic and that the interest rate r is equal to the time preference rate δ. The optimal rule in this case is such that the change in the level of consumption from one period to another is expressed as:[19]

$$c_t - c_{t-1} = \frac{r}{1+r}(y_t - \overline{y}). \tag{4}$$

The interpretation of this result is as follows: since all income above the average $\overline{y}$ is strictly transitory,[20] the increase in consumption generated is equal to the largest fraction of this transitory component that can be supported indefinitely. This increase is the yield obtained by investing the transitory component $y_t - \overline{y}$ in a perpetual bond (console) that pays interest rate coupons equal to r. A negative shock leads to an analogous drop in consumption.

The expressions that correspond to the level of consumption and to the fund accumulated at period t are given by:[21]

$$c_t = \overline{y} + \frac{r}{1+r}\sum_{i=1}^{t}(y_i - \overline{y}), \tag{5}$$

$$A_t = \sum_{i=1}^{t-1}(y_i - \overline{y}). \tag{6}$$

The average level of consumption with or without the optimal stabilization fund just described is the same; however, income uncertainty is considerably lower with a fund. An argument similar to the one at the close of the previous section leads us to conclude, based on (5), that when the optimal stabilization fund is implemented, the annual cost of the risk is a fraction $r^2/(1+r)^2$ of the corresponding cost if the fund did not exist. Analogously, we can show that the net present value of the reduction in risk obtained by means of a stabilization fund is equal to a fraction $1/(1+r)$ of the net present value of the total cost

---

[17] We assume that income during period t is known when choosing consumption during this period; that is, we assume there is no uncertainty with respect to current income when deciding to what an extent resources in the fund should be increased or depleted.

[18] In the second section, we study the case in which the country can save but has no access to credit.

[19] For a derivation, see for example, Blanchard and Fischer (1989, p.285).

[20] Let us recall that we have assumed that revenues are independent across periods.

[21] The expressions that follow assume that the stabilization fund is implemented beginning in period $t=1$.

of risk in the absence of any stabilization instrument. For example, for the parameters considered in the previous section, a stabilization fund is "worth" 0.85 percent of GDP the first year; its net present value is equal to 9.4 percent of GDP.

Financial Instruments in a Simple Case

A second strategy for dealing with primary commodity price fluctuations is to utilize financial instruments. We shall again consider the situation described at the end of the previous section, in which all income uncertainty derives from volatility in the (international) price of the main export product.

Selling Futures

We first consider the case in which the only mechanism whereby consumption can be smoothed is by selling a fraction of the primary commodity's output on a futures market one period in advance. The country can sign a contract in period t that commits it to selling a given volume of the good in period $t+1$ at a predetermined price. If the country sells all of its output on the futures market, it knows one period in advance exactly what its income will be.

We assume that the futures market is unbiased, so that the price agreed to in period t, for the sale of the product in the next period, is the expected value of this price based on the information available at the time the contract is signed. Since, moreover, we have assumed that prices are independent and identically distributed, the future price will be equal to the corresponding historical mean, $\bar{p}$. The revenues the country receives on average do not depend on the fraction of its output sold on the futures market; however, the larger this fraction, the lower will be the uncertainty in consumption (as measured by the corresponding coefficient of variation). The expression derived in (2), then, leads to the conclusion that the optimal strategy is to sell all of the production on the futures market. In that case, the uncertainty regarding consumption completely disappears, and the benefit associated with a futures market is equal to the total cost of risk.

Selling Copper Bonds

Next, we consider the case in which the only mechanism available to smooth earnings is the sale of (convertible) one-period commodity bonds, and there is the possibility of saving at a fixed rate equal to r. The country can sell a bond in period t that commits it to delivering (the equivalent of) a unit of its export good in period $t+1$. Assuming again that, the commodity bond market is unbiased, the sale price of these bonds will be equal to $\overline{p} / (1+r)$, where r is the international interest rate and $\overline{p}$ the average price. In equilibrium, the expected yield from investing one dollar in a commodity bond is equal to the yield obtained by investing that dollar at a fixed rate.

If the country decides in period $t = 1$ that, henceforth, it will sell commodity bonds for all of its production, its earnings from period $t = 2$ forward will be constant and equal to $\overline{y} / (1+r)$. In period $t = 1$, it will receive earnings equal to $y_1 + \overline{y} / (1+r)$. Since we have assumed that $r = \delta$, it is optimal to maintain consumption constant from $t = 1$ on. This can be accomplished if the "additional" income received in period $t = 1$, y_1, is invested so as to finance additional consumption equal to $ry_1 / (1+r)$ in each period. Consequently, a commodity bond makes it possible to completely smooth consumption from the moment it is first sold. The benefit from these bonds will be greater than the total cost of risk, for not only are earnings fluctuations eliminated, but the average level of consumption grows as well. The increase in the average level of earnings is due to the fact that commodity bonds not only are useful to stabilize income but also are debt instruments: in the period when they are first sold, the country receives income both from the sale of its current production on the spot market and from the sale of commodity bonds, whose principal will have to be paid in the following period.

Discussion

The conceptual framework in the previous two subsections, in which the performance of stabilization funds and sales of futures and commodity bonds were evaluated, is particularly simple since it sets aside a number of considerations that are important in practice. In this subsection, we shall briefly discuss the main issues that should be taken into account when the time comes to implement the instruments just described—issues that were not taken into account in the previous sections.

Correlation among Shocks

We have assumed that shocks are independent from one period to the next and that, consequently, all income above average is purely transitory, and therefore there is no reason to assume that it will persist.

Conclusions change drastically if there is persistence in the transitory shocks faced by the economy. Primary commodity price shocks are typically not independent from one period to another. For example, if a commodity's price is above its long-run value in a given period, this situation is more likely to persist in subsequent periods than it is to be reversed.

Below, we consider the case in which the commodity price follows a first order autoregressive process with a positive correlation coefficient equal to ρ. We shall also assume that production remains constant from one period to another. Thus, the optimal consumption rule associated with the stabilization fund is such that:[22]

$$c_t - c_{t-1} = \frac{r}{1+r-\rho}(y_t - \bar{y}). \qquad (7)$$

The equation above shows that the higher the correlation between the shocks of successive periods—that is, the closer ρ is to one—the higher the fraction of the transitory earnings from a given period that it is optimal to spend immediately. The lower the probability that earnings in subsequent periods will be low, the lower the incentives to save in periods of high earnings.

Consequently, the benefits from the stabilization fund described in the second section 2 decrease as the correlation between successive shocks increases. The same holds true for the futures and copper bonds described in the third section. The coefficient of variation of income V_p increases as the correlation between the shocks increases (ρ is greater): V_p is equal to ρ times the coefficient of variation for the case in which stabilization mechanisms are not utilized.

In the extreme case ($\rho = 1$), in which earnings show no tendency of reverting toward a mean value—that is, where earnings follow a random walk— equation (7) shows that the consumption rule that maximizes the welfare of the representative individual is such that:

$$c_t - c_{t-1} = y_t - \bar{y}. \qquad (8)$$

In this case, stabilization funds are absolutely useless for improving the welfare of the representative consumer. Since all shocks are permanent,[23] there is no better alternative than completely adjusting consumption levels to the new level of revenues after every shock.

Similarly, for the futures and copper-bond instruments considered in this chapter, the coefficient of variation for the earnings series does not diminish, and thus, the welfare of the representative consumer does not improve, when prices follow a random walk. Since, in this case, the best predictor of the price

---

[22] See, for example, Blanchard and Fischer (1989).
[23] The best predictor of future earnings is present earnings.

of the next period is the price of the current period, the degree of volatility of futures prices and commodity bonds is equal to that of the spot price. It is important to mention that there are reasons—which have no bearing on the volatility of the price series and, thus, are not captured by the conceptual framework of this chapter—why the sale of both futures and copper bonds has a positive impact, even when prices exhibit random-walk behavior. In the case of futures, it is possible to know what the income of each period will be one period in advance; with copper bonds, the benefit derives from the additional funds obtained during the period when they are first issued.

The above discussion shows that for stabilization mechanisms actually to be useful, either the shocks to the economy must have a transitory component, or the instruments designed must be more sophisticated than those described in this chapter. We shall see examples of both in later chapters.

This section also illustrates how important it is to be able to determine when a shock is transitory and when it is permanent—or, ideally, to be able to disaggregate any shock into the sum of a transitory and a permanent component. It is also important to determine how long a given shock will last—that is, its degree of persistence.[24] Incorrectly identifying the nature of a shock can prove extremely costly. During the past two decades, positive shocks to the Latin American economies have generally been considered permanent, and negative shocks, transitory, when the true nature of shocks was exactly the opposite.[25] Except in cases like that of the oil-price shock resulting from the invasion of Kuwait, which was clearly transitory, a point to bear in mind when designing stabilization mechanisms is how they determine the nature of the shocks that affect an economy.

Country Risk and Sovereign Risk

If it were possible to borrow without limits at the international interest rate, stabilization mechanisms would be unnecessary. Much of their importance lies in the fact that precisely when credit is most needed, the possibilities for developing nations to obtain it are typically lower. Thus, for example, during the debt crisis, the majority of Latin American countries had no access to voluntary credit. Moreover, as some of these countries regained access to the voluntary credit markets, they had to pay an additional premium when contracting debt because of the "country risk."

In this section, we consider the effects of limited access to credit and the

---

[24] The distinction between a transitory shock that lasts 10 years and a permanent one is more semantic than real.

[25] The statement is attributable to Max Corden.

problems associated with "sovereign risk:" the creditor country has no collateral to collect should the debtor country default on the debt contracted.[26]

The classic example of a stabilization fund examined previously assumes that the country has unlimited access to credit.[27] As mentioned earlier, this assumption is hardly realistic. When designing a fund, it is important to consider the fact that debt capacity is limited in practice. Furthermore, if we focus our attention on stabilization funds that do not resort to borrowing, these funds will not depend on third countries, which is a desirable property.

Selling futures contracts presents virtually no problems of sovereign risk, since the differences that arise due to price changes are settled on a day-to-day basis through "margin calls." In the case of copper bonds, however, it is particularly important to consider the effects of sovereign risk, since it will translate into lower prices than those obtained under the assumption of unbiased markets. With these instruments, it is the buyer who bears all the risk. If the country that sells the bonds decides not to honor its contractual obligation, the buyer incurs a loss equal to the amount paid. The greater the probability (perceived by the buyers of commodity bonds) that the country will not honor its commitments, the lower the price at which the respective bonds will be sold. If the country risk is very high, the resulting penalty may be high enough to block completely the possibility of placing these bonds on the market. By the same token, the fact that the country honors its international obligations will cause the country risk to decrease, making the possibility of selling commodity bonds more attractive.

There are several mechanisms whereby a country can provide guarantees to the creditors that buy its commodity bonds. First, these instruments could be created and underwritten by independent international agencies like the Inter-American Development Bank and the World Bank. Second, the monies deposited in a stabilization fund could be utilized as a guarantee against the commodity bonds floated by the country. What makes this alternative attractive is the negative correlation between a country's incentives to spend its stabilization fund and the importance of sovereign risk. Sovereign risk is higher when the commodity price is higher; however, at such times, the country has no incentive to spend its stabilization fund because it is saving for the time

---

[26] It is true that the majority of Latin American countries have honored their debt service obligations, motivated possibly by the threat of being excluded from the international financial system if they do not. However, the problem of sovereign risk continues to be relevant if we note that forcing debtor countries to honor their commitments involves costs to the creditor countries.

[27] Moreover, equation (6) shows that the level held in the fund follows a random-walk process; thus, it is certain that either the level accumulated or the amount owed will eventually grow without limits.

when prices will fall. If a country guards against risk by combining commodity-bond issues with a stabilization fund, it should bear in mind that the resources accumulated in the fund must be large enough to guarantee the financial instruments issued.[28]

Political considerations

A series of political considerations must be addressed when designing the stabilization mechanisms studied in this essay. A stabilization instrument can fail in practice if it neglects to take into account the behavior of those in charge of implementing it or those who can interfere in its operations.

In the case of a stabilization fund, two issues must be considered in this respect. First, there is the possibility that the current administration will utilize the resources held in the fund during election periods to help ensure that it remains in power. Second, there are the pressures from widely diverse sectors to spend the funds. In a developing country, the unsatisfied needs are so many that it is not easy to justify the existence of "idle" resources.

The risk that the government will spend the fund during election periods can be avoided by establishing precise rules for both accumulating and spending the resources in the fund. In particular, the items of expenditure and the conditions under which they may be spent must be clearly defined. To keep these regulations from making stabilization-fund operations excessively rigid, the possibility of modifying fund operations when the majority of the political sectors are in accord can be left open. This will be the case, for instance, if modifying the fund's operational rules requires legislation, in which case any change has to be approved by the parliament.

One way of dealing with pressures to spend the monies saved in a stabilization fund is for the operating rules of the fund to form part of an agreement between the country and a multilateral agency like the World Bank or the Inter-American Development Bank.[29] For example, the multilateral agency could serve as the underwriter of the commodity bonds floated by the country, requiring, in exchange, that the country reduce some of its risk by implementing a stabilization fund. The saving and spending criteria of this fund should be acceptable to both parties.

A second alternative to preventing the fund from being inappropriately spent

---

[28] The higher the country risk, the higher the relative importance of the stabilization fund. For this purpose, the money in the stabilization fund should be deposited in international banks. However, this may not be politically viable.

[29] This is the case with the Copper Stabilization Fund implemented in Chile.

is based on convincing leaders of public opinion, and public opinion in general, that the people most affected by transitory shocks are the lower-income sectors and that, therefore, these are the sectors that will be harmed the most in the long run if the resources in the fund are utilized for their short-term benefit.[30]

It would appear that dampening the effects of commodity price fluctuations through the sale of financial instruments does not pose the risks just described for the stabilization funds. Yet if the state produces the good being exported, this will be true only if decision making by the executives of the state-owned enterprises is sufficiently independent of the government. Otherwise, it may happen that during election periods, a higher-than-usual number of bonds will be sold (even if the associated risk premium increases), with the object of raising fiscal expenditures and increasing the likelihood that the governing coalition will be reelected.

It is also worth noting that when a state enterprise sells financial instruments, the political costs to its executives are higher every time prices rise above the value stipulated at the time of sale than the benefits received from selling above the resulting ex-post price. This is due to the fact that the public (and sometimes the national comptroller) interpret futures sales at prices below the ex-post spot market as "speculative" activities. Therefore, when evaluating the performance of executives of state enterprises that produce the primary commodities, one of the variables that the government should consider is fluctuations in the income generated by these enterprises. Otherwise, the respective executives will have no incentive to reduce the risk associated with commodity price fluctuations.

Analysis of Stabilization Funds

A mechanism traditionally suggested for mitigating different types of fluctuations is stabilization funds; such a fund was the key component of the World Bank structural adjustment program implemented in Chile in 1985. Following a description of Chile's Copper Stabilization Fund (FEC) currently in operation, this chapter presents a series of alternative criteria for obtaining accumulation funds that do not exhibit the shortcomings of the FEC. Had these criteria been applied, the performance of such funds would have been more satisfactory than that of the FEC.

---

[30] While this alternative appears less feasible than the previous one, it should be noted that with regard to inflation, the above mentioned objective of raising the consciousness of public opinion has been achieved in Chile.

The Copper Stabilization Fund

The Copper Stabilization Fund (FEC) was established as part of the structural adjustment loan (SAL) between Chile and the World Bank in 1985.[31] The document cites the objectives of stabilizing both the exchange rate and fiscal revenues deriving from the sale of copper. In practice, this fund began to record deposits—in a special account opened for this purpose in the Central Bank— only in 1987. The sums to be deposited in the FEC are calculated as follows:

- A reference price is established that corresponds to an estimated "trend price" for copper. The information available on how this price is calculated is contradictory. Some documents indicate that it is negotiated year to year by the government of Chile and the World Bank. Others maintain that it is equal to the average spot price of the six previous years on the London Metal Exchange.[32] Since differences between the reference prices associated with these two specifications have been small in practice, and since what is useful for the purpose of our analysis is that this price constitutes an approximation of the long-term price, we shall not linger to try and discover which definition is the one actually employed.
- At the quarter's end, the reference price is compared with the one secured by CODELCO. When the price obtained by CODELCO is higher by four cents or less, no deposit is made. If the difference is more than four cents but less than 10 cents, 50 percent of the margin over four cents goes into the FEC. All of the difference above 10 cents goes into the FEC. If the price is less than the reference price, we have rules analogous to the earlier ones—this time to decide how much should be drawn from the fund instead of how much should be deposited. In this case, the marginal propensity to spend is nil for the first four-cents' difference, 0.5 for the next six cents, and 1 for differences over 10 cents. The price differential is multiplied by the total copper exports of CODELCO, minus foreign copper purchases that may have been made to satisfy any existing contractual obligations. If the price of copper is above the reference price, the difference calculated according to the rules described above gives rise to a deposit by the National Treasury into the fund account at the Central Bank. If the price differential is negative, the treasury may withdraw the corresponding amount in the following quarter, with the sole condition that there be a positive balance in the account.

---

[31] This section is based on information obtained from the Central Bank and COCHILCO.
[32] Based on this specification, the average reference prices in 1987, 1988, 1989, and 1990 were US$.64, $.75, $.79, and $.85, respectively.

The table below shows the balance in the fund at the end of each year from 1987 to 1990.[33]

Table 2.1. Evolution of the Balance in the FEC
(in millions of US$)

Year	1987	1988	1989	1990
Balance	26	352	1,028	1,895

Since copper prices have been on the rise during the period under consideration, the total resources accumulated in the FEC have grown over time. Withdrawals from the FEC correspond to US$263 million to pay the external debt and US$363 million at the time of the "fruit crisis."[34] Although for accounting purposes the FEC has evolved in the manner described, in practice, the government has used the fund to pay the debt incurred with the Central Bank during the crisis of 1982-1984.[35] If the debt payment by the government is taken into account, the available balance in the FEC at the close of 1990 is only US$554 million.[36] If the objective of the fund is to dampen fluctuations in fiscal spending, this is the relevant figure; on the other hand, if its objective is to prevent exchange rate fluctuations, then the prepayment of the domestic debt has no effect on the availability of reserves, and the quantities in Table 2.1 are those that are relevant.

Whether the objective is to stabilize the real exchange rate or prevent fluctuations in fiscal expenditures, the FECs saving-spending rule is inadequate, for it does not take into account the level of resources accumulated when deciding how much to spend or save. Given any reference price, the lower the balance held in the fund, the greater the incentives to save. Any saving rule

---

[33] Source: Central Bank, Chile.

[34] In early 1989, the FDA temporarily prohibited Chilean fruit imports into the United States, after allegedly finding two tainted grapes in one shipment.

[35] These payments correspond to a transfer of foreign exchange by the government to the Central Bank. The importance of this transaction lies in the fact that the Central Bank—which is autonomous in Chile—is less susceptible to pressures to spend the additional revenues generated during a copper price boom.

[36] In fact, the Central Bank has different names for the two funds: the one concerned with the payment of the domestic debt is the Fiscal Compensatory Facility for Copper Revenues, while the other, in the spirit of the SAL agreement that gave rise to the FEC, is the Central Bank's Compensatory Facility for Copper Revenues.

should consider both the current price and the amount held in the fund when deciding how much money to save-spend. It is therefore not surprising that the balance in the FEC grew beyond what is reasonable and led to a new interpretation of the rule permitting part of the accumulated fund to be spent.

A second criticism of the FEC derives from the fact that the incentives to save in the fund should depend not only on the difference between the current and the long-run price; they should also consider the expected evolution of copper prices in the short run. If current prices are higher than those expected in the immediate future, it is advisable to save in order to be able to resort to the fund when copper prices fall. Alternatively, if the current price is less than what is expected in the years to come, the incentives to save are considerably less, for copper revenues will grow in the future. The FEC's rule incompletely incorporates these considerations by comparing the current price of copper with an estimate of the long-run price, failing to take into account that the more distant the time when it will be necessary to spend these savings, the less desirable it will be to save in times of boom. It is not enough to know the difference between the current price of copper and its long-run value; it is also relevant to know the expected length of the price cycle at the moment the decision is taken on how much to save in the fund. We conclude that the prices to be considered when defining the reference price should include those anticipated for the immediate future. To do this requires a model with a good forecasting capability, a question that we shall return to in the section that follows.

In sum, we consider the saving rule of the FEC unsatisfactory for two reasons: first, because it does not take the balance in the fund into account when deciding how much to save or spend; and second, because it does not consider expectations regarding short-term future prices when setting the reference price.

A Stabilization Fund with Access to Credit

In both this section and the next, we assume that the relevant variable to stabilize is the fiscal expenditures that derive from CODELCO's profits.[37].

We begin by considering what is the optimal stabilization fund when the country has unlimited access to external credit. While this is an extreme case,

---

[37] The qualitative aspects of the conclusions are the same if the foreign exchange reserves derived from copper exports are considered. CODELCO's profits are estimated as the difference between sales' revenues and the sum of (a) its operational costs, and (b) US$500 million (in 1988 values) assigned to depreciation and investment. This latter figure was obtained by regressing CODELCO's profits on its operational profits.

it illustrates some facts that prove useful when we study a more realistic fund in the next section.

Whatever the stochastic process that generates copper prices, if we keep the rest of the assumptions from the previous section, the optimal spending rule satisfies the well-known certainty-equivalence property. The optimal level of spending in each period is equal to a fixed fraction of total wealth, which, in turn, is equal to the sum of the present value of expected earnings and to the level saved in or debited to the fund. Thus, the optimal level of consumption (C_0) in period $t = 0$, is given by:[38]

$$C_0 = \frac{r}{1+r}\left(E_0\left[\sum_{t=0}^{+\infty}(1+r)^{-t}\, y_t \right] + A_0 \right), \qquad (9)$$

where E_0 denotes the expected value, based on the information available at the beginning of period $t = 0$, A_0 the balance available in the fund at $t = 0$, r the interest rate, and y_t earnings (or income) during period t.

The optimal savings fund, then, operates as if there were absolute certainty regarding future income streams. This rather undesirable property is because of the assumption of a quadratic utility function, which rather unsatisfactorily describes behavior under uncertainty, for it implies an increasing absolute risk aversion—that is, a greater willingness to pay to avoid uncertainty as income levels rise.[39]

As already noted, the optimal fund will accumulate nothing if copper prices follow a random-walk process. Indeed, the data indicate that it is impossible to reject this hypothesis.[40] Consequently, if a savings fund is to be beneficial, an econometric model is needed whose predictive capability is better than that of a random-walk process. Forecasting the price of copper is particularly difficult since the majority of models do not have a predictive power significantly better than that of a random walk. One exception is the model developed by Vial (1987) and variations on this model.[41] The average (absolute) forecast error using this model is approximately 30 percent less than that obtained with a random walk. An even more important characteristic that we shall make use of in the section that follows is that this model is quite reliable when forecasting copper price cycles—that is, when predicting whether the price has reached a

---

[38] For a derivation, see, for example, Blanchard and Fischer (1989, p. 286).

[39] The quadratic utility function is so popular in the literature because it leads to explicit expressions for the optimal saving and consumption rules.

[40] This statement is valid when considering annual data from 1960 to 1990 and when considering monthly figures for various time periods.

[41] The main characteristics of this econometric model can be found in Appendix 1.

peak or a trough and, thus, whether copper prices will rise or fall over the next few years.

The table below shows what the trend would have been for the annual year-end balances for the stabilization fund defined in (9):[42]

Table 2.2 Optimal Fund with No Credit Constraints
(in millions of US$)

Year	1985	1986	1987	1988	1989	1990
Balance	−423	−939	−1,118	−662	317	976

Initially, the price of copper is below its anticipated future value, making the optimal course of action to incur debt to keep spending levels approximately constant. However, starting in 1987, the outlook is less promising, and therefore, the fund begins to pay the debt contracted in earlier periods, attaining a surplus beginning in 1989. Table 2.3 contrasts the fiscal revenues and expenditures that would have been realized with the fund described:

Table 2.3 Revenues and Expenditures with the Fund
(in millions of 1988 US$)

Year	1985	1986	1987	1988	1989	1990
Revenues	385	349	685	1,354	1,727	1,359
Expenditures with the Fund	773	804	808	872	761	739

As expected, when access to credit is unlimited, the optimal fund is highly successful in smoothing variations in fiscal expenditures that arise from changes in CODELCO's profits received by the government. Each year, the country spends a fixed fraction of its wealth; variations in the level of spending derive from (1) price fluctuations (present and anticipated), and (2) fluctuations in the level accumulated or spent by the fund. However, as stated

---

[42] Predictions of future production levels are assumed equal to the highest level of production in the previous three years; the discount rate is equal to 10 percent; and the international interest rate corresponds to that of the LIBOR.

previously, the assumption of unlimited access to credit is hardly realistic. Below, we consider the reverse scenario, where there is no access to credit whatsoever.

A Stabilization Fund with No Access to Credit

In this section, we consider a stabilization fund under more realistic conditions. We assume that there is no possibility of resorting to debt so that, at all times, the level held in the fund, A_t, should be larger than or equal to zero.[43] We also assume that the instantaneous utility function of the representative individual has a constant elasticity of substitution (and thus, relative risk aversion) and that the time preference rate δ is higher than the international interest rate r.[44]

Now, spending in period t cannot be greater than the funds available — that is, the cash on hand—in that period, which we shall denote as $x_t = A_t + y_t$.

When solving the representative agent's utility maximization in period t, the usual Euler condition has to be modified to incorporate the constraint of non-negativity in the balance of the fund. This leads us to:[45]

$$u'(c_t) = Max \left[u'(x_t),\ \Gamma E_t u'(c_{t+1}) \right],$$ (10)

where $\Gamma = (1+r)/(1+\delta)$ and E_t denotes the expected value based on information available at the beginning of period t. Since expenditures cannot be larger than cash on hand (x_t), marginal utility cannot be less than $u'(x_t)$. This constraint is binding if the marginal utility at x_t is larger than the anticipated marginal utility (duly discounted) in the next period; otherwise, the marginal utilities are equal, as in the case in which access to credit is unlimited. If future income is expected to increase there are incentives for increasing current income, yet this is possible only if the available balance in the fund is positive. This limitation is not present when there is access to credit since, in that case, it would be enough to incur debt to consume more. To take advantage of situations like the one just described, it is necessary to save more than would normally be saved were there access to credit. The condition expressed in (10) reflects this additional incentive to save.

---

[43] The analysis that follows can be extended to the case where the debt capacity is limited and fixed *a priori*.

[44] This last assumption is particularly valid in developing countries. We continue assuming that the only source of income fluctuations derives from the export revenues of a given product.

[45] This result is from Deaton (1991).

In what follows we explore the implications of (10) in more detail. We first consider the case in which income in different periods is equal to the sum of the historical mean $\bar{y}$ and a transitory shock $y_t - \bar{y}$ that has zero mean and is independent and identically distributed from one period to another. Given an accumulated fund equal to A_t at the start of period t, and current year income equal to y_t, the available funds $A_t + y_t$ should be split between a fraction to be consumed c_t and a fraction to be saved (at an interest rate r). The fund accumulated at the start of period $t+1$ will then be equal to $A_{t+1} = (1+r)(A_t + y_t - c_t)$.

Although it is not possible to derive explicit expressions for the optimal saving and consumption rules, they can be obtained through numerical methods.[46] Even though optimal rules depend on specific parameters such as the degree of risk aversion and the interest rate, they all have certain similarities. Among these common features is the fact that the optimal level of consumption in a given period depends only on the amount of cash on hand, that is on the sum of the existing fund at the beginning of the period and the current period's income, and not on each of these quantities taken separately. Moreover, if the funds available in a given period are under a certain threshold value x^*, the optimal course is to spend all the resources available, thus exhausting the stabilization fund.[47]

Figure 2.1 shows the typical shape of the optimal consumption rule, which specifies consumption in period t, c_t as a function of cash on hand during that period, $A_t + y_t$.

If cash on hand available in a period is below a certain critical value x^*, the entire fund is spent. The lower the level of resources in the fund at the start of a period, the more likely it is that the entire fund will be spent during that period. Likewise, the higher income is in a given period, the less likely it is that the fund will be exhausted. Moreover, the threshold below which the fund is exhausted grows as either the degree of risk aversion or income uncertainty decrease.

The marginal propensity to consume α will be approximately constant and less than one when resources available are above x^*.[48] The lower the degree of risk aversion and the smaller the variance of income, the higher this propensity.

---

[46] See Deaton (1991).

[47] This property is derived from Deaton and Laroque (1992).

[48] In what follows, we intentionally assume that this propensity is constant. This is a good approximation and has the advantage of providing a simple rule that can be understood by the general public. Using well-known numerical dynamic optimization techniques to obtain the optimal rule leads only to a minor improvement, at the cost of having political authorities and the general public view the fund as a "black box."

Figure 2.1   Consumption Function

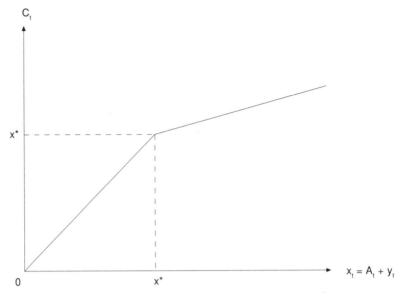

Next we consider the case in which there is a certain degree of persistence in transitory shocks. More specifically, we assume that income follows a first-order autoregressive process with a positive correlation coefficient. In this case, the fact that income is above average during a given period indicates that, while there is a tendency for it to return to the mean, it is highly probable that it will remain above average for several periods. The higher the correlation coefficient, the larger is the degree of persistence of transitory shocks in the following periods.

Given a price process of this type, the optimal strategy depends both on current income and the level of resources accumulated in the fund. For each level of current income, there is a function like that of Figure 2.1, with particular values of x^* and α, which determines the optimal spending level for every amount of cash on hand. The higher the current income, the higher the future income is expected to be, and thus, the lower the incentives to save. Thus, both the threshold value x^* below which the fund is exhausted, and the marginal propensity to consume (when income is above x^*) grow as current income is larger.[49] In fact, the extreme case, in which the stabilization fund reports no benefit ($x^* = \infty$ and $\alpha = 1$), corresponds to the case in which income

---

[49] The conclusions in this paragraph are based on Deaton (1991).

follows a random walk. When all shocks are permanent, a stabilization fund is useless for dampening the negative impact of income fluctuations.[50]

Below, we adapt the optimal spending strategies just outlined to the particular elements that determine the price of copper.[51] The copper price series has undergone several cycles during the last three decades. Even though these cycles are irregular both in their duration and amplitude, we can construct a stabilization fund analogous to those described earlier, as long as we can determine whether we are in the ascending or descending phase. Thus, for example, if copper prices are expected to rise in the future, the incentives to spend the balance in the fund will be high. Conversely, if copper prices are expected to fall, it will be desirable to accumulate resources in the fund with the object of spending those savings when the drop occurs. Also, the longer the average duration of the copper price cycle, the lower are the incentives to save and the benefits that accrue from a stabilization fund.[52]

The above considerations motivate proposing the following copper stabilization fund:

- Toward the end of year $t-1$, we classify year t as a year whose future looks better or worse than the present, depending on whether the Vial model predicts that the price at t, P_t, will be significantly lower or higher than the average price expected for periods $t+1$ and $t+2$.[53] Otherwise, we say that the future price is expected to be similar to the current price.
- With each of the above scenarios, we associate a consumption function like the one in Figure 2.1. The marginal propensity to consume is large when the price of copper is expected to rise in the future and small when it is expected to fall. The consumption functions are illustrated in Figure 2.2.[54]
- When calculating the national budget at the close of year $t-1$, the rule just described is used to determine fiscal expenditures (of copper earnings)

---

[50] The assumption in Deaton (1991), according to which income is known at the start of each period, is important for the validity of the previous assertion; otherwise, the analysis in this section would have to be modified. It would be necessary to incorporate the costs to the government of errors committed in predicting current earnings when calculating the national budget. In this essay, we do not consider this question when determining the optimal savings rule; rather, we incorporate it in an *ad hoc* manner when implementing these rules.

[51] In what follows, we place special emphasis on finding simple saving rules that, while not necessarily optimal, conform to a series of desirable properties.

[52] This is due to the fact that the discount rate is higher than the interest rate.

[53] Denote the price predicted by the Vial model for period t and the average of prices predicted for $t+1$ and $t+2$ by P_t and $\bar{P}_t$, respectively. We say that the future looks better than the present if P_t is less than 0.9 $\bar{P}_t$ and worse if P_t is larger than 1.1 $\bar{P}_t$.

[54] For simplicity, we have taken equal threshold values x^* in the three cases. This is because the Vial model is applicable only for years since 1985. With more information, x^* would be higher if the future price were expected to be higher.

during year t. Fiscal revenues considered are those estimated based on the price forecast at time period t.[55]

- Since fiscal revenues from copper are not known when calculating the national budget, the level of spending determined by the fund will be unattainable if actual revenues are much lower than anticipated.[56] We shall assume that, if possible, the balance available in the fund is used to compensate for the prediction error. Otherwise, the entire fund is consumed and actual expenditures are less than budgeted.

Tables 2.4 and 2.5 show the path of the balance in the proposed fund and the corresponding expenditures in two cases. In the first of these, the marginal propensities to spend are relatively low when the available funds are above the common threshold of US$500 million; in the second, they are relatively high.[57] Moreover, we assume that the balance initially available in the fund is zero, that the money deposited receives no interest, and that the average price of copper in 1991 is equal to US$1.10 per pound.

The evolution of both funds is similar. In the first period (1985-1987), available funds are low and the cycle is considered to be in the ascending phase; thus, all resources are spent and the fund maintains a zero balance. In 1988 and 1989, current earnings rise significantly, and future prices appear to be equal to current prices. Consequently, a major portion of the additional resources in the fund are saved. Beginning in 1990, the descending phase of the cycle starts, and the fund begins to be used to partially offset the effects of the drop in prices. As is to be expected, the lower the marginal propensity to spend, the greater the average balance in the fund.

Both funds indicate, for different reasons, that part of the corresponding balance should be spent in 1992. In the case of the fund with a low marginal propensity of consumption, the reason to spend is that the levels accumulated are already extremely high; in the case of the fund with a high propensity to spend, it is precisely the magnitude of this propensity that explains why a decision is made to spend part of the fund.

If the initial balance in the fund is positive—say, equal to US$500 million—it is spent during the 1985-1986 period in both cases.[58] This is an inherent

---

[55] The amount produced is assumed to be equal to the highest production level of the last three periods. Production costs are determined on the basis of the information supplied by CODELCO. The future looked better than the current year at the beginning of 1986 and 1987, worse at the beginning of 1990, 1991, and 1992, and the same at the beginning of 1988 and 1989.

[56] This fact can be incorporated into the fund's mechanism; we are leaving this for future research.

[57] The corresponding values are 0.2, 0.4, and 0.6 in the first case, and 0.5, 0.7, and 0.9 in the second.

[58] Once the fund is exhausted, its evolution is the same as that described in the tables.

**Figure 2.2   Consumption Functions for the Proposed
           Stabilization Fund**

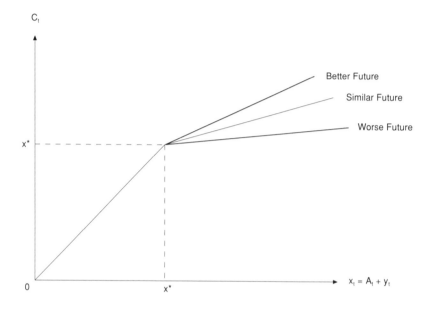

Table 2.4 Low Propensity to Spend
(in millions of 1988 US$)

Year	1985	1986	1987	1988	1989	1990	1991	1992
Income	385	349	685	1,354	1,727	1,359	1,109	
Real expenditures	385	349	685	917	983	891	910	
Fund balance (beginning of year)	0	0	0	437	1,187	1,649	1,848	1,639

Table 2.5 High Propensity to Spend
(in millions of 1988 US$)

Year	1985	1986	1987	1988	1989	1990	1991	1992
Income	385	349	685	1,354	1,727	1,359	1,109	
Real expenditures	385	349	685	1,229	1,127	1,249	1,118	
Fund balance (beginning of year)	0	0	0	125	725	835	826	426

characteristic of stabilization funds when access to credit is limited: they are frequently exhausted. However, periods when this occurs are such that the benefits of exhausting the fund are greater than the anticipated benefits of retaining part of the resources in order to smooth future fluctuations.

It would be desirable to evaluate how the proposed stabilization evolves over longer periods, selecting those propensities to spend that maximize some appropriate criterion. This is not possible, however, since the econometric model on which the copper price predictions are based is applicable only for years since 1985. Despite this constraint, we believe that the type of rule proposed in this section satisfies a series of desirable properties that the FEC lacks. First, it takes into account both the expected earnings and the level accumulated in the fund when choosing the spending level for a given period. This provides a mechanism that, in contrast to the FEC, prevents over-accumulation. Second, the proposed fund looks at expected future prices to determine the phase of the cycle in which the price of copper currently resides. This offers advantages over the reference price defined for the FEC.

Stabilization Fund for Fiscal Expenditures[59]

Stabilization policies require a careful analysis of the benefits and costs associated with shocks to a country's economy. To choose mechanically policies that minimize the fluctuations of a given aggregate variable may lead to socially undesirable results.

For instance, the effect of transitory shocks on the fiscal revenues of a country in which the state is the main owner of the particular resource (Chile, Mexico, and Venezuela, for example) will translate into fluctuations in one or more of the components of public expenditures: public investment, social expenditures, and public sector salaries. This motivates a careful discussion of the impact of variations in the three components of public expenditures just mentioned on welfare:

- Investment in general, and public-sector investment in particular, has a strong component of irreversibility, because a significant fraction of investment is embodied in capital that is specific to the project in question. Thus, the social cost of reducing the level of public investment,—especially if it leads to halting ongoing projects—[60] is greater than the benefits associated with increasing this investment during periods of high fiscal revenues, even if the economic authority is risk neutral. This justifies

---

[59] Many of this section's issues are considered in more detail in Engel and Mondschein (1993).
[60] As occurred in several Latin American countries during the early 1980s.

being cautious when starting new projects and should be taken into account when designing stabilization policies.

- It is reasonable to assume that the political cost associated with reducing the level of social expenditures is higher than the benefits associated with an increment in such spending. This is especially true if we consider that reductions in social spending typically occur in moments of crisis; thus, the sectors that benefit the most from these stabilization policies find themselves in a particularly vulnerable situation.[61] Consequently, as with public investment, there is an important asymmetry between the costs of reducing social spending and the benefits associated with increasing it.
- The effects of increasing and decreasing public-sector salaries are similar to those described for social expenditures, although there is possibly less asymmetry between the corresponding benefits and costs.

The above discussion leads to the following maximization problem that the economic authority solves from period to period. Denoting by G_t and Y_t the fiscal expenditures and fiscal revenues of year t, and by A_t, the resources held in the fund at the start of year t, at time $t = 0$ the economic authority selects that flow of government expenditures that solves:

$$\max \sum_{t=0}^{} (1+\delta)^{-t} E_0 \left[U\left(G_t, \sum_{s\geq 1} \gamma^s G_{t-s}, (G_{t-1} - G_t)_+ \right) \right], \tag{11}$$

$$\text{subject to } G_t \leq A_t + Y_t, \qquad t = 1, 2, 3, \ldots \tag{12}$$

where E_0 denotes the expected value based on the information available in $t = 0$. The instantaneous utility function U is increasing in its first argument, that is, that other things being equal, a larger level of current expenditure is more desirable. It is also increasing in the second argument that measures the value of fiscal expenditures in previous periods, duly discounted by the coefficient of depreciation γ. Even if current fiscal expenditures are low, the higher the investment in social expenditures in earlier periods, the greater the welfare of the population. The utility function is decreasing in the third argument of the equation, which is equal to the drop in fiscal expenditures should there be such a drop, and equal to zero otherwise. This component is the novel aspect of our approach, because there will be a tradeoff between the benefit of raising welfare by raising spending levels today and the cost of increasing the probability that it may be necessary to cut spending in the future.

The stochastic constraint, to which the above maximization problem is

---

[61] See, for example, Raczynski (1988).

Figure 2.3   The Stabilization Fund without Uncertainty

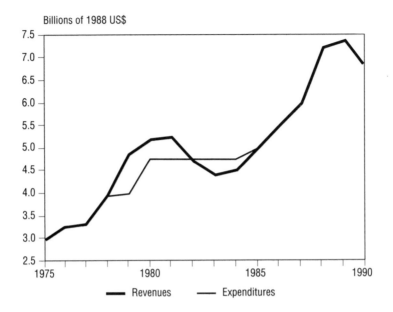

Billions of 1988 US$

Revenues   Expenditures

subject, derives from the fact that there is no access to credit; thus, expenditures in each period cannot exceed the amount of cash on hand (the sum of current earnings and the resources held in the fund). It is this constraint that makes it particularly hard to solve this problem. A variety of alternative solutions consider different compromises between (1) how close the problem actually being solved is to the problem of dynamic programming implicit in the above formulation, and (2) how realistic the assumptions are concerning expectations about the corresponding stochastic variables.[62] In general, this approach is useful when devising stabilization funds, as long as the uncertainty about the future evolution of fiscal revenues is not too large. Below, we present a possible approach, the details of which can be found in Appendix 3.

We assume that the utility function is linear in each of its arguments,[63] which, after certain algebraic operations, leads to the following equivalent maximization problem:

---

[62] Among these options are the utilization of "chance constraints," substituting the constraints with the assumption that debt can be incurred at a cost that grows with the size of the debt, and solving the dynamic programming problem after having discretized the state variable. The latter approach, combined with statistical techniques to find a tractable expression for the resulting optimal policy, is developed in Engel and Mondschein (1993).

[63] This allows us to separate the effects of asymmetries in the utility function as discussed above from risk aversion.

$$\max \sum_{t \geq 1} (1 + \delta)^{-t} E_0 \left[G_t - b \left(G_{t-1} - G_t \right)_+ \right], \tag{13}$$

subject to the constraint in (12). The positive constant b depends both on the rate of depreciation γ and on the tradeoff between the benefits of increasing current expenditures against the cost of increasing the likelihood of a future drop in this variable.

Figure 2.3 shows the evolution of fiscal revenues in Chile from 1975 to 1990 and what the optimal level of spending would have been had these revenues been known beforehand.[64] The path of fiscal expenditures would have exhibited no drop, and the stabilization fund would have accumulated resources during the 1978-1981 period, spending these savings during the recession of 1982-1984. The cumulative decline in spending from one year to the next totals $950 million in 1988 U.S. dollars, while the sum of the resources accumulated in the fund during the period reaches $2.375 billion in 1988 U.S. dollars. For example, if the parameter b is equal to 5, the benefit from the "ideal" stabilization fund during that period is equal to $2.375 billion 1988 U.S. dollars.[65]

In practice, not enough information is available to implement a fund like the one described above. When deciding how much to spend and how much to save in each period, it is necessary to know the economic authority's degree of uncertainty regarding future fiscal revenues and how costly it is to modify the budget once it has been approved. Quantifying this degree of uncertainty is beyond the scope of this work. However, we can present two extreme cases that illustrate the fact that a fund based on the conceptual framework presented in this section is justified, when the uncertainty regarding future fiscal revenues is not too high. Figures 4 and 5 correspond to scenarios with low and high uncertainty about the future trajectory of fiscal revenues.[66] Where uncertainty is low, the stabilization fund prevents drops in fiscal spending. However, in contrast to the fund without uncertainty, the average available balance in the fund is considerably higher—$780 million in 1988 U.S. dollars. Where uncertainty is high, the associated benefits are of little import. The worst of the recession in 1982 is prevented, but the average available balance exceeds $1 billion in 1988 U.S. dollars.

---

[64] We assume $b > 2.5$.

[65] This figure is similar to the one obtained in section one, although the basis for its calculation is more satisfactory. It goes without saying that as b varies, very different results are obtained. In general, the cost of uncertainty for the fund considered in this section is equal to the difference between b times the sum of decreases in government revenues and those resources accumulated in the fund.

[66] See Appendix 3 for details.

Figure 2.4   The Stabilization Fund with Low Uncertainty

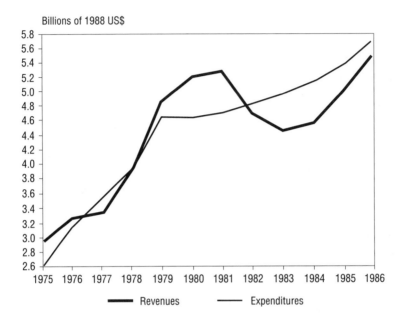

Figure 2.5   The Stabilization Fund with High Uncertainty

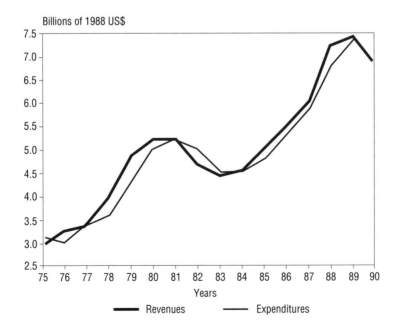

Financial Instruments for Stabilizing Prices

Forwards and Futures Contracts

Forwards Contracts

A forwards contract consists of an agreement between two parties to buy or sell a given product at a future date (established in the present), at a certain price (also stipulated in advance). At maturity, if the observed market price (spot price) is higher than the price contracted (forwards price), the buyer reaps a profit equal to the difference between the two prices. If the spot price is lower, the opposite occurs. The party that sells the forwards contract agrees to deliver the product specified in the contract to the buyer at the preset price (forwards price). This type of contract is frequently used to hedge against the risks involved in holding assets whose prices vary over time. The usual procedure is to realize opposite transactions in the forwards and spot markets: if a producer holds a given asset (or buys it on the spot market), then he will sell the same amount on the forwards market at a given price. When the contract expires, the producer sells his product at the forwards price; this allows him to guarantee the future return at the time he enters into the contract.

Two characteristics of forwards contracts are worth noting. First, when the contract is signed, no transfer of money takes place between the parties. Second, forwards contracts carry the risk of default or noncompliance. It may well be that the party that agrees to deliver the product will not fulfill his end of the bargain.

The markets for commodities forwards contracts are generally not very liquid, especially in the case of contracts with maturities of over three months. However, the London Metal Exchange is an exception to this rule. For three-month contracts, the commodities with high liquidity are aluminum, copper, lead, nickel, and zinc.

Futures Contracts

Futures are very similar to forwards. However, there are some differences that should be emphasized. To begin, futures contracts are highly standardized. The product to be traded must meet certain specifications for the contract to be valid—that is, a certain quantity and very specific quality of the product, exact dates, delivery sites, etc. For this reason, in 95 percent of the cases, the parties that take positions in these markets cancel their original contract, taking the opposite position before it expires. The second difference is that these types of transactions are carried out solely through authorized exchanges controlled by a clearing house. Another difference is that with futures, losses or gains are settled with the clearing house on a daily basis, using the closing price of the day as the point of reference. This significantly reduces the risk of default or noncompliance in the original futures contract. Finally, this type of contract requires a certain guarantee in the form of a deposit of money or securities (called the "margin" of the futures contract).

The same operations can be carried out with futures as with forwards—hedging or speculation, for example. However, because of the standardization clauses, futures contracts are more liquid. For instance, if we take the New York Commodity Exchange (COMEX) and consider the liquidity of some of the various coppers futures (with different expiration dates) for July 16, 1987, and July 16, 1991, we have:

Table 2.6

Expiration	No. of contracts in effect	
	7/16/87	7/16/91
July	4,168	2,751
September	46,273	15,421
December	24,533	6,484
March	5,898	1,958
May	1,128	1,364
July	582	1,150
December	241	568

As can be seen, there is a substantial variation in the number of contracts sold between the two dates, especially in 60-day and six-month contracts. It should be mentioned that in COMEX, the volume of each copper contract is 25,000 lbs. The contracts with the highest liquidity are those with maturities of three and six months.

In order to study how to stabilize copper export earnings, a case of particular interest to Chile, only futures and not forwards will be considered. In any case, the prices of both contracts are practically equal—and the equality is strict, if interest rates are deterministic (Duffie, 1989).

As indicated, not only do futures markets enable economic agents to protect themselves from the effects of unanticipated price fluctuations, they also provide opportunities for speculation. However, our interest centers on the insurance role played by futures. Typically, this is accomplished by taking opposing positions in the spot and futures markets. To illustrate the mechanism whereby futures contracts stabilize a producer's earnings, for example, we shall use a simple model that assumes that consumers do not speculate on the futures market (McKinnon, 1967; and Newbery and Stiglitz, 1985). We shall assume that the producer produces a good $q = \overline{q}\theta$, where $\overline{q}$ is the expected production and θ a multiplicative error, with $E\theta = 1$ and Var $\theta = \sigma^2$ (which makes the coefficient of variation in production equal to σ).

We assume that the producer covers himself by selling a quantity h on the futures market. Thus, his uncertain earnings are expressed as:

$$y = p\overline{q}\theta + (f - p)h,$$ (14)

where p is the price at which the producer can sell his product on the spot market at the end of the period and f is the future price known now. We shall assume that $p = \overline{p}\Phi$, where $\overline{p}$ is the expected price at the end of the period and Φ is a multiplicative error ($E\Phi = 1$ and Var $\Phi = \sigma_p^2$, which makes the coefficient of variation in prices be σ_p) The producer's problem is to maximize his expected profits with respect to h. As is well known, the mean-variance approach is valid if the utility function has a coefficient of absolute risk aversion A that is constant. If, moreover, we assume that the errors θ and Φ follow a bivariate normal distribution, then the problem is equivalent to maximizing (Newbery and Stiglitz, 1985):

$$W = E(y) - \frac{1}{2}A\,Var(y).$$ (15)

From the first order condition, it follows that the optimal volume to be sold on the futures market is:

$$h = \frac{f - \overline{p}}{A\,Var(p)} + \frac{\overline{q}\,Cov(p, p\theta)}{Var(p)},$$ (16)

where A is the coefficient of absolute risk aversion $(-u''(R)/u'(R))$, R is the initial wealth of the producer, and $u(\ )$ the utility function. Equation (16) shows how the optimal hedge breaks down into a purely speculative component, which disappears in an unbiased futures market $(f = \overline{p})$, and a hedging component, which depends solely on the covariance of income not covered with the price. The difference $\overline{p} - f$ is called "normal backwardation" (a term attributable to Keynes), and in our theory, it is simply a risk premium. It should be borne in mind that these results represent a simplification of the futures markets.

If we assume that r is the correlation coefficient between the price and volume q, it can be shown that (Newbery and Stiglitz, 1985):

$$h = \overline{q}(1 + r\sigma / \sigma_p) + \frac{f - \overline{p}}{A\overline{p}^2 \sigma_p^2}. \tag{17}$$

This result generalizes the reasoning advanced in Chapter I, that if the price is the only source of risk when output is certain and the futures market is unbiased, the producer will sell all of his output on the futures market. Another interesting case occurs when there is uncertainty both in the price and in output, $r = -1$, the futures market is unbiased, and the elasticity of demand is $\varepsilon (= \sigma / \sigma_p)$; then:

$$h = \overline{q}(1 - \varepsilon). \tag{18}$$

If the elasticity is $\varepsilon = 1$, the producer will be perfectly covered and will sell nothing on the futures market. It should be stressed, however, that this result (18) corresponds to a very special case, seldom encountered in practice. Moreover, the condition of an unbiased market is not realistic, either; nevertheless, these assumptions make it possible to obtain results under ideal conditions, which serve as a benchmark for real-life situations.

In this example, the producers are the ones who cover themselves; however, consumers can also do the same by buying on the futures market. The exception to this rule is the final consumers, since, unlike producers, their consumption is diversified in various products.

Returning to our previous example, we can calculate the ratio between the income risk of the producer, measured as the variance in his earnings, with and without futures transactions. For this, the variance of expression (14) can be taken, and, assuming an unbiased market, it gives the following result:

$$Var(y^f) = \overline{q}^2 \left[Var(p\theta) - Cov^2(p, p\theta) / Var(p) \right]. \tag{19}$$

Without trading on the futures market, the risk in income is:

$$Var\, y = \overline{q}^2 Var(p\theta). \tag{20}$$

The ratio between (19) and (20) is:

$$\frac{Var\, y^f}{Var\, y} = 1 - \lambda^2. \tag{21}$$

where λ is the correlation coefficient between the price and the unhedged income. If we consider a simple case in which $r = 0$ (the correlation between the price and the volume), this expression is simplified to (Newbery and Stiglitz, 1985):

$$\frac{Var\ y^f}{Var\ y} = \frac{1}{1 + 1/\varepsilon^2\left(1 + \sigma_p^2\right)}. \tag{22}$$

This means that if the demand elasticity is approximately equal to one (which is the case for Chilean copper), then the producer cuts his risk in half simply by selling on the futures market.

Futures Contracts as Price Stabilization Mechanisms

It has been amply documented that, with the possible exception of oil (Gardner, 1989), stabilizing the prices of raw materials by means of international agreements has not been successful. It has been postulated that, when it is impossible to stabilize consumption, for example, through credits and loans or through stabilization funds, then it is possible to stabilize income partially, therefore reducing the need to smooth consumption vis-à-vis income. If the reason behind fluctuations in export income is the price instability of the export good, then international price stabilization would seem an attractive means of stabilizing earnings. The problem with this approach is that it lowers the average price of the commodity and, more importantly, export earnings (Newbery and Stiglitz, 1985; Williams and Wright, 1992) This is why a country that seeks to stabilize variations in export earnings resulting from high price volatility should resort to strategies that employ the futures or forwards markets or other types of financial instruments. For the time being, we shall deal with the futures markets.

To see what role the futures markets can play in stabilizing export earnings, we shall proceed along the lines developed by Kletzer, Newbery, and Wright (1990). Let us consider the following notation:

p_t = the cash price or spot price of copper in period t,
F_{tj} = the future price for period t, in period j,
b_t = $p_t - F_{t,t}$: the contemporary base in period t,
f_t = $F_{t,t-1}$: the future price at the start of period t,
$f_{t+1} - f_t$ = the intertemporal base.

In the literature on futures markets, the base risk refers to two different types of risk that a producer undertakes: the contemporary base risk and the intertemporal base risk. The first occurs when a producer who has sold futures contracts to cover his production liquidates his position, repurchasing the contracts at maturity, and then sells on the physical market. The risk materializes because the spot price at maturity and the futures price on that same day are not necessarily equal (there may be differences in the quality of the product, transportation costs, etc.). Countries that export raw materials generally do not encounter this kind of risk. However, they do have to face the second kind, as we shall see below. Thus, in what follows $b_t = 0$ ($p_t = F_{t,t}$). The following notation shall be used: $Ex_t = E_{t-1}x_t$ and, in addition, an unbiased futures market ($f_t = E_{t-1}p_t$) shall be assumed.

In the example below, it is important to specify which type of serial correlation the price of the export good—in this case, copper—exhibits. There is sufficient evidence to indicate that copper prices follow what is known as a random-walk process. This was detected by using a periodicity of weekly, monthly, and quarterly prices. If annual prices are employed, only a slight discrepancy is detected concerning the random walk hypothesis—which reinforces the idea that this hypothesis is fairly reasonable (Basch, 1992). The prices were taken at the close of each period in question and deflated with the U.S. Wholesale Price Index (copper prices are from New York's COMEX exchange). Thus, we have:

$$p_t = p_{t-1} + u_t, \qquad (23)$$

where u_t is an independent and identically distributed process, with a mean of zero and a variance σ_u. The equation can also be expressed as

$$p_t = f_t + u_t ; \ f_t = p_{t-1}. \qquad (24)$$

We shall assume that f_t is the spot price anticipated for the close of period t, with information available up to the beginning of this period. In an unbiased futures market, f_t corresponds to the future price observed at the start of t. What is referred to as the intertemporal base risk is $f_{t+1} - f_t = p_t - p_{t-1} = u_t$, and it can fluctuate considerably from period to period. In general, it is not possible to hedge entirely against this base risk, but as we shall see, the risk can be significantly lowered. Even in the case in which the futures markets have a maximum horizon of one year, for example, an insurance strategy can be designed that allows the producer to hedge for longer periods, implementing what is known as a sequential securities strategy (rollover hedging).

Rollover hedging works by selling more futures contracts than are needed for a hedge of a single period and then using the difference to finance transactions for the subsequent period. Obviously, this does not produce a perfect guarantee, since the amount to be hedged within two periods will depend on the production at the time, which in turn will depend on the next futures price—something that is unknown at the beginning. Nevertheless, as seen in section one, the costs associated with price instability increase directly with the square of the coefficient of variation of export earnings. By lowering the risk by a certain fraction, the costs of the risk are reduced by a larger fraction.

To illustrate the benefits entailed in a strategy of rollover hedging, we consider a producer whose earnings are:

$$y = pq - \frac{1}{2}cq^2, \tag{25}$$

and who, moreover, has a coefficient of absolute risk aversion A that is constant. Coefficient c reveals that the costs are quadratic in q. Although the costs are considered quadratic, which is somewhat arbitrary, the results obtained will not differ essentially from those that would have been obtained had another cost specification been assumed. It can be shown (Kletzer, Newbery, and Wright, 1990), that the producer maximizes his utility, producing

$$q = \frac{\overline{p}}{c\varphi}, \qquad \varphi = 1 + 2R\sigma_p^2, \qquad R = \frac{A\overline{p}^2}{2c}, \tag{26}$$

where R is the coefficient of relative risk aversion and σ_p is the coefficient of variation of the price p. It can be seen that the effect of perfectly stabilizing the price implies $\sigma_p = 0$, and thus, changing φ to 1. If the producer is able to sell unbiased futures contracts (an assumption that simplifies the discussion), he will be able to bring about perfect price stabilization by selling q futures contracts. The value of this strategy for the producer, in terms of the increment in the assured equivalent income generated, is $2R\sigma_p^2$. Now, if we assume that we have an unbiased futures market and that the producer faces the problem of a horizon of two periods (two years, for example), the producer has two alternatives for protecting himself against the risk involved. The first is to sell his production $q \ (= \overline{p}/c)$ on the futures market at the beginning of the first year and later to do the same thing at the beginning of the second year. The present value of the of the producer's certainty-equivalent utility, ignoring terms in σ_p that are greater than σ_p^2, is expressed by:

$$V = \frac{\overline{p}^2}{2c}\left\{1 + \beta(1 + \sigma_p^2) - 2R\beta^2\sigma_p^2\right\}, \tag{27}$$

where β is the time discount factor.

The second strategy, rollover hedging, consists of selling $2q$ futures contracts at the beginning of the first period and then q contracts at the beginning of the second. Naturally, the contracts are liquidated at maturity. The expression equivalent to (27) is:

$$V = \frac{\overline{p}^2}{2c}\left(1 + \beta\left(1 + \sigma_p^2\right)\right). \tag{28}$$

The advantage of the second strategy over the first is approximately 19 percent, if reasonable values for Chile of $\beta = 0.9$, $\sigma_p^2 = 0.1$, and $R = 2$ are assumed. Furthermore, the advantage of this same strategy over not using the futures market is 120 percent. These gains, in terms of the certainty-equivalent utility, are due mainly to sharp reductions in the earnings variance. It can be seen that the reduction, in terms of variance between the two insurance strategies (ignoring terms in σ_p greater than σ_p^2) is:

$$\Delta Var = q^2 \beta^2 Var(p). \tag{29}$$

In addition the reduction, in terms of the earnings variance, between not using the futures markets and employing the first strategy of selling simple contracts is proportional to σ_p^4—that is, very small. Therefore, it becomes highly attractive to resort to the futures markets when employing the rule of rollover hedging.

This same concept can be extended to the case of n periods. That is, the idea is to now sell nq_t on the futures markets at the start of period t, when production q_t is constant. Then, in period $t+1$, these contracts are liquidated, q_t is sold on the spot market, and contracts are sold again this time for $(n-1)q_t$. This process is then repeated until period $t+n$. It is possible to insure oneself for a long-term horizon, but this would incur higher transaction costs. Kletzer, Newbery, and Wright (1990) derive a formula for the value of the marginal benefit for each additional contract. It should be taken into account that as the number of contracts sold increases, future transaction costs rise, as do the benefits from risk reduction. Specifically, the ratio between the marginal benefit and cost of extending the period of coverage from $n-1$ to n is:

$$\frac{\beta^{n+1} R \sigma_p^2}{(1+\beta)\mu}, \tag{30}$$

where μ represents the cost of each additional futures contract. Clearly, the marginal benefit diminishes as the horizon of coverage lengthens.

If we consider a situation in which $R = 1$, $\sigma_p^2 = 0.1$, $\beta = 0.9$, and $\mu = 0.003$ (Gardner, 1989), then the number of quarterly contracts that a producer like Chile would have to sell for a given fixed quarterly output (assuming that there is no risk in the level produced) is $n = 26$. This implies that the optimal strategy for a country like Chile consists of selling 26 times a given quarterly output on the futures market. The rollover cycle would be completed after 6.5 years. Naturally, this limits the amount of copper that Chile can insure in the futures markets, for if we assume a liquidity on the order of 45,000 contracts in three-month futures for New York's COMEX market, then Chile will be able to cover only approximately 20,000 tons (8 percent of its quarterly production).

Similarly, if we consider the London Metal Exchange, with a liquidity of 140,000 tons of copper in three-month contracts daily, we can cover roughly 5,380 tons a day, which represents a total of 336,260 tons a quarter (Chile's output during this period is approximately 250,000 tons). Chile alone, therefore, would corner (or nearly corner) these markets in this type of transaction, making it unfeasible to insure 100 percent of its production. All of this in addition to the fact that were Chile to embark on this strategy, it would seriously affect international copper prices, thus invalidating the above reasoning. The actual amount that Chile could cover in this fashion in a given period is clearly inferior to its output during that period.

One last aspect of caution should be mentioned. If the exporting country faces certain restrictions on international credits, sequential hedging operations become riskier. This is because futures contracts require a daily margin of guarantee to ensure that contracts are met. Since these contracts are for large volumes, there is a risk of noncompliance should the country be faced with credit rationing. Naturally, this risk diminishes as the amounts sold on the futures market also diminish. In the particular case of Chile, the bulk of copper exports is in the hands of CODELCO (a state enterprise), an institution so solvent in the eyes of international creditors that the regulatory agencies of the futures markets do not require it to pay the daily margin. Obviously, CODELCO does not sell futures volumes as large as would be required in an optimal rollover scheme.

Historical Price Simulations [67]

It is interesting to run a simulation exercise based on historical prices to determine the effectiveness of a sequential rollover strategy for the sale of futures. The idea is to use three-month futures contracts on the London Metal Exchange, initially selling four of these futures contracts for some nominal volume (in this exercise, one pound of copper), later to pay them at the end of a quarter. A pound of copper is simultaneously sold on the spot market (this could hypothetically become the quarterly production of copper), and three contracts are again sold, also to be settled at the close of a quarter. This procedure is repeated until the last quarter, when one futures contract is canceled and one pound of copper is sold on the spot market. The net flows at the end of each quarter are then added up algebraically, without taking into account the interest rate or the commissions paid for the futures transactions.

---

[67] This part is taken from the master's thesis "Alternativas para estabilizar los retornos de divisas en Chile: el uso de bonos ligados a bienes primarios," by Héctor López M., for the degree of Master of Industrial Civil Engineering from the University of Chile.

The total flow is contrasted with what would be obtained if only the spot price were used—that is, if the four pounds of copper were sold at the spot price observed in the market. This gives us the following table for this strategy:

Table 2.7

Quarter	Flow with Futures	Flow without Futures
1	$4(F_{0,1} - p_1) + p_1$	p_1
2	$3(F_{1,2} - p_2) + p_2$	p_2
3	$2(F_{2,3} - p_3) + p_3$	p_3
4	$1(F_{3,4} - p_4) + p_4$	p_4

where $F_{t,t+1}$ is the futures price observed at the start of period $t+1$ (the end of period t) for the price of copper at the end of $t+1$—that is, at the end of quarter $t+1$; p_t is the spot price observed at the end of quarter t; and $(F_{t,t+1} - p_{t+1})$ is the contemporary base observed in the market at the end of period $t+1$. This strategy begins in March 1976 and is continued over the next 13 years, ending in March 1989. The cumulative flows for each year appear in Table 2.8, as do the means, variances, and the quotients of both the means and the variances.

According to Table 2.8, under the futures rollover strategy, the variance declines by 64 percent and the mean of the total flows declines by 5 percent. The 5-percent decrease in the level of the means is the cost of stabilizing export earnings by 64 percent with respect to their original levels. Although it is not trivial to establish a simple relationship between the flows with and without rollover, it can be seen that the greatest discrepancies between them (observed in 1987 and 1988) occurred when copper prices, which had been at a rather depressed level, sharply increased.

Commodity-linked Bonds

As previously discussed, futures markets have two disadvantages: the length of the contracts is very short (the maximum length is currently around two years), and the contracts most frequently traded are generally not liquid enough to allow Chile to cover a significant portion of its copper export earnings. In view of this, issuing copper bonds—that is, bonds linked to copper—appears to be an alternative worthy of consideration.

A copper bond is similar to a zero-coupon bond (a pure discount bond), for it promises the delivery of a given quantity of copper to the purchaser of the

Table 2.8

Year	Flow with Rollover	Flow without Rollover
1976	383.0	311.2
1977	296.7	284.2
1978	322.1	389.1
1979	422.7	494.1
1980	499.9	430.5
1981	428.8	366.5
1982	344.6	363.8
1983	406.4	328.0
1984	312.8	321.5
1985	336.4	319.5
1986	305.8	326.5
1987	330.1	474.5
1988	405.4	649.2
Mean	368.8	389.1
Variance	3,688.9	10,244.1
Quotient between Variances	0.36	
Quotient between Means	0.95	

instrument (strictly speaking, it promises the monetary equivalent of the basket of copper at the copper price at maturity). More interesting for our purposes of stabilizing earnings are bonds linked to the price of copper. These are bonds whose final value (principal) or interest payments are denominated in units of copper (or the final value of some appropriate futures contract). Thus, for example, a country might float a bond that pays an amount equivalent to 10 tons of copper in December futures contracts every year for 10 years, with a final payment of 25 contracts, all for an initial payment of US$750,000. The buyer of this type of instrument typically has the option of receiving its par value, or the basket of copper in this case. This copper bond therefore includes an option to buy (a "call" option, in the options jargon) for the purchaser (Cox and Rubinstein, 1985). A case of a bond linked to copper that has actually been implemented is one in which the payments of interest and principal are made in equal installments, where the value of each installment is linked to the monetary equivalent of a certain basket of copper.

This type of instrument has a long history. As far back as 1863, the

Confederate States floated bonds payable in cotton (O'Hara, 1984). In 1945, the French government used bonds indexed to the cost of electric energy to compensate for the nationalization of its electricity providers. Later, in 1973, France issued a gold bond (the Giscard) in the amount of US$1.5 billion. Recently, there have been bonds payable in silver (Sunshine Mining), gold (Peggold), oil (Standard Oil Company), and coal (Semirara Coal Corporation of the Philippines). In 1989, a private Mexican company issued copper bonds with a 38-month maturity to the Banque Paribas. Finally, it is interesting to point out that in Chile, there was a bond issue backed by gold to finance the La Coipa gold mining project through the Chase Manhattan Bank.

With respect to bonds linked to commodities and futures, it should be emphasized that these mechanisms can be utilized by both private and public agents. However, the previous discussion of stabilization funds refers mainly to fiscal revenues, which, of course, include the taxes paid by private copper producers.

Copper Bonds in Light of Sovereign Risk

To simplify the treatment of copper bonds, we shall assume that they are pure discount instruments for a single period (zero-coupon bonds), which at maturity pay a given basket of copper or its monetary equivalent. We shall also assume that the buyer of these bonds is a competitive agent who is risk neutral. To open the discussion, let us assume that there is no risk of default.

In this scenario with the further assumption that these instruments can be issued indefinitely, at the present value of their expected price at the close of the period, copper bonds have the same insurance characteristics as optimal futures contracts with the same price. If we have the situation in which: (1) copper exports represent approximately 45 percent of total exports, on average; (2) the coefficient of variation of the output and of the price of copper are both 30 percent; and (3) we assume that the correlation between the price and the output is zero then through ratio (22) we have $Var\, y\, (b.c.)/Var\, y = 0.52$, where $Var\, y\, (b.c.)$ corresponds to the variance in earnings when copper bonds are issued. If there are no other mechanisms to stabilize earnings, copper bonds will cut the annual cost of risk nearly by half; this, as we have said, is the amount that consumers are willing to pay for stable consumption. In the case in which only price uncertainty is present but the coefficient of variation of earnings remains the same, earnings are completely stabilized ($Var\, y\, (b.c.) = 0$). Thus, in this latter scheme, the stream of earnings (which we are assuming to be equal to the stream of consumption in each year) can be completely stabilized by selling copper bonds for the entire output (which is assumed to entail no risk). Thus, the country attains constant earnings and consumption, passing any difference deriving from copper price variability to the creditor (Wright and Newbery, 1989).

In this simplified illustration, in which only demand risk (copper price uncertainty) is present, it remains to be analyzed which factors motivate the debtor country to fulfill its end of the agreement when issuing copper bonds. In other words, it would be interesting to know what conditions would produce a situation of default in the long term. It is clear that when the price of copper is depressed, there are fewer incentives not to pay, for it is the issuing country that benefits in this case. However, in the reverse situation when prices are high, what is not gained is $y_t - \bar{y}$, where y_t is the income that the country would have received without the copper bonds and $\bar{y}$ is the stabilized income. Therefore, what must be compared is $(y_t - \bar{y},)$ plus the present value of expected future consumption without the issue of bonds, and the present value of expected future consumption with the issue of bonds. If the first figure is greater than the second, then there will be incentives not to pay.

It should be mentioned that there is a radical difference between a loan granted to an enterprise or an individual and a loan granted to a country: the creditor of the sovereign country does not have at his disposal the necessary guarantee for the credit, since the assets of the debtor country are within that country's borders (Keynes, 1924; Eaton and Gersovitz, 1981). This is why country risk or sovereign risk merits special treatment. The literature mentions three mechanisms that creditors can employ to compensate for the lack of adequate guarantees for their credits. The first is the immediate suspension of additional loans from the moment the country fails to meet its obligations; the second is intervention by force in the debtor country; and the third is interference in the trade of the country in arrears.

To see what happens when a country issues bonds backed by some raw material, let us consider the case above in which the only risk is from the demand side, with the product set at $\bar{q}$. Let us assume that price p has a multiplicative error $\varnothing$ ($p = \bar{p}\varnothing$), such that $\varnothing$ can take two values: $\varnothing = \pm v$, each with a probability of 1/2. Hence, the coefficients of variation of prices and earnings are equal to v. We shall assume, moreover, that the utility function of the debtor country is quadratic in earnings, and that $\bar{y}$ (equal to the expected consumption for each period) and $\bar{p}$ are normalized to 1. Thus, as stated in the first section, the annual cost of the risk of stabilizing consumption is exactly equal to $Rv^2/2$. Its present value is simply $Rv^2/(2\delta)$, where δ is the time preference rate.

Let us consider now the situation in which a fraction $(1 - \alpha)$ of the output $(0 < \alpha < 1)$ is allocated to cover the payment of a copper bond issued in the previous period. Here, the consumption of each period is being financed through the placement of copper bonds and that fraction of output α that does not go toward payment of these bonds. In a case where $\varnothing = 1 + v$, there will be incentives not to honor the debt contracted. Consumption for the period, should the debt contracted in the previous period be paid, is $[(1-\alpha)/(1+\delta)+\alpha(1+v)]$. This must be contrasted with the consumption that would be obtained in a situation of default: $1+v$. The differential represents the temptation not to pay; it is approximately equal to $v(1-\alpha)$. The default situation is the decision that maximizes the expected utility of the country, if this amount happens to be greater than the present value of the additional cost of the implied risk. If the bonds cover a fraction $1-\alpha$ of output, then the risky part of output corresponds to a fraction α of it, and the coefficient of variation of earnings is equal to αv. This makes the difference equal to $Rv^2(1-\alpha^2)/2$. Default is produced when $\delta > Rv(1-\alpha)/2$. Hence, it can be inferred that complete insurance ($\alpha = 0$) is feasible only if $\delta < Rv/2$, and moreover, that a necessary condition for a partial insurance is that $\delta < Rv$. Therefore, to the degree that the coefficient of variation of earnings v, R, and the fraction α not covered tend to increase, the discount rate δ that produces the condition of default will increase accordingly (Kletzer, Newbery, and Wright, 1990).

Dynamic Stabilization Strategies with Bonds Linked to Copper

It is interesting to examine how the ideas described above can be implemented to stabilize a country's earnings. The following simple example is taken from Kletzer, Newbery, and Wright (1990) and involves a country whose earnings are derived entirely from the exports of a single product. Furthermore, there is considered to be no uncertainty in production, and the only income uncertainty is attributable to prices. These are assumed to have a multiplicative error $\varnothing(p = \bar{p}\varnothing)$, such that $E\varnothing = 1$ and $Var\varnothing = \sigma_p^2$ and, moreover, are independent and identically distributed over time (these assumptions are strong, but simplify the discussion). In addition, consumption in this country is considered to be equal to the mean value of output discounted one period. The following strategy can thus be implemented, beginning in period 0, where income is y_0: first, invest the amount βy_0, where $\beta = 1/(1+r)$, and r is the interest rate (assumed to be equal to the investment yield), which is assumed constant for all periods; then place a pure bond (backed by the commodity that the country exports) for the value of the entire output, at a price $\beta \bar{y}$. This is how an even consumption level for all periods of $r\beta y_0 + \beta \bar{y}$ is attained that is independent of the future price values of the export product.

This simple, but intuitive, result can be extended to the case of a country experiencing credit difficulties that is forced to float this type of bond to finance the costs of producing its only export product. The country is assumed to lack access to the futures markets, for any of the reasons previously outlined. Pure bonds (that do not pay coupons) are issued that mature at the time output is realized. The obligation of the issuing country is to pay the creditor the price of the good when the instrument matures. Let us suppose that the profit to the country after one period is π, B is the price of the bond at the time of issue, Q the number of bonds issued, q the volume produced after one period, and finally, $c(q)$ the cost function. Thus, the profit (which is a random variable because the price is) at the end of one period is expressed by

$$\pi = (1+r)(QB - c(q)) + p(q - Q). \tag{31}$$

That the funds obtained by issuing bonds should be greater than or equal to production costs is implicit; any difference is invested at a risk-free interest rate r. Furthermore, it is assumed that the issuing country pays the creditor a higher premium for the anticipated risk than the risk-free rate r. Specifically, it is postulated that:

$$\frac{\overline{p}}{B} > (1+r). \tag{32}$$

Hence, the mean and the standard deviation of the country's net earnings are expressed by:

$$u = (1+r)(QB - c(q)) + \overline{p}(q - Q), \tag{33}$$

$$\sigma = |q - Q|\sigma_p.$$

If we assume that the volume produced is fixed and the bonds cover the entire production $(Q = q)$, then

$$u = (1+r)(QB - c(q)), \tag{34}$$

$$\sigma = 0.$$

This outcome can be replicated for all periods, resulting in the same consumption indefinitely, as in our earlier example. Ball and Myers (1991)[68] show how to analyze various alternatives for the maximization of the anticipated utility in this context, using different combinations of q and Q. Basically, they perform a graphic analysis in a mean-standard deviation space. They show that if the producer is very risk averse and the risk premium on the bond price is not very high, then $q = Q$ and the producer is completely covered. To the degree that the level of risk aversion falls and the risk premium rises, Q

---

[68] Based on the results of Meyer (1987).

decreases. Finally, if the risk premium is high enough and the producer is not too risk averse, then $Q = 0$ as long as there is the possibility of incurring debt through conventional means.

In both examples, it is assumed that it is possible to invest at a fixed rate and place bonds backed by primary commodities. It should be noted that if the funds invested at the risk-free interest rate can be used as a guarantee, it becomes much easier to place the bonds in the country where the deposit is made.

After examining cases in which a complete stabilization of the country's export earnings, and thus consumption, can be achieved, the question arises of what happens if there is a possibility of noncompliance on the part of the debtor country. The answer is that complete stabilization cannot be achieved through the issue of this type of bond. Furthermore, Kletzer, Newbery, and Wright (1990) show that when the default constraint is binding, other stabilization mechanisms, such as the sale of forwards or futures, or simply resorting to the credit markets to solicit a loan, must also be discarded for these ends.

To respond to the question of which contract would permit an optimal stabilization of earnings (stabilization of consumption in the case in which earnings are derived solely from exports), we shall follow the approach of Worral (1987) and Kletzer (1988) when the default constraint is binding. Here, it is assumed that the prices of the export good in any period can take one of the values in a discrete set of prices: $p_t(s) = p(s)$, with $p(1) < p(2) < ... < p(S)$. Thus, the country's earnings are $y(s) = p(s)q$, $s = 1,2...S$. According to Worral the optimal contract should depend in some way on the price of the export good and on the scheduled payments of a credit b_t. These would be agreed upon in each period and would depend on the observed price in $t+1$. These payments are denoted by $M_{t,s} = M\big(y_t - m_t; p_{t+1}(s)\big)$, where y_t, m_t are the levels of earnings (at the observed price p_t) and the debt payment in period t, respectively; b_t and $M_{t,s}$ are calculated through dynamic programming, where the function to optimize is V:

$$V\big(y_t - m_t\big) = Max\Big\{u\big(y_t - m_t + b_t\big) + E\big[V\big(y(s) - M_{t,s}\big)\big]\big/(1+r)\Big\}. \quad (35)$$

Function V should be maximized by finding a debt level, and its payment function, subject to the constraint that the debtor country does not wish to fall into arrears under any circumstances, since this would imply having no access to credit in the future. This restriction is the constraint of perpetual nonarrears:

$$V\big(y(s) - M_{t,s}\big) \ge u\big(y(s)\big) + E\big[U(y)\big]\big/r. \quad (36)$$

where r is the risk-free rate that we are assuming to be equal to the time preference rate δ, u, the utility function of period t, and U the utility function of the remaining periods. Another constraint that debt b_t should satisfy is that there should be no opportunities for arbitrage for risk-neutral creditors:

$$b_t = E\left(M_{t,s}\right)\big/(1+r). \tag{37}$$

The first order condition is expressed by (Kuhn-Tucker):

$$u'(c_t) = \left(1+\mu_s\right)V'\left(y(s) - M_{t,s}\right), \; s = 1, 2, .., S. \tag{38}$$

where $c_t = y_t + b_t - m_t$ is the consumption in t and μ_s is proportional to the Lagrange multiplier corresponding to the default constraint in situation s. Obviously, μ_s is zero if the constraint is not binding.

Worrall (1987) demonstrates that the solution to this problem consists of an optimal debt and a payments function such that they establish a lower limit to the net earnings of the next period, $y(s) - M_{t,s}$, equal to the net earnings of period $t, y_t - m_t$. The payments function for higher earnings satisfies constraint (36) with strict equality holding. Consumption $y(s) + b_{t+1} - M_{t,s}$ is also found to increase with $y(s)$.

A concrete way of implementing Worrall's dynamic programming is through a scheme in which Chile issues (pure) copper bonds for a single period. Actually, the creditor issues a credit b_t to Chile and sells the country a put option that covers a fixed quantity of copper q_f, to be paid in $t+1$, with a striking price agreed to at t equal to

$$K_{pt} = \left(y_t - m_t + b_t(1+r) + Z_{pt}\right)\big/q_f. \tag{39}$$

It should be noted that a "put" is an option that gives the right to sell a certain product at a certain predetermined price (striking price) on a certain date (Cox and Rubinstein, 1985). The value of the put at t, called the put price, is paid by Chile in the period $t+1$, when the option is exercised or expires. This price is obtained through the condition that the creditor cannot perform any arbitrage:

$$Z_{pt} = E\left[Max\left(K_{pt} - p_{t+1}, 0\right)\right]. \tag{40}$$

A zero coupon copper bond that has a horizon of a single period and whose payment may be effected by means of a given basket of copper (q_f), or its monetary equivalent (as the issuer of the bond—in this case, Chile—so chooses), is equivalent to the flows that would be produced in a case in which a creditor sells Chile a put option and also grants it a loan b_t at the risk-free interest rate r.

In the following period $t+1$, if the situation s produced is such that $p_{t+1} < K_{pt}$ then Chile exercises its option to sell, delivering a volume q_f of copper at the striking price, or performing an equivalent monetary transaction. Thus, Chile will receive a net yield of $K_{pt}q_f - b_t(1+r) - Z_{pt}$, and the creditor receives $m_{t+1} = M_{t,s} = y(s) - y_t + m_t$, which is also equal to:

$$m_{t+1} = q_f\left(p_{t+1} - K_{pt}\right) + b_t(1+r) + Z_{pt}. \tag{41}$$

It should be noted that this quantity may also be negative, since $p_{t+1} < K_{pt}$. In this situation, it happens that Chile's net earnings in $t+1$ are equal to those it received in t, that is:

$$y_{t+1} - m_{t+1} = y_t - m_t. \tag{42}$$

Thus, Chile would again replicate the strategy for period $t+1$, in terms of the credit b_t and the put option that it implemented in t.

In addition, if the price in $t+1$ is such that $p_{t+1} \geq K_{pt}$, then the put option expires without being exercised, and Chile has to pay the creditor the sum expressed by $m_{t+1} = b_t(1+r) + Z_{pt}$, which is always positive. In this case, q_f is sold on the market at the price p_{t+1}, such that the net earnings are:

$$y(s) - m_{t+1} = q_f\left(p_{t+1} - K_{pt}\right) + \left(y_t - m_t\right) > y_t - m_t. \tag{43}$$

In period $t+1$, the process is repeated, but now a loan b_{t+1}, which is smaller than b$_t$, is solicited, and a put is bought at a price $Z_{p,t+1}$, with a striking price $K_{p,t+1}$ greater than K_{pt} to raise the floor for minimum net earnings to $y_{t+1} - m_{t+1}$ (greater than the net earnings in t). Through this mechanism, a substantial stabilization of Chile's net earnings and, hence, consumption is achieved. Moreover, consumption is always growing. This type of instrument is different from other observed versions of commodity bonds, in which the option to receive either the basket of goods or the monetary value is held by the creditor and not the debtor. In the case in which Chile buys a put option, the risk posed by low copper prices is reduced, with a high proportion of the favorable outcomes in prices being maintained.

The analysis described above can be broadened to include another factor that would make the stabilization program more attractive to creditor and debtor alike. It basically consists of allowing the debtor country to help finance both the purchase of a put option and the debt service not linked to the primary good by selling the creditor a call option (Cox and Rubinstein, 1985). This is an instrument that grants the right to buy a certain good at a predetermined price (the striking price) in a set period of time. If the debtor country structures its debt linked to the primary good to contain a call option for the creditor, both creditor and debtor can share the benefits of an increase in the price of the raw material. This call option, naturally, has a value, called the premium (Z_{ct}), which will allow the initial cost of the debt to be reduced. An instrument of this type, which consists of a credit and two options—the purchase of a put and the sale of a call—is known in the literature as a collar (Hull, 1989). We shall see that when a copper bond includes a collar, there is greater stabilization of the country's net earnings than in the case above, furthermore, allowing the creditor to share the benefits of possible copper price increases with Chile.

This new financing scheme for Chile could function as follows. In period t, the creditor grants a credit b_t at the risk-free interest rate r, sells Chile a put option at Z_{pt} and buys a call option at Z_{ct}. Both operations are on a volume q_f of copper. It shall be assumed that Z_{pt} and Z_{ct} will be paid in $t+1$, when these options expire. The striking price of these put and call options would be, respectively:

$$K_{pt} = \left(y_t - m_t + b_t(1+r) + Z_{pt} - Z_{ct} \right) / q_f,$$ (44)

$$K_{ct} = \left(\alpha(y_t - m_t) + b_t(1+r) + Z_{pt} - Z_{ct} \right) / q_f,$$

where $\alpha > 1$. Prices Z_{pt} and Z_{ct} are determined by the condition that arbitrage cannot be carried out with these instruments:

$$Z_{pt} = E\left[Max(K_{pt} - p_{t+1}, 0) \right],$$ (45)

$$Z_{ct} = E\left[Max(p_{t+1} - K_{ct}, 0) \right].$$

In period $t+1$, the situation s may be such that there are three mutually exclusive alternatives for the price of copper:

$$p_{t+1} \le K_{pt}.$$ (i)

In this case, the put option is exercised and the call is not. The debtor country delivers q_f, or equivalent transactions, in exchange for K_{pt}, and pays a net sum of $b_t(1+r) + Z_{pt} - Z_{ct}$. The net earnings received by Chile are:

$$K_{pt} q_f - b_t(1+r) - Z_{pt} + Z_{ct} = y_t - m_t,$$ (46)

and the payment received by the creditor is $m_{t+1} = y(s) - (y_t - m_t)$, which is also equal to:

$$m_{t+1} = q_f(p_{t+1} - K_{pt}) + b_t(1+r) + Z_{pt} - Z_{ct},$$ (47)

which hypothetically could be negative.

$$p_{t+1} \geq K_{ct} \tag{ii}$$

Here, the opposite of (i) occurs: the call is exercised and the put is not. The creditor exercises his right to buy the volume q_f of copper at K_{ct}. Chile receives a net return of:

$$K_{ct}q_f - b_t(1+r) - Z_{pt} + Z_{ct} = \alpha(y_t - m_t), \tag{48}$$

and the creditor receives a payment of $m_{t+1} = y(s) - \alpha(y_t - m_t)$ which is also equal to:

$$m_{t+1} = q_f(p_{t+1} - K_{ct}) + b_t(1+r) + Z_{pt} - Z_{ct}. \tag{49}$$

It can be shown that this quantity is always positive.

$$K_{pt} < p_{t+1} < K_{ct}. \tag{iii}$$

In this case, both options expire without being exercised. Chile sells q_f on the market, obtaining net earnings of

$$q_f p_{t+1} - b_t(1+r) - Z_{pt} + Z_{ct}, \tag{50}$$

and pays the creditor the net sum of

$$m_{t+1} = b_t(1+r) + Z_{pt} - Z_{ct}. \tag{51}$$

As in the above case, in which Chile purchased a put option, this mechanism can be replicated in period $t+1$, so as to raise the minimum net earnings to $y_{t+1} - m_{t+1}$, when this latter quantity is greater than $y_t - m_t$. It is interesting to note, in this case, that Chile's net earnings are bounded on the upper end by $\alpha(y_t - m_t)$ and on the lower by $(y_t - m_t)$ in period $t+1$.

These last results can also be depicted graphically. Given that Chile's net earnings were $(y_t - m_t)$ in period t, they correspond to Figure 2.6 in period $t+1$.

If this instrument is replicated under identical conditions over time (sequential rollover), without altering the lower and upper boundaries, something similar to Figure 2.7 will be obtained, where the continuous dotted lines represent the net earnings of the debtor country (Chile) over time. The dotted lines—above $\alpha(y_t - m_t)$ and below $(y_t - m_t)$—basically represent what the creditor receives when the price of copper moves outside the range (K_{pt}, K_{ct}).

Figure 2.6

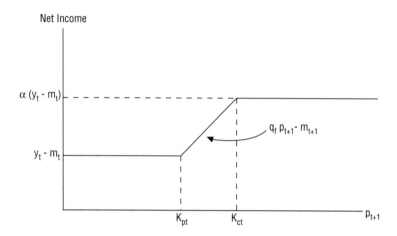

When the price falls within this range, the creditor receives $b_t(1+r)+Z_{pt}-Z_{ct}$. Thus, the discontinuous dotted lines graph the "prices" and "costs" of this strategy for the creditor.

From Figure 2.7 we see that if $K_{pt}=K_{ct}$ for all periods, then Chile will have net earnings that are constant over time equal to (y_t-m_t). This is because in this case, $\alpha=1$. It is interesting to graph the payments m_{t+1} that the creditor would receive in period $t+1$. This appears in Figure 2.8.

Figure 2.7

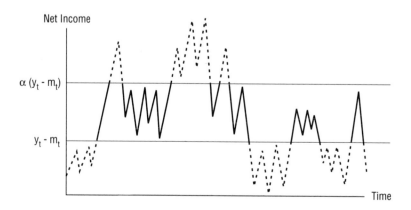

Figure 2.8

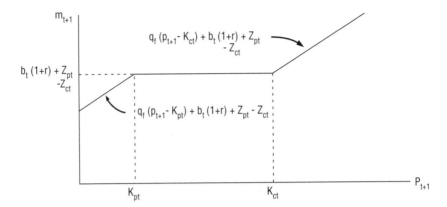

It should be noted that, depending on the value of the copper price in period $t+1$, what the creditor receives in this period when $p_{t+1} < K_{pt}$ — that is, $q_f(p_{t+1} - K_{pt}) + b_t(1+r) + Z_{pt} - Z_{ct}$ — could turn out to be negative.

With regard to these copper bonds, it is relevant to know ex ante the expected value of the flows that both the sovereign country and the creditor would receive. To render the discussion more concrete, we shall assume the simplest case of a "put" copper bond—that is one composed of a pure discount bond for a single period, plus the purchase of a put option by Chile. To put it formally, the relations that define this situation are contained in the expressions (39-43). This same analysis can be performed for "call" and "put-call" copper bonds (Basch, 1992).

To make the results more realistic, we shall consider the country risk to be reflected in a rate s that is greater than the risk-free rate r. It can be demonstrated that Chile's expected net earnings would be:[69]

$$E(y_{t+1} - m_{t+1}) = p_t(1+r) - b_t(1+s) + (s-r)(p_tA_1 - K_{pt}A_2). \qquad (52)$$

Terms A_1 and $A_2 (> A_1)$ are related to the probability that p_{t+1} is greater than K_{pt} and can be calculated analytically, using the stochastic calculus techniques employed by Black and Scholes (1973). The first two terms correspond to Chile's expected net earnings in a situation of normal debt, without considering the purchase of a put. It can be shown (Basch, 1992) that the amount stipulated by equation (52) is less than that of its counterpart without the purchase of options. However, the ex-ante variance is also less. The cost incurred to reduce

---

[69] See Appendix 2.

the expected variance depends on: s, r, p_t, K_{pt}, and the volatility of the price to be stabilized.

Similarly, the expected debt payment that the creditor will receive can be calculated:

$$E(m_{t+1}) = b_t(1+s) + (s-r)(K_{pt}A_2 - p_t A_1).$$ (53)

The amount is greater than what the creditor would obtain if he did not sell Chile a put. The ex-ante variance, as expected, is also greater. Similar results are obtained in the case of call and put-call copper bonds (Basch, 1992).

Stabilization Using Copper Bonds, with Historical and Stochastic Simulations [70]

As in the case of futures, with regard to the rollover strategy, it is interesting to run some simulation exercises on an ex-ante basis, this time using bonds linked to copper. Simulations for three types of bonds will be run: a simple bond with a put option, a simple bond with a call option, and finally, a simple bond with a put and a call option.

The copper bonds in this exercise will be more general than those in the previous section, since they are not zero-coupon bonds. As with the zero-coupon bonds, the sovereign risk will be explicitly taken into account. It is included by means of a discount rate that reflects the discount of the external debt notes of the debtor country (in this case, Chile). In contrast, bonds will be considered in which the value of each coupon consists of a given nominal quantity W that is kept constant during the life of the instrument ("face value"), plus the final payment of the put and call options. The methodology followed is that of Schwartz (1982) and Fall (1986), later broadened by López (1991). If K_p and K_c are the respective striking prices of the put and call options, the value of each coupon at time t_i (for the case when the copper bond comes with both a put and a call option) is determined by:

$$d(t_i) = W + Max(0, p(t_i) - K_c) - Max(0, K_p - p(t_i)),$$ (54)

where W is the nominal value of the coupon paid in each period and $p(t_i)$, the price of copper in period t_i. The total value of the copper bond at the time of issue is simply the present value of the total coupons d_i determined in (54). If there are n periods in which coupons are paid, this value will be:

---

[70] These results are taken from the thesis for the degree of Master of Industrial Civil Engineering from the University of Chile, "Alternativas para estabilizar los retornos de divisas en Chile: el uso de bonos ligados a bienes primarios," by Héctor López M.

$$B(t_0, t_n) = \sum_{i=1}^{n} WQ(t_0, t_i) + \sum_{i=1}^{n} C(t_0, t_i) - \sum_{i=1}^{n} P(t_0, t_i), \qquad (55)$$

where Q represents the present value of a pure discount bond, issued at t_0 and paying \$1 at maturity in t_i; C, the present value of the call option sold by Chile to the creditor, with a striking price of K_c and expiration at t_i; and P the present value of the put option purchased by Chile from the creditor, with a striking price of K_p and expiration at t_i. It should be noted that both options are on the same basket of copper. A bond described by (55) does not provide for payment of the principal at maturity, for it has already been amortized in equal installments. Thus, W consists of interest, plus part of the principal. An instrument of this type allows the issuer to control basically four parameters that affect the price of the bond at the time of issue: the coupon rate W, striking prices K_c and K_p, and the volume of the raw material to be included in the basket under consideration (copper, in the case of Chile). It should also be mentioned that values C and P are basically determined by the Black-Scholes formulas (1973) for valuing European options. Schwartz (1982) shows that adding the assumption of stochastic interest rates does not greatly alter the traditional results. This is also confirmed in López (1991). Moreover, in the Black-Scholes equations, it was assumed that copper price volatility is not stochastic; however, the typical equations were corrected in (55) to include a deterministic convenience yield (Fall, 1986). This convenience yield (δ) is a return obtained by investors for having physical possession of the raw material. It is known that δ is inversely proportional to the volume of the good stored. Thus, the return that investors actually demand for having the raw material in their possession is

$$\alpha = \alpha_s + \delta, \qquad (56)$$

where α_s is the log return of the copper price, which as previously noted, follows a random-walk process. This was demonstrated for prices at the end of the week, the end of the month, and the end of the quarter for the period 1976 to 1989 (Basch 1992).

The first simulation was run for an 18-month put-call bond on a basket of one pound of copper. The striking prices K_c and K_p were calculated as ±5 percent of the observed price of copper (in logarithmic terms) at the respective time of issue. The nominal coupon W, paid quarterly, was set equal to p_t at the time of issue. The normal bond, with which this copper bond is contrasted, is constructed in a manner such that it has the same present value and maturity as the copper bond, with amortizations based on a floating rate process. The historical simulation begins in March 1976 and continues, issuing an instrument every three months, until the last issue in March 1986. The mean value of the quotients of the variances of quarterly flows between the bond with options and the normal bond, is 0.513. That is, the variance of the flows can be reduced to one-half, no matter when the instrument was issued. Later, 100 Monte Carlo simulations were run to generate copper price series and quarterly risk-free interest rates for an 18-month period beginning in March 1989. These were generated from a multivariate ARIMA (0,1,0) series for log p_t, and ARIMA (1,1,0) for log r_t, where r_t is the rate for three-month U.S. Treasury bonds. It should be mentioned that the processes for generating these series are consistent with the postulates used to derive the Black-Scholes formulas (1973). The result of the mean of the quotients between variances is 0.678 (that is, there is a 33 percent reduction in the average variance).[71] When three-year instruments were employed, the Monte Carlo simulation yielded a mean quotient of the variances of 0.433 (a 57 percent reduction).

Simulations were also run for copper bonds with only a put option and with only a call option. In these cases, the maturities were for three years, with the striking price equal to the price of copper at the time of issue. The results of the mean of the quotient of variances m (*Var b.c./Var b*) appear in Table 2.9.

Table 2.9. Results of m(Var b.c./Var b)

	Put Bond	Call Bond
Historical Simulation	0.527	0.102
Monte Carlo Simulation	0.767	0.175

Finally, a simulation strategy was considered that took the cyclical movements of copper prices into account. Intuitively, it would appear to be easier to place bonds linked with copper on the market (with the call option, for example) when prices are "low," rather than when they are perceived by the community to be "high." This is because copper prices are more likely to rise in the first case than in the second, producing greater benefits for the creditor who buys the call option. It should be noted, however, that if the price of copper follows a random walk process, which is validated in our results, then this reasoning is fallacious. In any case, the exercise was made with the striking prices of the call and put options defined as $\overline{p}_{10} \pm \sigma_{10}$. In this expression σ_{10} corresponds to the standard deviation of the logarithm of the real prices of copper for the 10 years before issue, and $\overline{p}_{10}$ is the antilogarithm of the mean

---

[71] These same results can be seen in the graphs in the final appendix.

of the same price series (copper prices were deflated according to the U.S. Wholesale Price Index, WPI). The nominal coupon was determined on the basis of $\bar{p}_1$ (the antilogarithm of the mean of the prices for the year prior to issue). These bonds with put and call options were issued every three months, beginning in March 1986, and they had three-year maturities. The result for m in this period is equal to 0.324 (a 68 percent reduction, on average). The parallel result for the Monte Carlo simulation is $m = 0.021$ (a 98 percent reduction). One factor that should be mentioned is how the present value of the quantities involved was calculated in all the previous results. Basically, we followed López (1991), in which, based on three-month U.S. Treasury bonds, a temporal structure for the interest rate was devised. To provide for the sovereign risk that these instruments entail, a nominal rate of 1 percent per year was used. It should be noted, however, that the three quantities considered in previous calculations—nominal coupons, puts, and calls—are treated differently. Nominal coupons W, paid quarterly, are discounted with the rates of the time structure for the inferred interest rate, plus 1 percent annually for country risk. In contrast, the puts that Chile buys are not discounted at all, for it is assumed that the creditor poses no sovereign risk, and that the calls that Chile sells carry only the discount equivalent to 1 percent per annum.

Analysis of the Stabilization Results Using Financial Instruments

Having performed a series of simulation exercises on an ex-ante basis, by employing strategies that involve both futures and bonds linked with the price of copper, it would be interesting to analyze which individual strategy or group of strategies is preferable. This is not an easy task, for any conclusion would be grounded on assumptions that may perhaps seem strong. In a strict sense, on a purely ex-ante basis—that is, before knowing how future copper prices evolve—the comparison between the different alternatives presented is somewhat useless. The reason is that the various types of bonds (either pure bonds or bonds in combination with options) were defined such that their net present values were equal to zero. Using this as our basis, we can hardly say that one alternative is superior to another. What remains to be seen is what the ex-post result would have been had Chile elected to employ one debt instrument over another. The same holds true for the analysis of the strategies involving futures markets. The only aspect that distinguishes the various alternatives is the cost of intermediation involved (i.e., the transaction costs), such as fees that must be paid to stock brokers or specialized agents when implementing any of these strategies.

We shall commence with a brief review, showing how this translates graphically (see appendix for graphs). To begin, Figure 2.9 in the appendix shows the main series used in running the simulations: the three-month interest rates corresponding to the U.S. Treasury bonds, the spot prices of copper, and the prices of 90-day futures contracts (both on the London Metal Exchange). Figure 2.10 of the appendix indicates the ex-post result obtained with a sequential hedging strategy as opposed to selling only on the physical market.

The ex-post results of the strategies that employ copper bonds begin with Figure 2.11 of the appendix. Here, and in Figure 2.12, are the cases in which Chile (the debtor country) buys a put option and sells a call option respectively. To understand these graphs, it must be realized that the simulation exercise in each case consisted of a sequence of copper bond issues, each with a three-year maturity, starting in July 1976 and ending in March 1986, for a total of 39 issues. For each instrument, it is possible to calculate the variance in the flows obtained for the case of a copper bond and for that of incurring normal debt. The quotient of these variances (calculated ex post) for each issue, appears in the upper part of the figures. Below are the present values of each case (copper bond and normal debt), also calculated with ex-post data. It should be noted that at the time of issue, the normal debt was calculated in such a way that it would have the same present value as the copper bond. Later, the debt was amortized quarterly, under a program of floating rates. Figures 2.13 and 2.17 of the appendix are identical to the two previous figures, except that the copper bonds are more complex. Here, they consist of the simultaneous purchase of a put and the sale of a call, with different striking prices. Figure 2.13 shows the case in which the striking prices vary according to each date of issue, to take into account the historical highs and lows of the copper prices of the 10 years before issue. In Figure 2.17, a fixed criterion is maintained, in which the striking prices of the options are set according to the copper price observed at the time of issue. Moreover, this latter case considers the placement of instruments with 18-month maturities. Figures 2.14 and 2.18 of the appendix show the bands of the two previous cases, which depict how the striking prices varied at the time each instrument was issued. These are indicated in the first case by $\bar{p}_{10} \pm \sigma$, and in the second by $p + \Delta$ and $p - \Delta'$. The value p corresponds to the value of the nominal coupon at the time the bond with a variable criterion is issued, while in the second case, it corresponds simply to the observed value of the price of copper at the time of issue.

Finally, Figures 2.15 and 2.16 in the appendix show how sensitive these instruments are to the precise time of issue (in this case, only the put-call bond with a variable criterion was considered). Both figures depict the case of a bond with a 10-year maturity and the effect that the variation in the price of copper between July 1976 and October of the same year has on the net yield obtained with each.

To rank the results obtained and decide which strategies were the best on an ex-post basis, we shall use a simple conceptual framework that permits an analysis of each, taking the mean and the variance of each exercise into account. By "mean" shall be understood the mean of the 39 values corresponding to the 39 present values of the total bond issues, each with three-year maturities (with the exception of the 18-month instrument). For each of these 39 issues, we can calculate the variance of the flows (each instrument has 12 flows). If we calculate the mean of all the variances, we obtain a sort of "average" variance for the flows that were obtained ex post. These are the means and variances that we shall consider.

Before presenting the respective results of means and variances, it is useful to clarify some aspects of equation (55), which was used to calculate the historical simulations of the different instruments analyzed. The first point refers to the fact that $B(t_0, t_n)$ is essentially a debt instrument—be it a "normal" debt instrument or a copper-bond linked with the price of copper—and with our choice of signs (positive, if the monetary flows are toward the debtor country and negative otherwise), it should be positive; if this were not so, it would be a loan. However, because of the conditions stipulated for defining the various instruments, it sometimes came to pass that the present value of the payment flows had a positive sign, so that $B(t_0, t_n)$ actually became a "negative" bond, or a loan if you will, with a negative sign. This occurs when the third term on the right side in (55) is greater than the sum of the other two, this sum always being positive. This can be confirmed by observing Table 2.11 of the appendix, in the columns corresponding to the present values of the copper bond and the normal debt: the signs change according to the observed prices of copper after 45 issues, each with 18-month maturities. Had we considered a copper bond of the call variety, for example, the signs would have always been negative, a fact corroborated in Table 2.10, below.

Table 2.10 Means and Variances of Financial Instruments

		Mean (M)	Variance (V)
1.1	Futures rollover	368.8	3,688.9
1.2	Sale on physical market	389.1	10,244.1
2.1	Put bond	90.9	166.9
2.2	Normal debt	79.8	265.7
3.1	Call bond	−65.4	22.7
3.2	Normal debt	−104.9	295.9
4.1	Put-call bond (variable band)	88.1	108.0
4.2	Normal debt	77.5	269.1
5.1	Put-call bond (fixed band)	2.3	31.5
5.2	Normal debt	11.4	148.4

To understand this table, the means and variances of each copper bond should be compared with its respective normal debt and, when examining the rollover strategy in the futures markets, with the sale of copper on the physical market. That is, strategy 1.1 should be compared with strategy 1.2; 2.1 with that of 2.2; 3.1 with that of 3.2; 4.1 with that of 4.2; and 5.1 with that of 5.2. The fact that $B(t_0, t_n)$ is occasionally a "negative" bond does not invalidate the exercise, for in such cases, the normal debt is also "negative," and, thus, the flows of both credits are compared in terms of the present value and the variance of the remittances toward the issuing country. We see that, based on these assumptions, there would be three dominant strategies with respect to normal debt: a put bond, a call bond, and a put-call bond with a variable band criterion. The other two strategies—futures rollover and a put-call bond with a fixed band criterion—do not present a conclusive picture. Once again, it should be underscored that these ex-post results correspond to the price evolution actually observed in the market. Another copper price sequence would perhaps produce different mean-variance results for these strategies. Consequently, it cannot be inferred from this which instrument is optimal. What can be said ex ante, is that these instruments will be able to decrease the variance in the flows in the vast majority of situations, as seen in Table 2.11 of the appendix (which shows the ex-post results of the means and variances corresponding to each of the 45 issues, in the case of both the put-call bond with a fixed band criterion and the normal debt).

Another aspect of these copper bonds should be noted. They are not strictly comparable to the transactions in the futures markets. The difference lies basically in the fact that these bonds are debt as well as hedging instruments, while futures are strictly hedging instruments. Copper bonds can be converted to pure stabilization instruments, simply by eliminating the debt portion leaving only the two options: the put and the call. In the literature, this strategy is called a "collar." Variations on this idea can be introduced—issuing options, for example, on the same volume of copper at different striking prices, such that the value of the put Z_{pt} is equal to the value of the call Z_{ct}. This combination of options produces a zero-cost strategy, which achieves a complete insurance at the striking price of the put, with a ceiling given by the striking price of the call. This is known as the Max-Min strategy. Another zero-cost alternative is the ZECRO (Zero Cost Ratio Option) strategy. Here, once again, the cost of the put is exactly offset by the sale of the call, but this time, both options have the same striking price. The volumes of copper on which these options are issued, however, are now different. The Max-Min and ZECRO strategies are two extremes on a continuum of zero-cost alternatives.

These examples serve to show the vast potential and flexibility of options strategies. Copper bonds retain the characteristics of these strategies, and they are also debt mechanisms. This is why they constitute an excellent vehicle for developing countries, which on the one hand, need to incur debt in order to grow, and on the other, must protect themselves against price shocks connected with the goods they export.

Finally, it is interesting to make some observations about the sovereign risk associated with a put-call copper bond. It can be shown (Basch, 1992) that the expected value of the temptation for the debtor not to honor the contractual commitment to the creditor is greater in the case of a copper bond than in that of a traditional debt with the same present value as the bond. The difference is essentially the value of the put, which is the insurance that Chile is buying to guarantee a minimum price for its copper. It can be assumed that the higher sovereign risk associated with a put-call bond is offset by a given floor created by the put option for the price that Chile will receive, together with a lower price variance. It can likewise be shown that a call bond—with a present value equal to that of a traditional debt paper—carries a country risk equal to that of the latter. It should also be mentioned that commodity bonds that have been traded on the market correspond precisely to this type of instrument (call bonds).

Conclusions and Policy Recommendations

This essay presents a series of strategies that Chile can employ to offset the negative shocks associated with copper price swings. First, it considers a variety of stabilization funds that do not have the shortcomings of the Copper Stabilization Fund (FEC) implemented in 1985. Second, it examines a series of financial instruments associated with the price of copper (copper bonds) that also have attractive features. These instruments are not merely alternatives but can be combined in such a way that the stabilization fund serves as a guarantor to the buyers of the copper bonds, thus reducing the well-known problem of sovereign risk. It is, therefore, not unreasonable to conceive of a strategy that involves the simultaneous implementation of a copper stabilization fund, together with transactions in the copper futures markets and the placement of copper bonds on the international capital markets. In this way, it does not become necessary to cover the totality of copper output in the futures markets; instead, there will be a diversification of mechanisms, through which the objective of stabilizing both fiscal revenues and foreign exchange income derived from exports can be achieved.

Stabilization Funds

The saving-spending rule originally implemented for the FEC is inadequate, for it does not consider the level of resources accumulated in the fund when deciding how much to spend or save. For a given price, the lower the balance in the fund, the greater the incentives to save; the FEC does not take this fact into account.

A second criticism of the FEC is that not only should the incentives to save in the fund grow with the difference between the current and the long-term prices, but the expected short-term copper prices should also be taken into account. If current prices are higher than those anticipated for the near future, it is advisable to save in order to be able to resort to the fund when the price of copper drops. In contrast, if the current price is lower than that anticipated for the coming years, the incentives to save are substantially lower, because copper earnings will grow in the future. Consequently, the prices to consider when defining the reference price are those anticipated for the future, not an average of historical prices.

This essay proposes two stabilization funds as alternatives to the FEC, both of which aim at stabilizing public expenditures.

The first fund offers the advantage of simplicity, without the shortcomings of the FEC. This fund utilizes Vial's (1987) econometric model for the copper market to determine whether the current price is in the ascending or descending phase of the cycle; this makes it possible to predict whether the price of the next period will be higher (and thus, the incentives to save, lower) or lower (in which case, it is more desirable to accumulate resources in the fund). Because of the fact that the fund is a self-insurance instrument, the relevant variable when deciding how much to spend or save is the "cash on hand"—that is, the sum of the balance held in the fund plus current earnings. This fund employs the following rule: if the available funds fall below a certain threshold level, the entire fund is spent. The marginal propensity to spend when available funds are above this threshold value will be larger: (1) the brighter the future appears (based on the predictions of the Vial model); (2) the higher the temporal discount rate; and (3) the lower the degree of risk aversion. The resulting fund behaves in a more reasonable manner than the FEC, avoiding the overaccumulation of resources that appears to have occurred in the Chilean fund during the ascending phase of the copper price cycle. In contrast to that of the FEC, the saving-spending rule of this fund takes into account both the level held in the fund and short-term copper price forecasts.

The second stabilization fund is based on a careful analysis of the asymmetries that exist between the benefits of increasing public expenditures and the costs of decreasing them: the monies utilized in public investment projects have an important specific component, and the political costs of reducing social expenditures and public sector salaries are greater than the benefits derived from increasing them. Each time the economic authority increases public spending, it should weigh the immediate benefit against the cost of eventually having to cease financing the respective item (e.g., leaving a port unfinished or reducing the pensions of retirees). This aversion to cutting future fiscal expenditures justifies a stabilization fund, even if earnings follow a random walk process. By solving the problem of dynamic optimization, a stabilization fund is obtained that considerably smoothes fiscal expenditures, as long as the uncertainty regarding fiscal revenues is not excessive.

Financial Instruments

Based on the results in the third section, it is apparent that bonds linked to copper offer significant advantages over other financial instruments, such as futures. These bonds allow a country like Chile, which is vulnerable to shocks to the price of its main export product, to transfer the inherent risks to the international capital markets on an ex-ante basis. Other financing mechanisms can achieve similar results, but from an ex-post standpoint—for example, falling into a situation of credit arrears, with all its attendant problems. As can be seen in Lessard (1989) and Fischer (Priovolos and Duncan, 1991), passing the risk to the international capital markets through commodity bonds constitutes a Pareto optimum situation. This flows from the fact that these instruments make it possible to stabilize consumption within the debtor country ex ante. Furthermore, they are related to exogenous and observable events that do not require the same degree of monitoring as do other mechanisms like futures contracts and direct investment, which are also capable of transferring risk on an ex-ante basis.

As mentioned in the third section, there are basically two major problems associated with these latter mechanisms. First, the liquidity in the international exchanges is not high enough to permit a rollover hedging strategy on a large scale. If Chile decided to implement such a strategy with a significant portion of its output, this decision would distort the structure of futures prices in copper contracts in a significant way, rendering these instruments ineffective as insurance mechanisms. The second problem, though not as important as the first, involves the fact that futures contracts are settled on a daily basis, until the decision is made to liquidate them. This could lead to situations in which Chile would be obliged to leave as margin on the contracts amounts that could at some point prove considerable. Naturally, these margins are directly proportional to the volumes traded. For example, in the period from 1976 to 1989, from one day to the next, there was a maximum rise of US¢10.71 in three-month futures contracts (with maturities in March 1980) on the London Metal Exchange. Had Chile sold its quarterly production (roughly 250,000 tons) in futures, using the rollover strategy, then on that day alone it would have had to increase its margin by US$ 58.9 million. Clearly, this is an extreme case, and Chile would probably have had favorable price movements in many periods. However, this fact, which was not explicitly mentioned in the discussion of the benefits deriving from futures contracts, makes the decrease in the variance of the net flows, or the increase (or perhaps decrease) in their expected values, biased.

The above discussion would seem to indicate that among the financial instruments for stabilizing earnings, commodity bonds would clearly be preferable—which leads to the question of why they have not enjoyed widespread acceptance in the international capital markets.

Where governments are concerned, it can be said that there are agency problems while acting as a broker when attempting to make use of the futures markets or float commodity bonds. In the ex-post scenarios that do not prove favorable for the issuing country, the government can be tagged with the label of speculator by its political opposition. It should be noted that this observation does not apply to private issuers. However, two main factors can explain why introducing these types of mechanisms has met with difficulties. First, there may be a biased perception about the sovereign risk posed by such instruments. Second, the creditor banks do not enjoy comparative advantages that enable them to deal with the risk posed by price volatility of primary commodities.

Let us first approach the question of sovereign risk. As Kletzer, Newbery, and Wright (1990) mention, the greatest risk of noncompliance in the case of a country that issues a put-call copper bond emerges when there is a sharp rise in prices. They are right if both principal and interest must be paid at maturity. However, this is not a frequent occurrence. On the contrary, the debtor country will typically wish to issue new bonds when the old ones expire, and if prices have risen, the country will obtain the new funds under more favorable conditions. Nevertheless, when bonds with put-call clauses are issued, their sovereign risk increases directly with the value of the insurance paid by the issuing country, both to maintain a minimum price for its export product, and to enjoy lower price volatility. It is not fully clear how the creditor country values the fact that the issuing country now faces a less volatile price for its commodity. Furthermore, in the case in which call bonds are issued and there is no price floor, the sovereign risk does not change with respect to that of a traditional debt. Therefore, if the debtor country has attained a level of acceptance in the voluntary credit markets, as in Chile's case, the sovereign risk of this type of instrument should not be a critically limiting factor in trading on the international market.

The second point is more delicate. It directly concerns how to induce creditor banks to increase their demand for such bonds. The mechanism that comes to mind is to convert the bonds to instruments that are tradeable in the secondary markets—that is, to "securitize" them. Secure and standardized assets would thus be created that would be freely traded in the secondary markets. This advantage becomes clear when comparing a "pure" copper bond that has been standardized with a copper bond that has also been securitized. Potential investors would obviously apply a greater discount to the "pure" bonds since, at some point, they will have to incur costs when utilizing the services of a commodity broker. However, having securitized bonds does not eliminate the problem entirely. Let us suppose, for example, that a bank grants a credit to a country like Chile on the basis of a securitized bond. To eliminate the risk inherent in the price of copper, the bank could sell copper futures. The problem with this course of action is that the bank would compound its risk concerning Chile instead of diminishing it. One way of solving the problem would be for the debtor to back these instruments, offering physical stocks of the commodity as a guarantee. Another way of gaining credibility for these bonds is for the underwriting agent to be perceived as a neutral party by the creditor banks. One formula is for the Inter-American Development Bank, the World Bank, or some other independent neutral international agency to act as the creator, underwriter, and overseer of these securitized bonds. As previously mentioned, when a stabilization fund is implemented, the fund could serve as the underwriter for the copper bond issues. Of particular interest is the negative correlation between the incentives to spend the existing resources in the fund and the sovereign risk of the country that manages it. The higher the price of copper, the higher the perceived probability of default (country risk) when a copper bond has been issued. However, in this situation there are no incentives to use the stabilization fund, which makes the guarantee for the bonds more solid.[72]

Although the problem of how to stimulate the demand for such bonds remains, they possess the benefits previously mentioned in the third section, which in our judgment are greater than their costs. This conclusion is supported (though based on postulates that are not as robust as one would like), by the tables in the appendix, where the benefits, in terms of the values of the means and variances of the flows corresponding to strategies that utilize copper bonds, are compared with incurring "normal" debt. In three of the four cases analyzed, the copper bond strategies completely overshadow their normal debt counterpart. Only in the case of an 18-month put-call bond with a fixed band criterion is the resulting situation not altogether clear. Another factor that should be taken into account when considering the floating of copper bonds is that such instruments can be exchanged for the old ("normal") debt contracted by Chile in the past. The old debt would be perceived by the banks as instruments that are not as attractive as the new debt (copper bonds) and as such would be transferred to Chile with a favorable discount, which would permit the country to reduce its external debt.

---

[72] Engel (1993) studies how to combine the sales of commodity bonds with a stabilization fund in a dynamic setting.

BIBLIOGRAPHY

Adams, F.G., J.R. Behrman, and S. Levy. 1989. The macroeconomic effects of primary commodity instability in Bolivia and Peru: A background paper. Presented at conference, Macroeconomic Effects of Primary Commodity Price Instability, April, IDRC, Santiago, Chile.

Aitcheson, J., and J.A.C. Brown. 1957. *The lognormal distribution*. Cambridge, England: Cambridge University Press.

Ball, R., and R. Myers. 1991. Hedging with commodity-linked bonds under price risk and capital constraints. In *Commodity risk management and finance*, eds. T. Priovolos and R.C. Duncan. Oxford and New York: Oxford University Press for the World Bank.

Basch, M. 1992. Market strategies to stabilize income in LDCs. Work in progress.

Behrman, J.R. 1987. Primary commodity instability and economic goal attainment in developing countries. *World Development* 15 (May):559-574.

Bertsekas, D.P. 1976. *Dynamic programming and stochastic control*. New York: Academic Press.

Bevan, D.L., P. Collier, and J.W. Gunning. 1987. Consequences of a commodity boom in a controlled economy: Accumulation and redistribution in Kenya 1975-83. *The World Bank Economic Review* 1:489-513.

Black, F., and M. Scholes. 1973. The pricing of options and corporate liabilities. *Journal of Political Economy* 81:637-659.

Blanchard, O., and S. Fischer. 1989. *Lectures in macroeconomics*. Cambridge: MIT Press.

Cox, J.C., and M. Rubenstein. 1985. *Option markets*. New York: Prentice-Hall, Inc.

Deaton, A. 1991. Saving and liquidity constraints. *Econométrica* 59 (no. 5):1221-1248.

Deaton, A., and G. Laroque. 1992. On the behaviour of commodity prices. *Review of Economic Studies* 59 (no.1):1-24.

Duffie, D. 1989. *Futures markets*. Englewood Cliffs, N.J.: Prentice Hall.

Eaton, J., and M. Gersovitz. 1981. Debt with potential repudiation: Theoretical and empirical analysis. *Review of Economic Studies* 48:289-309.

Engel, E. 1993. Combining commodity bonds with stabilization funds to reduce income uncertainty. Harvard University. Work in progress.

Engel, E., and S. Mondschein. 1993. A fiscal expenditures stabilization fund. Harvard University and MIT. Work in progress.

Fall, M. 1986. Commodity bonds: A financing alternative. Master's thesis, Sloan School of Management, MIT.

Gardner, B.L. 1989. Rollover hedging and missing long-term future markets. *American Journal of Agricultural Economics* (May): 311-318.

Gelb, A. 1979. On the definition and measurement of instability and the cost of buffering export fluctuations. *Review of Economic Studies* 46:149-162.

Hausmann, R. 1990. Dealing with negative oil shocks: The Venezuelan experience of the eighties. Paper presented at the Conference on Temporary Shocks, Oxford, September.

Hull, J. C. 1989. *Options, futures, and other derivative securities*. 2d ed. Englewood Cliffs, N.J.: Prentice-Hall.

Kauffman, D. 1991a. Determinants of the productivity of projects in developing countries: Evidence from 1200 projects. Background Paper, *World Development Report 1991*. Washington DC: The World Bank.

————. 1991b. The forgotten rationale for policy reform: The productivity of investment. Background Paper, *World Development Report 1991*. Washington, DC: The World Bank.

Keynes, J.M. 1924. Foreign investment and national advantage. *The Nation and the Athenaeum* (August 9).

Kletzer, K.M. 1988. *Sovereign debt renegotiation under asymmetric information*. Discussion Paper N°555, June, Yale University Economic Growth Center.

Kletzer, K., D. Newbery, and B. Wright. 1990. *Alternative for smoothing the consumption of primary commodity exporters*. Working Paper 558, December, The World Bank.

Labys, W. 1986. Contribution of stock-flow adjustments to long run commodity modeling. Paper presented at Project LINK Meeting, Bangkok.

Lessard, D.R. 1989. Financial risk management needs of developing countries: Discussion. *American Journal of Agricultural Economics* (May):534-35.

López, H. 1991. Alternativa para estabilizar los retornos de divisas en Chile: el uso de bonos ligados a bienes primarios. Master's thesis, Department of Industrial Engineering, University of Chile.

McKinnon, R.I. 1967. Future markets, buffer stocks, and income stability for primary producers. *Journal of Political Economy* 75 (December):844-61.

Meyer, J. 1987. Two-moment decision models and expected utility maximization. *The American Economic Review* 77:421-30.

Newbery, D.M., and J.E. Stiglitz. 1985. The theory of commodity prices stabilization: A study in the economics of risk. Oxford: Clarendon Press.

O'Hara, M. 1984. Commodity bonds and consumption risks. *Journal of Finance* 39: 193-206.

Petzel, T.E. 1989. Financial risk management needs of developing countries: Discussion. *American Journal of Agricultural Economics*:531-533.

Priovolos, T., and R.C. Duncan, eds. 1991. *Commodity risk management and finance*. Oxford: Oxford University Press.

Raczynski, D. 1988. Social policy and vulnerable groups: Children in Chile. In *Adjustment with a human face: The country studies*, eds. A. Giovanni, R. Cornia, and F. Jolly. Oxford: Clarendon Press.

Schwartz, E. 1982. The pricing of commodity-linked bonds. *The Journal of Finance* 37 (no. 1, May):525-39.

Valdés, R. 1991. *Nuevos instrumentos financieros: una introducción a futuros y opciones*. Serie Docente N°4, CIEPLAN.

Vial, J. 1987. An econometric study of the world copper market. Ph.D. thesis, University of Pennsylvania.

————. 1989. *El mercado mundial del cobre. Antecedentes para un análisis sistemático*. Colección Estudios CIEPLAN N°26, June, Santiago.

Vial, J., and R. Valdés. 1991. *Patrones de consumo de cobre: Determinantes del consumo del cobre por sectores en EE.UU*. Colección Estudios CIEPLAN N°32, June, Santiago.

Williams, J.C., and B.D. Wright. 1992. *Storage and commodity markets*. New York, N.Y.: Cambridge University Press (in press).

Worrall, T. 1987. *Debt with potential repudiation: Short-run and long-run contracts*. Discussion Paper in Economics Series A, N°186, University of Reading.

Wright, B.D., and D.M.G. Newbery. 1989. Financial instruments for consumption smoothing by commodity-dependent exporters. *American Journal of Agricultural Economics* (May):511-516.

Glossary

Ex	:	Expected value of the random variable x. It sometimes refers to the historical average of x.
$E_t x$	:	Expected value of variable x with information available up to time t.
$Var\ x$	:	Variance of variable x.
$Cov\ (x,y)$	:	Covariance between variables x and y.
V_x	:	Coefficient of variation of variable x.
R	:	Coefficient of relative risk aversion.
A	:	Coefficient of absolute risk aversion.
δ	:	Time preference rate.
r	:	Risk-free interest rate. It is almost always assumed that $r = \delta$.
β	:	$1/(1+r)$
X_+	:	X if $X \geq 0$ 0 if $X < 0$
Γ	:	$(1+\delta)/(1+r)$
A_t	:	Level accumulated in a stabilization fund at the beginning of period t.
c_t	:	Consumption of the "representative individual" during period t.
y_t	:	Earnings in period t.
x_t	:	Funds available in period t.
G_t	:	Fiscal expenditures in t.
λ	:	Coefficient of correlation between price and earnings.

APPENDIX 1

A MODEL OF THE COPPER MARKET [73]

The model of the world copper market described here has been conceived as an instrument to make medium-term projections of the main market variables (price, consumption, inventories, etc.), as well as to evaluate the effects of different scenarios concerning the evolution of the world economy on the copper market.

Description of the Model

This model, developed by CIEPLAN over the past two and a half years, represents a development of the Vial model (1987) and follows the tradition of the "standard model of basic goods." In this latter model, structural aspects in the determination of supply, demand, and copper inventories are emphasized, and price plays the role of equalizing the supply and demand for inventories (Labys, 1986).

The model consists of a total of 151 variables, 82 of which are endogenous. Of these latter, 34 are determined on the basis of behavioral equations estimated econometrically, and the remainder correspond to identities or transformations of variables.

With respect to the world supply of copper, a distinction is made between primary production of refined copper, which has its origins in mining production or in solvent extraction, and secondary production, which derives from the recycling of old copper scrap.

Primary production of refined copper at the world level is related linearly to world mining production and production by means of solvents, expressed in equivalent units of fine copper. Production by means of solvents is assumed to be exogenous, and mining output is obtained from the sum of the output of the United States, Canada, Chile, Peru, Zambia, Zaire, South Africa and Namibia, the Philippines, China, Bulgaria, Czechoslovakia, Hungary, East Germany, Poland, Romania, the former Soviet Union, and "the rest of the world." Of this group, only the first eight are obtained endogenously, the explanatory variables being each country's capacity (exogenous) and labor costs and energy prices (both in terms of copper).

Secondary production is divided between the United States, Japan, Europe, the newly industrializing countries, China, the former Soviet Union, Hungary, Poland, Czechoslovakia, East Germany, Romania, Bulgaria, and "the rest of

---

[73] This has been developed by Joaquín Vial, a researcher at CIEPLAN.

the world." The general model for each country expresses the consumption of refined copper as a function of industrial output and the current and lagged values of copper, aluminum, and energy prices—each relative to the prices of the industrial goods. In the case of the United States, information was available on consumption by categories of final use, which made it possible to estimate sectoral demand functions.[74]

The change in inventories occurs because of the difference between consumption and global supply, with the price equation closing the entire system. The price of copper in London, expressed in constant dollars, depends on the discrepancy between the actual Inventories-Consumption ratio and that of the trend, the real value of the dollar vis-à-vis other currencies, and on the real interest rate.

The equations of the model were estimated using annual data from the 1965-1989 period.

Evaluating the Properties of the Model

The model is simultaneous and nonlinear and is solved by utilizing iterative numerical solution techniques (Gauss-Seidel). The SIMPC program for microcomputers, developed by Don Econometrics for the LINK Project, is used for this purpose.

The dynamic simulations for the 1981-1990 period yield acceptable results, demonstrating the model's ability to predict the price cycle that actually emerged in this period.

The sensitivity of the simulation results to various disturbances has been analyzed in some detail. The deterministic simulation results show the existence of an inverse relationship between energy prices and the price of copper, as well as a positive relationship between aluminum and copper prices. Similarly, a positive linkage can also be observed between industrial output and the price of copper. Another feature worth noting is the presence of long periods of adjustment to shocks, which appears to be a distinctive characteristic of this market (Vial, 1989).

---

[74] For further background on these estimations, see Vial and Valdés (1991) and Vial (1989).

APPENDIX 2

EXPECTED VALUE OF THE "PUT" COPPER BOND

To derive equations (52-53), the price of copper is assumed to follow an Ito diffusion process:

$$dp = \alpha_p p dt + \sigma_p p dz_p , \qquad (A.1)$$

where p is the price, α_p the expected geometric yield of copper per unit of time, σ_p is the standard deviation of the copper yield between t and $t+dt$, and finally, dz_p is a standard Gauss-Wiener process (or standard Brownian process). For the purposes of our calculations, α_p and σ_p are constants. The form of (A.1) is based on the hypothesis that the price of copper in the spot markets has a stationary lognormal distribution (Black and Scholes, 1973). This assumption is in full agreement with the empirical evidence (Basch, 1992). To further simplify the calculations, we shall assume that the convenience yield δ of copper is zero. This simplification does not substantially alter the results (Fall, 1986).

What must be calculated to obtain the expected value of the net earnings that Chile would receive were it to incur debt through "put" copper bonds is basically the probability π that p_{t+1} is greater than K_{pt} and $E(p_{t+1}|p_{t+1} \geq K_{pt})$. Employing the assumption of lognormality of the copper price:

$$p_{t+1} = p_t \exp(\mu + \sigma_p Z), \qquad (A.2)$$

where μ is the expected logarithmic yield per unit of time ($= \alpha_p - \sigma_p^2 / 2$) and Z is a variable with a normal standard distribution. We can calculate these quantities. The results are:

$$\pi = Pr\left(p_{t+1} \geq K_{pt}\right) = N\left(h - \sigma_p\right), \qquad (A.3)$$

$$\pi E(p_{t+1}|p_{t+1} \geq K_{pt}) = p_t e^r N(h), \qquad (A.4)$$

where $N(.)$ is the cumulative density function of Z, r the risk-free interest rate, and h determined by

$$h = \left(\log\left(p_t / K_{pt}\right) + r + \sigma_p^2 / 2\right) / \sigma_p \qquad (A.5)$$

$E(m_{t+1})$ is calculated with the same equations. These equations lead to:

$$E(y_{t+1} - m_{t+1}) = (p_t - b_t)e^s + p_t(e^r - e^s)N(h) + \tag{A.6}$$

$$+K_{pt}(1 - e^{s-r})(1 - N(h - \sigma_p)),$$

$$E(m_{t+1}) = b_t\, e^s + p_t(e^r - e^s)(1 - N(h)) + \tag{A.7}$$

$$+K_{pt}(e^{s-r} - 1)(1 - N(h - \sigma_p)),$$

Equations (52) and (53) correspond to expressions (A.6) and (A.7), respectively, where in these latter, a powers series expansion is carried out, since it is assumed that r, s, and $s\text{-}r$ are small.

APPENDIX 3 [75]

SOLUTION TO THE PROBLEM OF DYNAMIC PROGRAMMING

There are several ways of obtaining approximate solutions to the problem of maximizing the objective function set forth in (13), subject to the constraint of (12). These solutions should ponder: (1) how near the proposed solution is to the solution of the dynamic programming problem, with (2) how realistic the assumptions are about the values of the future earnings series.

One of the main sources of difficulty in resolving this problem is that the constraints are stochastic in nature. The proposed methodology deals with the problem through the "chance constraints" method—that is, instead of requiring that these constraints be satisfied with certainty, it is assumed that they are satisfied with a high degree of probability (in this work, the probability was assumed to be 0.80). Combining this assumption with that of normality for the distribution of future earnings (with means and variances that depend solely on variables known at the time the problem is solved), the stochastic constraints become "usual" linear constraints.

The approach considered in this work addresses the problem of dynamic programming ("open loop") by means of a "closed loop" approach, whereby, in the current period, the sequence of optimal decisions for a given horizon is obtained without taking into account additional information that will be available when making future decisions.[76] To remedy this, the "rolling horizons" methodology is utilized, implementing only the solution that is related to the following period. Next period, the problem is solved again, incorporating the respective data on earnings; this process is repeated for each successive period.[77]

Below we explain how it is possible to reduce the problem to a sequence of linear programming problems by utilizing the approximations just described.

If $\left(G_{t+1} - G_t \right)_+$ is expressed as the difference between two positive variables, linear programming results make it possible to show that at all times, only one of these variables is basic. Furthermore, a simple algebraic calculation shows that $\left(G_{t+1} - G_t \right)_+$ will be equal to the first variable considered in the previous difference. By combining this fact with the approximations described earlier, the original problem has been reduced to solving a sequence of standard linear programming problems, each of which determines the expenditures of the current year, as well as the level of resources in the fund at the beginning of the subsequent year.

---

[75] The methodology described in this appendix was developed by Susana Mondschein.

[76] See, for example, Bertsekas (1976).

[77] The length of the horizon considered was seven years.

We complete the description of the methodology employed by specifying how the distributions of future earnings were determined, based on the information known at the time each of the above maximization problems was solved. In the scenario with high uncertainty, it was assumed that the fiscal revenues process exhibited random walk behavior (with a positive drift); the respective mean and variance were estimated on the basis of the available data.[78] Thus, the mean of the revenues t years hence will be equal to the last revenue available, added to t times the average growth rate of this revenue. The variance of this random variable will be equal to t times the variance of the respective random walk. In the scenario with low uncertainty, it was assumed that the mean of revenues in future years is equal to true revenues, and that the variance of these revenues is equal to that of the case with high uncertainty.

---

[78] It goes without saying that in reality, the economic authority has more information on expected future revenues.

Table 2.11 Means and Variances for a Put-call Bond and Normal Debt

Date of issue	Present Value		Variance	
	P-C bond	N.D.	P-C bond	N.D.
76.3	−78.2	111.3	2.4	30.3
76.4	12.7	9.0	16.3	28.6
77.1	−37.2	−46.5	13.8	14.2
77.2	−13.6	−24.1	39.2	20.1
77.3	28.2	31.5	41.8	73.4
77.4	47.0	81.8	19.4	171.3
78.1	53.6	90.6	22.4	139.3
78.2	64.9	117.9	6.5	97.6
78.3	73.4	142.9	9.3	390.3
78.4	80.7	128.0	8.7	323.2
79.1	63.7	87.2	47.0	313.4
79.2	3.2	13.9	160.6	345.0
79.3	65.6	85.4	38.8	427.6
79.4	19.0	34.8	135.1	570.4
80.1	−157.9	−238.2	.0	234.0
80.2	−49.6	−79.3	61.0	199.9
80.3	−77.0	−101.1	36.3	171.4
80.4	−79.1	−118.1	11.3	126.5
81.1	−38.5	−70.9	31.1	128.3
81.2	−40.3	−65.4	28.0	109.5
81.3	−44.5	−66.3	16.0	61.3
81.4	−28.0	−45.7	22.1	25.8
82.1	−10.2	−25.4	27.9	10.1
82.2	5.9	1.6	43.7	47.8
82.3	25.0	23.1	52.3	79.4
82.4	12.7	15.6	56.8	98.7
83.1	−26.7	−37.0	70.0	129.8
83.2	−71.4	−88.0	32.2	98.9
83.3	−79.9	−93.4	1.3	21.9
83.4	4.4	−7.3	13.0	12.6
84.1	8.8	−2.0	16.4	9.9
84.2	−6.5	−13.7	17.4	12.9
84.3	26.6	26.6	13.6	14.7
84.4	34.3	33.1	7.2	17.0
85.1	1.2	2.3	13.7	33.8
85.2	−34.0	−21.7	13.1	32.4
85.3	−36.9	−26.0	7.1	19.5
85.4	5.0	3.9	12.5	17.2
86.1	1.0	1.7	63.6	49.1
86.2	14.1	27.5	101.9	148.4
86.3	45.5	102.7	43.0	307.9
86.4	59.5	140.4	24.4	269.9
87.1	71.7	169.3	7.0	160.7
87.2	87.3	221.5	1.2	490.3
87.3	99.2	200.0	8.1	590.3

Figure 2.9a Interest Rates and Spot Prices Copper from 1976 to 1989

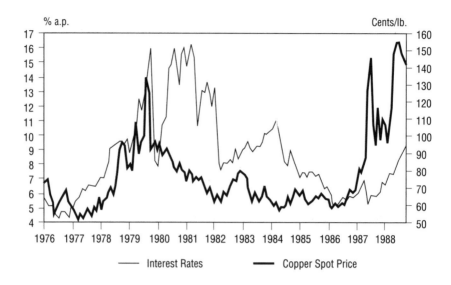

Figure 2.9.b Three-month Futures Copper Prices

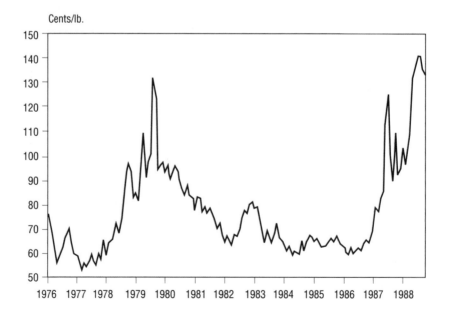

**Figure 2.10   Rollover Strategy with Futures
1976–1989**

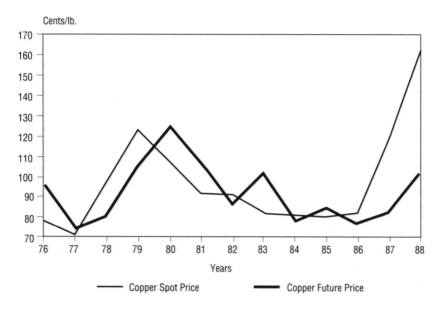

Cents/lb.

Years

——— Copper Spot Price   ▬▬▬ Copper Future Price

Figure 2.11.a Historical Simulation: Put Bond

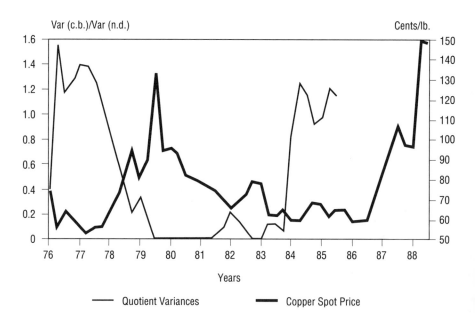

Var (c.b.)/Var (n.d.)   Cents/lb.

Years

— Quotient Variances   ▬ Copper Spot Price

Figure 2.11.b Present Ex-post Values

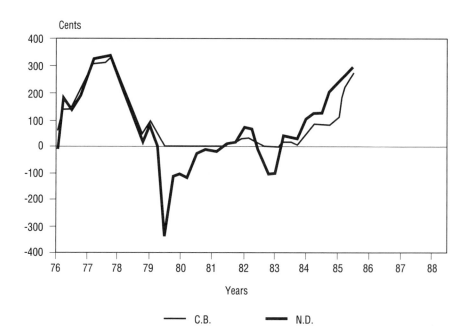

Cents

Years

— C.B.   ▬ N.D.

Figure 2.12.a Historical Simulation: Call Bond

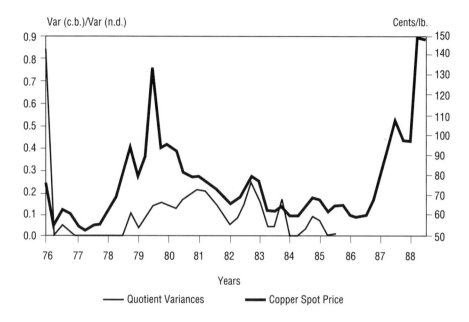

Figure 2.12.b Present Ex-post Values

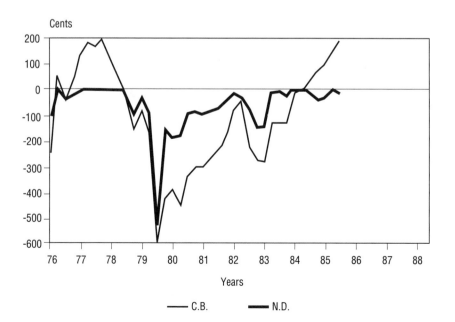

Figure 2.13.a Historical Simulation: Put-Call Bond with a Variable Band

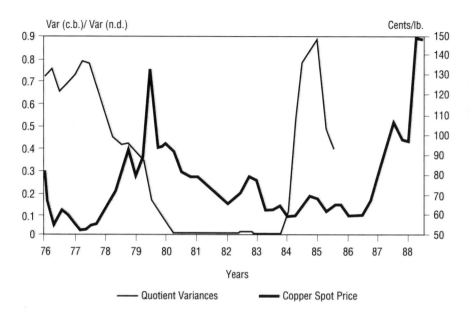

Figure 2.13.b Present Ex-post Values

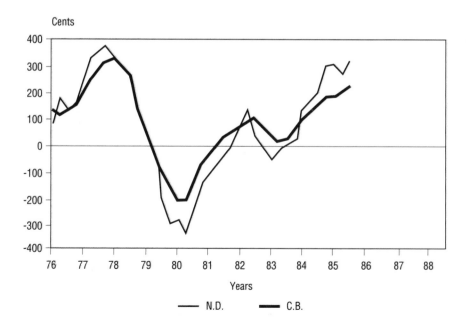

Figure 2.14 Profile of Put-Call Bands with a Variable Criterion

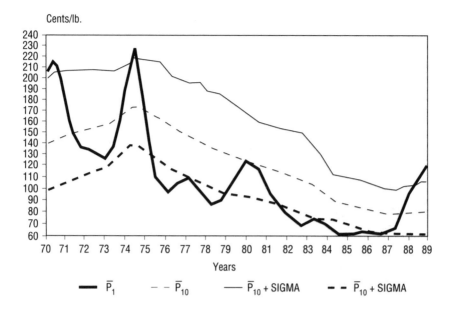

Figure 2.15.a Historical Simulation: 10-year Put-Call Bond, Issued in 1976 (3rd quarter), with a Band of ±10%

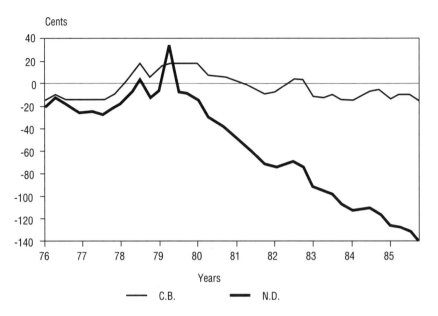

Figure 2.15.b Copper Spot Price

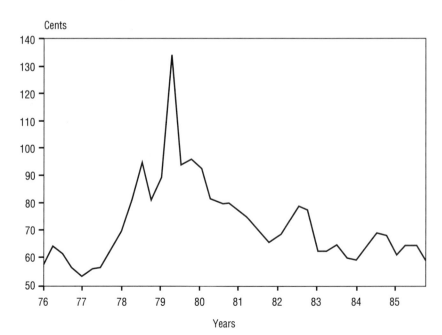

Figure 2.16.a Historical Simulation: 10-year Put-Call bond, Issued in 1976 (4th quarter), with a Band of ±10%

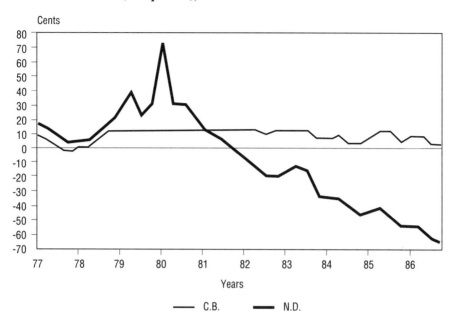

Figure 2.16.b Copper Spot Price

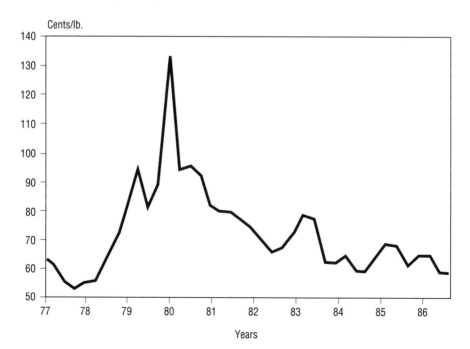

Figure 2.17.a   Historical Simulation: 18-month Put-Call Bond, with a Fixed Band

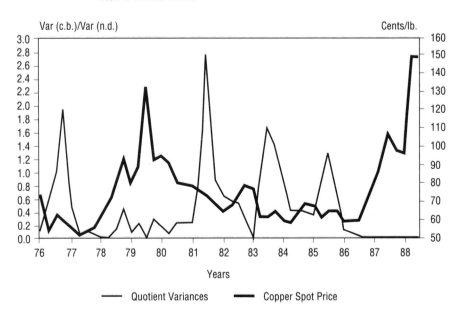

Figure 2.17.b   Present Ex-post Values

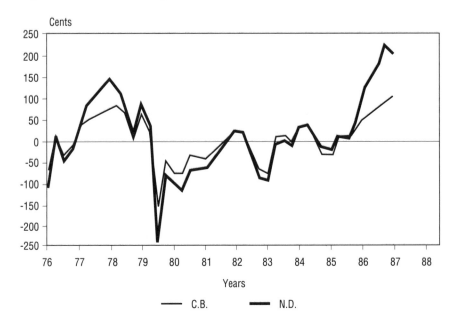

**Figure 2.18   Profile of Bands for a Put-call Capital Bond with a
Fixed Criterion**

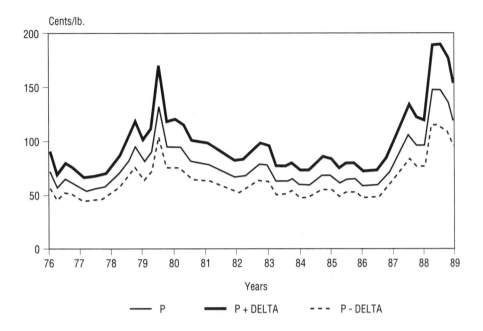

CHAPTER THREE

AN OPTIMAL SPENDING RULE FACING OIL INCOME UNCERTAINTY (VENEZUELA)*

Ricardo Hausmann
Andrew Powell
Roberto Rigobón

Introduction

The Venezuelan economy is characterized by the importance of oil income as the main source of foreign exchange and of fiscal revenues. In fact, oil exports account for over 80 percent of total exports while taxes paid by the oil industry constitute over 70 percent of ordinary fiscal revenue. Figure 3.1 shows the evolution of oil exports per capita in constant 1990 dollars. As can be seen, this income has been particularly unstable since the early 1970s. In fact, as shown in Table 3.1, the volatility of oil exports per capita, as measured by the standard deviation of the log differences, increased significantly in the 1970s and has remained at rates above 30 percent per year since. As a share of nonoil GDP (NOGDP), oil shocks averaged 11.8 percent during the 1970s and 5.2 percent in the 1980s (Figure 3.2).

Furthermore, as we shall argue below, this volatility has had very significant social costs: adjusting to such an unstable source of revenue has not only made it difficult to spend the fiscal resources efficiently but has produced important macroeconomic adjustment costs while causing the policy regime to collapse several times.

* The authors are grateful for the comments and the suggestions of Miguel Basch, Eduardo Engel, Montague Lord, Patricio Meller, and Juan Antonio Morales.

Table 3.1. Log Differences of Real Oil Exports Per Capita
(Percentages)

	1950–1959	1960–1969	1970–1979	1980–1989
Mean	0.6	−1.8	3.1	2.9
Standard deviation	20.7	14.1	35.5	30.2

Source: International Financial Statistics for Venezuelan oil exports and for the U.S. WPI and Central Bank of Venezuela for population.

This paper analyzes the problem of oil revenue uncertainty from different theoretical vantage points and formulates a concrete and coherent policy proposal. The second section states the problem of oil income instability and uncertainty. It distinguishes between the costs associated with each of these concepts. The section ends with an estimation of the macroeconomic costs suffered by the economy during the adjustment to the two major negative shocks of the 1980s. In the third section we argue that there is room for government policy in order to deal with the problem. We develop our case from two perspectives. First, we study the strategic interaction between the government's choice of spending and household's portfolio decisions in the context of oil income uncertainty. We establish an inefficiency and show that some form of insurance is welfare enhancing, even if all agents are risk neutral. We then study the consequences of collective choice as a means to decide on oil income allocations. We show that, in the absence of a rule, it is unlikely that consumption smoothing would take place, given the strategic interaction of players in a rent-seeking game.

The fourth section revues the different alternative solutions to the problem depending on the existence of certain markets and institutional mechanisms. It studies the sale of oil reserves, hedging through futures and options markets and economic "diversification." The main argument is that the absence or shallowness of markets makes it difficult for Venezuela to transfer efficiently a significant fraction of its oil risk. We therefore conclude that the best strategy involves an optimal spending-and-saving rule, which is implicitly a form of self-insurance through a stabilization fund. The fifth section reviews the different optimal saving rules found in the literature given the different nature of the uncertainty involved and other assumptions. To determine the relevant model we study the stochastic process followed by oil prices and exports and establish that it is non-stationary in its trend. According to the literature, for such a process, if no adjustment costs are assumed then it is not optimal to save in order to smooth consumption.

The sixth section presents a model for optimal saving for a non-stationary

**Figure 3.1   Per Capita Real Oil Exports
            (at 1990 prices)**

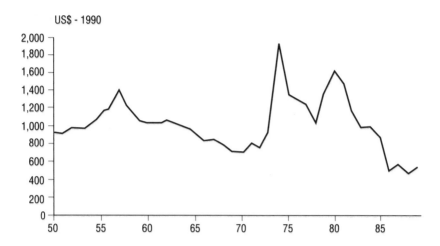

**Figure 3.2   Yearly and Cumulative Real Oil-export Shocks
            as Percentage of Nonoil GDP**

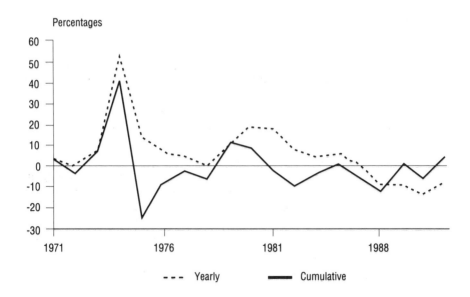

Martingale process with liquidity constraints and adjustment costs. We find an explicit spending rule and, in the seventh section, use econometric and Monte-Carlo methods to choose the relevant parameters. The eighth section analyzes the dynamic properties of the spending rule proposed and shows that it has a unique and stable steady state equilibrium and that the convergence towards it is smooth. It also presents a framework in which to decide on the initial fund level when the rule is adopted. The ninth section analyzes the reduction in uncertainty achieved by the spending rule. It shows that not only three fourths of the variance in spending, as compared to that of oil income, is eliminated, but that the remaining instability is highly predictable, so that the reduction in uncertainty is even larger. The tenth section shows ex-post simulations for Venezuela, assuming that the fund would have been adopted in 1972. We contrast fund levels with the international reserves actually held by Venezuela and conclude that the proposed approach would have avoided much of the troubles of the 1980s. The final section deals with the institutional aspects of the creation of a stabilization fund in Venezuela that would employ our optimal spending rule.

The Problem: Oil Income Instability and Uncertainty

The Costs of Uncertainty and (Known) Instability

Imagine that some godly angel had descended on Venezuela in 1970 to announce, with certainty, the path that oil exports would follow in the next 20 years. How would history have diverged from the actual experience? Notice that in this question we have not affected the degree of instability in oil revenues, only its uncertainty.

If future income is known, it is easy to plan spending. In fact, according to the standard permanent income hypothesis, the agent subjected to this highly unstable but known source of revenue would simply calculate the net present value of the income stream and would then spend smoothly, equating the discounted marginal utilities of consumption in each period. Income instability would not translate into spending instability at all. It would all be reflected in changes in the holdings of financial assets. If borrowing were called for, financial intermediaries would not have much of a problem in evaluating the risks involved, since the future stream of revenue is known with certainty. Hence, known instability should not be much of a social problem.

Given this case as a benchmark, let us study now the costs generated by uncertainty. In this case, agents would try to estimate the net present value of their expected but unknown income stream. Standard individual choice theory tells us that if the agent is risk averse, the expected utility derived from that uncertain income stream will be smaller than the utility generated by a known income stream equal to the expected value of the original stream. This means that there is a certainty equivalent income lower than the expected income that will generate the same level of utility. Such an agent would be in the market for an insurance policy that would transfer the risk to some other agent. If no such market exists, the agent would save a fraction of his income in order to protect himself from the low utilities derived in low income scenarios. Hence, on average, spending and the utility derived from it would be lower than in the case of certainty. This constitutes the standard theory of the costs of uncertainty.

Newbery and Stiglitz (1981, pp. 72-76) develop an approximate measure of the percentage risk premium (ρ) that an agent would be willing to pay in order to eliminate the uncertainty in his revenue (Y). The formula can be written as:

$$\rho = \frac{1}{2} R \sigma_Y^2$$

where R is the coefficient of relative risk aversion and σ_Y is the coefficient of variation of the income stream. Using our figures for per capita real exports for the period 1970-1989, we find that percent, and assuming $R = 1$, this gives us an estimate for ρ of 7.5 percent. This means that agents would be willing to forgo 7.5 percent per year of expected oil revenues or about 3 percent of NOGDP in order to guarantee a certain level of income.

Now, with uncertainty, agents will be changing their spending as they reassess their expected income stream. Thus, in 1974 Venezuela found out that it was wealthier than it had previously thought while in 1986 it discovered just the opposite. These reassessments call for changes in spending that may be significant at the aggregate level if the income flow and its volatility are high enough, as is the case for oil in Venezuela. Hence, aggregate uncertainty will cause changes in aggregate spending.

We will now argue that these changes in expenditures will cause further costs to the economy and that our previous estimate of the uncertainty cost in terms of utility losses due to risk aversion is only a small part of the total picture. The reasons have to do with the costs of mobilizing resources in order to accommodate the changes in spending. Let us see.

Imagine a three-sector economy in which capital is fixed but labor is mobile. The three sectors are oil, other tradeables, and nontradeables. If oil income unexpectedly rises, this will call for an increase in domestic spending of all goods. The increase in the demand for tradeables can be accommodated through a rise in imports, given the added availability of oil-generated foreign exchange. However, the increase in the demand for nontradeables must be met domestically and this will require an expansion in employment in the sector.

If the economy started at full employment, this increase will be achieved only by reducing employment and output in the tradeable sector. The price signal that will achieve this resource reallocation is a real exchange-rate appreciation. The movement of labor between sectors is likely to have output costs as workers remain temporarily unemployed between jobs.

Under a negative shock, the decline in domestic demand for nontradeables will reduce employment in that sector but demand for labor in the tradeable sector will grow only if there is a real depreciation. In the mean time, unemployment is likely to be high, causing output losses.

Consider now the problem of allocating investment in this economy. If oil income is expected to be high, nontradeable activities will offer better returns. In contrast, if oil income is expected to fall, tradeables will be the best option. Since, ex ante, agents do not know which of these two situations will occur, they will attach an oil-related risk premium to investments in either sector. In an open economy, the risk-adjusted return on capital will tend to equal world rates. Given this, the volume of investment in the economy will be lower than would have otherwise been the case, causing a slower rate of growth in the nonoil economy.

Finally, the revision of spending levels usually implies losses as the acquisition of certain assets in one period may be shown to be inadequate in future periods as income expectations change. Also, certain expenditures that take time may be stopped, slowed down, or inefficiently accelerated as the revenue stream unfolds.

An Estimate of the Macroeconomic Costs Involved

The social costs of oil income instability became particularly evident in Venezuela during the 1980s. GDP per capita, which increased by 234 percent from 1950 to 1980, or 4.0 percent per year, had a cumulative fall of 18.1 percent between 1980 and 1989. The currency, which had been only moderately devalued once in over a century, depreciated tenfold between 1983 and 1989. The yearly inflation rate, which had averaged 3.4 percent for the period 1950-1980, reached 84 percent in 1989. The foreign debt, which was negligible in 1974, totaled 54 percent of GDP or more than three years of exports by 1989.

Obviously these results were not due exclusively to the instability in oil revenue, but they were clearly influenced by the fact that oil exports, which had reached US$24 billion at 1990 prices in 1980, fell to 10.2 billion in 1989, a decline of 66.4 percent in real per-capita terms, or of 17.7 percent of 1980 GDP.

The fall followed the two well-known positive shocks of the 1970s and came in two rather discontinuous steps. The first shock in 1982-1983 was linked to OPEC's attempts to defend oil prices by cutting output. It reduced the real value

Table 3.2. Efficiency of the Adjustment to the First Shock
(As percentage of trend nonoil GDP)

	1982	1983	1984	1985
External shock	9.8	12.8	11.6	15.9
Primary absorption costs	7.8	11.8	10.4	15.4
Secondary adjustment costs	1.5	7.9	11.7	11.1
Total adjustment costs	9.4	20.7	23.3	28.2
Actual adjustment	0.8	33.9	30.8	32.9
Excess adjustment	−7.9	11.0	6.1	3.7

Note: Primary adjustment cost is equal to the external shock minus the initial output absorption gap.

of exports (at 1990 prices) from US$22.4 billion a year for 1979-1981 to US$15.9 billion for 1983-1985. The second shock took place when prices collapsed in 1986 and reduced real exports to US$9.5 billion for 1986-1989. Relative to 1980 GDP, these two negative shocks amounted to reductions in the real value of exports of 8.5 percent and 8.2 percent respectively.

As mentioned above, a cut in external income requires the economy to reduce domestic spending (also called absorption) or increase output in order to return to balance of payments equilibrium. We are interested here in finding out how costly this process was in Venezuela during the 1980s. To do this we adopt the following framework based on Corden (1988) and Meller (1990). We shall distinguish among three concepts of adjustment costs.

Primary adjustment cost is the optimal and unavoidable decline in absorption required to return to external balance. If all domestic output were perfectly tradeable, then adjustment costs would simply equal the external shock minus whatever excess of income over absorption existed at the moment of the shock. However, since not all output is perfectly tradeable, part of the fall in absorption may not go to improve the trade balance but to reduce nontradeable output. In this case, the economy does not remain at full employment, and output falls below trend, generating a further cut in income and absorption. We refer to this additional effect as secondary adjustment cost. Finally, we should distinguish these two costs from the actual adjustment costs incurred each year, which may be above or below the sum of the two previous effects depending on whether the economy has over- or under-adjusted, leaving an unwarranted surplus or deficit. We will measure these costs in Tables 3.2 and 3.3. Notice that primary adjustment costs may be positive or negative depending on the sign of the shock. However, secondary adjustment costs will be positive as they reflect the losses in resource reallocation which will happen independently of the sign of the shock.

The efficiency of adjustment to the 1982-1983 shock is analyzed in Table 3.2. There we compare the actual values of NOGDP to a counter-factual in which the economy exhibits homothetic growth of 3 percent per year, including its real oil revenue. We chose a low growth rate because the economy was very close to full employment in 1981 and productivity trends had been negative. Anyway, a more optimistic counter-factual would only make the adjustment even more inefficient.

Table 3.2 shows the results of our calculation. The first row measures the external oil shock with respect to its 3 percent growth trend, in units of trend NOGDP. The second row deducts from the external shock an amount equal to the initial output absorption gap (i.e., the current account surplus), which we take to be equal to two percentage points of NOGDP in 1981. This row indicates the unavoidable disabsorption costs of the shock if it is to establish external balance.

The third row shows the difference between actual NOGDP and trend NOGDP in units of trend NOGDP. This represents the loss of output given the path taken by the economy that we consider to be the secondary adjustment cost. If adjustment would be costless, this measure would be zero. In the fourth row we sum the primary and secondary adjustment costs and call it total adjustment costs.

In the fifth row we indicate how much actual absorption differed from the 3-percent trend, measured in units of trend NOGDP. The final row indicates the difference between total adjustment costs and the actual adjustment which took place. If the difference is positive, then there is excess adjustment expressed in terms of a balance of payments surplus. If the difference is negative, then the economy is reducing its net foreign assets in order to finance absorption and has consequently adjusted insufficiently.

Notice that secondary adjustment costs were quite substantial, averaging over 11 percent of NOGDP in 1984-1985 and representing a half of actual adjustment costs by 1985. In other words, for each percentage point of income lost through declines in oil exports, the economy lost an additional point through disruptions in output from trend. These large secondary adjustment costs are broadly consistent with developments in the labor market in which unemployment increased by six percentage points between 1981 and 1985.

Similar though somewhat different results were obtained after the 1986 shock. To perform our calculations we take 1985 as our base year and assume a counter-factual in which output, absorption, and real external oil income follow a 4 percent homothetic growth rate. The fact that unemployment was higher in 1985 than in 1981 leads us to assume a slightly higher counter-factual growth rate than in the first shock. We also assume an initial output absorption gap of two percentage points of NOGDP given the size of the current account surplus in 1985.

Table 3.3.   Efficiency of the Adjustment to the Second Shock
(as shares of trend nonoil GDP)
(percentage)

	1986	1987	1988	1989
External shock	9.9	8.5	12.6	9.0
Primary absorption costs	7.9	6.2	11.3	6.8
Secondary adjustment costs	−2.0	−3.5	−5.2	8.3
Total adjustment costs	5.8	2.5	5.5	15.7
Actual adjustment	0.5	−1.7	−6.1	17.9
Excess adjustment	−5.0	−4.1	−11.0	1.9

Note: Primary adjustment cost is equal to the external shock minus the initial output absorption gap.

Table 3.3 shows that by 1988, primary absorption costs were 11.3 percentage points of trend NOGDP. Interestingly, secondary adjustment costs were negative. The economy grew at rates higher than 4 percent because the government did not cut spending, allowing the current account to deteriorate while unemployment returned to its natural rate. Hence, actual adjustment costs were negative so nonadjustment did not have output costs.

However, as adjustment became inevitable in 1989 in the midst of a balance of payments crisis, we see an increase in the secondary costs of adjustment of 13.5 percent of NOGDP, leaving output 8.3 percent below the trend. Underadjustment was eliminated, leaving a small excess adjustment of 1.9 percent of NOGDP. For the period as a whole, actual adjustment costs amounted to 17.9 percent, 46.4 percent of which were secondary (i.e., inefficient).

Thus adjusting to changes in absorption because of oil income variability generates significant secondary costs that have represented losses of the same order of magnitude as the external shocks themselves (about 10 percent of NOGDP). Notice that these costs do not include the utility losses caused by the uncertainty (say, 3 percent) or the decline in the rate of growth caused by lower investment rates or by expenditure revisions (not estimated). If all these factors are considered, the uncertainty and instability of oil income clearly becomes a major social problem.

Is This a Public Policy Issue?

The fact that uncertainty has social costs need not imply that there is room for improvement through government action. The government seldom has an informational advantage over markets, and these may be more efficient answers to problems of risk and uncertainty. Thus, in the case of coffee price uncertainty, agents will be reacting through their consumption and savings decisions to the changes in market conditions, and it may well be that the resulting instability, though costly, is optimal.

However, things are different when the recipient of the volatile income is the government. First, while in the case of coffee many autonomous and atomistic agents are involved in the spending decisions, in the case of oil it is the government's single choice that will be relevant. This already implies a role for government action. Furthermore, since public fiscal decisions will affect household behavior, strategic interactions will take place causing further inefficiencies that can be addressed through public policy. Secondly, the government, or better yet Congress, is not a single monolithic unit but instead a group of agents that decide collectively. The perils of social choice may hamper efficient decisions unless constrained by some rules. In this section we will develop more fully these two arguments to justify explicit government action to deal with oil revenue uncertainty.

Governments and Households: Strategic Interactions

In this subsection we will develop some implications of the strategic interaction between the government and households based on related work by Hausmann, Powell, and Rigobón (1991). Imagine the following situation. The government must decide how much to spend in the next period before it knows how much it will earn. It does know the probability distribution of its income stream, and this information is public.

Households must then decide on the composition of their portfolio, knowing the government's spending commitment but not its income. Domestic assets yield liquidity services while foreign assets are protected from the inflation tax.[1] Finally, the value of income is revealed (or in game-theoretic jargon, nature moves deciding income). If the government spending commitment exceeds available resources, the price level will jump to clear the market for goods causing losses to holders of domestic currency. We assume that the government fixes spending in nominal terms so that it also shares in these losses. If, by contrast, income is higher than budgeted spending, then the price

---

[1]   We need to assume that domestic assets yield liquidity services since they would otherwise be return-dominated by foreign assets making them worthless. Hence we include it in the utility function. This approach has been explored by Kouri (1976), Obstfeld (1981), and Calvo (1981). For a review see Dornbusch and Giovannini (1990).

level remains constant and reserves will be left for future consumption.[2] We assume that the government and households maximize the same utility function composed of three factors: private consumption, liquidity services, and public goods.

This setup constitutes a Stackelberg game that can be resolved by finding first the households' optimal portfolio choice contingent on the government's spending commitment and then the government's optimal spending. The resulting equilibrium can be contrasted with that obtained by a social planner[3] that maximizes the same utility function but that can decide both variables simultaneously.

We establish the following propositions:

- Proposition 1. Households will have a lower demand for money function than the social planner. This follows from the fact that money becomes an asset whose value is contingent on the realization of oil income and the government spending commitment. It is as if money involves a "put" option on the oil income with a "strike price" equal to the spending commitment. If income is higher than the commitment, money has a constant value and the put option is worthless. Otherwise, it will loose value by an amount proportional to the government deficit. These losses serve to finance the government in periods of low income. Hence, money demand will be a decreasing function of planned government spending since this variable increases the value of the put. However, since households are atomistic they do not consider the inflation tax they pay individually as increasing the availability of public goods, a fact that the social planner does take into account. Hence, households value money less than the social planner and will have a lower demand function for money for any given level of government spending.
- Proposition 2. If the government is in the upward sloping part of the inflation tax Laffer curve, it will commit a higher level of spending than the social planner. Since demand for money is lower than in the social planner's equilibrium for any level of government spending, there will be too much private consumption and too few public goods in the low income scenario. To balance this, the government will fix a budget that will attempt to minimize this distortion. If it is in the upward sloping part of

[2] We assume the rate of interest on these assets to be lower than the social rate of time preference so that leaving a budget surplus is socially costly.
[3] The social-planner problem constitutes the Pareto-optimum equilibrium of the economy. If the equilibrium in the Stackelberg game is different, then it is inferior and opens the door for improvements through public policy.

the Laffer curve, it will set a higher spending commitment than the social planner.

If these two propositions hold, then:

* Proposition 3. There will be less money in the economy. This follows from the joint proposition that the spending-contingent demand for money is lower and that government spending is higher.
  Expected inflation will be higher. This follows from the fact that nominal government spending is higher while money demand is lower requiring a higher inflation rate.
  International reserves will be lower. This follows from the fact that real government spending will be higher when income is high, thus leaving smaller surpluses.
* Proposition 4. All these distortions increase with the variance of oil income. In fact, as the variance is reduced, the solution to the Stackelberg problem converges to the Pareto-optimum equilibrium.
  Money demand is a decreasing function of the variance of oil income. This follows from the option-like nature of money. As the variance increases, the expected value of the losses in cases of low income goes up while no benefit accrues to the money holder in cases of higher income. Thus, in net terms, it makes money more costly to hold, reducing its demand.
  Hedging is welfare enhancing even in the case of risk neutrality. Socially it is optimal to reduce the variance, and hedging is a way to do this. This will induce households to increase their money holdings, thus reducing the government's spending commitment and obtaining a Pareto-superior equilibrium. Since in the previous propositions risk neutrality pays no role, it will also be true in this case.

Thus, the presence of this strategic interaction between the government's spending decisions and household portfolio reactions generates important distortions that justify hedging or other risk reducing measures taken by the government.

The Perils of Collective Choice

In democratic setups, such as Venezuela's, spending decisions are not taken by a dictator but by Congress. This involves the use of majority decision rules which, ever since Arrow (1951), have been found to be wanting. Log-rolling, pork-barrel politics, and other such inefficient games have been analyzed in the Public Choice literature (see e.g., Mueller [1988]).

Oil revenues, as most other fiscal resources, will eventually be appropriated by individuals. Roads pass through particular neighborhoods, highway construction contracts are given to specific firms, drinking water runs into private homes and some children receive free education of varying quality. However, these agents do not have preestablished claims on those resources. In fact, property rights on oil revenues are obtained by participating in a costly and dynamic political process. No right can be taken for granted but will always be subject to challenge by other agents. To illustrate some of the relevant implications of these considerations, imagine the following scenario.

Assume that agents receive oil rents by participating in a political process that requires effort. The greater the effort spent, the greater the reward. However, effort is more effective for a particular agent when others are not asking for their share. Just as in the rent-seeking literature (Krueger [1973], Tollison and Tullock [1980], Bhagwati [1982]), the equilibrium of such a situation requires that the marginal disutility of effort equal the marginal benefit. Entrants will force expected rent-seeking profits down to zero, and the whole effort involved will be socially unproductive.

Consider, in this setup, a positive oil shock. Let us assume that socially the Pareto efficient solution is to save most of the additional income in the short-run in order to avoid adjustment costs. The question is whether such savings will be achieved in a democratic environment. The present model attempts to illustrate why it would not, thus explaining why countries tend to have great difficulty in managing positive shocks.

The main dynamic driving the result is that if one agent reduces his level of rent-seeking effort in order to allow resources to be saved, he raises the effectiveness of the effort put in by other agents, thus creating incentives to increase their influence activities.

To illustrate this, assume that there are two agents and each must decide whether to try to obtain a share of the rent or instead to stay calm and allow resources to be saved for future use. Call these two actions e (for effort) and s (for save). By assumption, if both save then the first best is obtained: resources will be available for future spending with fewer adjustment costs. However, if player 1 saves, it is in the interest of player 2 to seek rent, since the lack of effort by player 1 will make player 2's endeavors more effective. This makes player 2 better off at the expense of player 1, who will then have incentives to ask for his share. If both seek rent, then resources will be distributed in a costly manner because of high adjustment costs and a socially inefficient outcome will be obtained.

This latter result can be shown to be the unique solution of this game. Without loss of generality, let us set the utility derived by both players when they play as zero. Effort generates a disutility equal to u while it allows the agent to obtain a rent that depends inversely on the effort put in by the other player. For example, if player 2 chooses s, then player 1's effort is rewarded with r_0. If instead, player 2 chooses e, then player 1's effort generates rent $r_1 < r_0$. Moreover, when at least one player does not chose s, then each must pay macroeconomic adjustment costs a, independent of his own action.[4]

For there to be an incentive for players to seek rent, we require $r_1 > u$ and $r_0 > u + a$. Also, for saving to be socially efficient we need $r_1 < u + a$. The resulting pay-off matrix is the following:

	s	e
s	0,0	$-a,\ r_0 - u - a$
e	$r_0 - u - a,\ -a$	$r_1 - u - a,\ r_1 - u - a$

Given these assumptions and constraints, the game boils down to the standard Prisoner's Dilemma. Action dominates s since $r_0 - u - a > 0$ and $r_1 - u - a > -a$. The unique Nash equilibrium of the game has both players choosing and obtaining $r_1 - u - a < 0$, a socially inefficient result. Hence, the solution to the game has both players engaging in rent-seeking activities making the outcome socially inefficient.

This opens the possibility that by constraining behavior through rules, the social optimum may be achieved. Stabilization funds can be thought of as constitutional saving rules in the tradition of Brennan and Buchannan (1985). This is a justification for stabilization funds based on political economy. It stems from the notion that collective choice will cause very little consumption smoothing because of the strategic interaction between rent-seeking agents.

The Solutions

In this section we explore the different solutions to the problem of oil income uncertainty assuming different institutional setups and market possibilities. We will argue in favor of adopting spending rules and stabilization funds by first considering and eliminating other (better) solutions.

---

[4]   For simplicity we are assuming that there is a single adjustment cost for all circumstances in which at least one player chooses e. Complicating this hypothesis will not affect the results.

A First Best: Sell the Oil Reserves

If the problem faced by the economy is that of an asset that generates an uncertain and highly volatile income stream that has undesirable effects, then the first best solution is to exchange a portion of the asset for a safer one in order to reduce the overall risk faced by the economy. The risky asset involved in the case of oil is the natural resource (i.e., the petroleum reserves) and not the other factors of production, such as capital and labor, which do not generate rents.

The problem can be treated as one of portfolio choice and can be simplified to the case of an optimal composition between the risky asset (oil reserves) and a riskless asset, say U.S. Treasury bills. To give an idea of the magnitudes involved, consider the following calculation. Venezuela has some 60 billion barrels of proven oil reserves excluding the huge bituminous shale of the Orinoco river (estimated at over 160 billion barrels of mostly heavy crudes). At current production rates, the reserve production ratio for traditional crudes is close to 70 years. The total extraction cost has averaged less than $4 a barrel. For argument's sake, let's double this figure to $8 a barrel. Prices for Venezuelan crude have averaged about $18 per barrel in 1991. Hence, the value of a barrel of oil underground is about $10 per barrel.[5] Thus, if a proper market for reserves existed, the 60 billion barrels of reserves would be valued at some $600 billion. If this wealth were invested in riskless assets, the income generated, assuming a nominal interest rate of 7 percent on 30-year U.S. Treasury bills, would be US$42 billion, about three times the current value of exports. And this income would not only be virtually riskless but would also not be exhaustible!

Given expected risks and returns of oil, it would be relatively straightforward to set up an optimal portfolio, given risk aversion and other costs of uncertainty. However, the underlying assumption in such a calculation is that there exists a "fair" or efficient market for oil reserves. But such a market does not exist. And for good reason.

To be able to sell the reserves, the government would have to oblige itself not to renationalize the company in the future, something that it has already done once in 1976. It would also have to credibly precommit its future oil tax policy, so that investors can reasonably estimate future cash flows, considering only the intrinsic oil risk. However, since such precommitment is not possible,

---

[5]   The fact that not all of the oil can be taken out immediately is not very relevant. According to Hotelling's rule, the price of oil must be expected to rise with the interest rate, since otherwise there would be incentives to speed up production. If the interest rate is close to the rate of time preference of some investor, then the present value of a barrel extracted in the future is very similar to its current price.

investors will charge an additional sovereign risk, thus lowering the price. Given this, the government will receive less than the real value of the asset, unless it effectively carries out the threat to tax or nationalize. This being the case, agents will assess an even larger risk. The problem of time inconsistency of optimal plans (Kydland and Prescott [1977], Calvo [1978] makes the market disappear. Hence, getting rid of the oil risk by selling oil reserves it not a viable alternative. What next?

Second Best: Hedging

If, for the reasons given above, the actual asset cannot be sold, then it may be optimal to transfer the risk to some other agent using contingent claims such as futures and options. If such markets exist, it is possible to calculate a hedge ratio that would optimally reduce the uncertainty in the income stream, given the costs involved[6] and the benefits from risk reduction. By selling the oil forward, selling futures, or selling calls to buy puts, it is possible to lock into a known oil price for a given period of time, thus eliminating any price uncertainty for that term.

There is a problem with this solution: even though markets exist, and have been growing very fast in recent years, they still do not go far enough in time nor are they liquid enough to deal with a relevant fraction of Venezuela's oil uncertainty. From a macroeconomic point of view, the problem is to reduce the uncertainty surrounding oil wealth (i.e., the net present value of all future flows). The first few months of these flows represent a very small fraction of overall wealth so that reducing uncertainty over them will not be of aggregate significance.

Most oil-related futures contracts negotiated in open exchange markets go out for less than a year (Table 3.4). Only the Light Sweet Crude Oil contract negotiated at the New York Mercantile Exchange goes for almost two years. Moreover, the markets are small compared to the volume of Venezuelan exports while their liquidity drops dramatically with the time to maturity. For example, the total number of contracts outstanding on April 9, 1991, on all openly traded oil related future contracts was 158.7 million barrels for one-month deliveries (May), 23.4 million for six-month deliveries (October) and 11.5 million for one-year deliveries (April 92). By contrast, the volume of Venezuelan exports per month amounts to some 60 million barrels (i.e., three times the total size of the six-month delivery market).

---

[6]   The market for derivative securities can be thought of as an insurance market. If contracts were actuarially fair, a risk averse agent would hedge completely. However, contracts are more costly than this benchmark, so agents would never hedge their risk completely.

Table 3.4. Volume of Futures Contracts
(million barrels per month)

	Crude oil NYM	Gas oil IPE	Brent crude IPE	Heating oil NYM	Gasoline NYM	Total
May 91	66.65	11.33	33.53	20.27	26.88	158.66
June 91	49.41	10.11	23.42	11.15	16.77	110.85
July 91	32.71	5.40	5.01	12.10	14.52	69.75
August 91	25.10	3.52	1.78	7.80	7.36	45.57
September 91	22.10	1.56	3.04	3.83	4.07	34.61
October 91	14.49	1.05	1.04	2.13	4.66	23.37
November 91	8.48	1.30		1.84	0.70	12.32
December 91	21.47	0.62		13.06	0.68	35.83
January 92	9.42	0.68		2.68	2.78	15.56
February 92	5.20			1.53	2.85	9.57
March 92	7.36			0.37	0.31	8.04
April 92	11.17			0.25	0.10	11.53
May 92	2.04			0.45		2.49
June 92	6.81					6.81
July 92	3.25					3.25
August 92	1.71					1.71
September 92	1.34					1.34
October 92	0.19					0.19
November 92	2.43					2.43
December 92	1.14					1.14
January 93	5.12					5.12
February 93	2.22					2.22

Source: The Wall Street Journal, Tuesday, April 9, 1991, p. C-14.
Note: Heating oil contracts were converted at the rate of 9.25 barrels per metric ton.

The market for futures options has similar problems. These go out only for three months, and the volume of contracts negotiated is of the order of 120 to 150 million barrels for all maturities (Table 3.5). This number must be contrasted to the 180 million barrels that Venezuela would export in that period of time.

The lack of liquidity in these markets implies that if Venezuela really attempted to hedge a sizeable fraction of its risk, it could not take prices as given. Knowing this, other market participants would take into account the possibility that Venezuela may attempt to move the market for its own advantage and would consequently include this aspect in their assessment of the risk associated with the traded securities, making hedging very expensive.

Table 3.5.   Volume of Open Futures Options Contracts for May-June-July 1981
(millions of barrels)

	Crude oil NYM	Heating oil NYM	Gasoline NYM	Total
Calls	121.20	6.39	17.13	144.736
Puts	104.39	4.60	11.17	120.160

Source: The Wall Street Journal, Tuesday, April 9, 1991, p. C-15.

Economic Diversification: A Nonissue

It is often argued that one way to deal with the problem of oil income uncertainty is through economic diversification. If oil became a smaller portion of the economy, then its volatility would be less important at the macroeconomic level. Thus, an active policy directed at limiting investment in the oil industry in favor of other sectors of the economy would be called for. There is a long standing debate in Venezuela surrounding this issue, and it has recently heated up given the large planned expansion of the oil industry.

Of course, it is nice to see other activities develop besides the oil industry, but this should not be called diversification in the sense of explicitly changing the composition of assets and investments in order to achieve some aggregate goal. The relevant question is whether there is space for an active policy geared toward promoting other sectors in a way that creates artificial limits to the growth of the oil industry. Is there really an efficient trade-off between oil and other activities? Do oil-rich economies really face a problem of choosing a (centrally planned) portfolio of investments between sectors? Is there a market failure that must be dealt with through government redirection of investment away from the oil industry?

We will argue that there is not. To see this, take the argument to its extreme: eliminate oil income uncertainty by getting rid of the oil income itself. This is obviously absurd, since such a move would not reduce the risk rate, only the level of activity. The underlying intention behind such a move is the hope that output in other sectors will grow enough so as to compensate for the loss in oil revenues. But will it?

By reducing the level of activity in the oil industry, it is possible to take capital and labor out of the oil industry and put it into the rest of the economy. Will nonoil output increase enough to compensate for the loss in oil income? The answer is no. The reason is that around equilibrium, the marginal productivities of factors will be equalized across sectors. Thus, the marginal move of capital and labor will leave the net contribution to total income of these two factors unaffected. However, there is a factor specific to the oil industry, namely oil reserves, which cannot be moved to other sectors and which will decrease its contribution to income without any countervailing effect. Hence, national income will fall.

The Pareto-efficient equilibrium implies an ex-post allocation of resources that would make the marginal rates of substitution between capital and labor equal across sectors and the marginal productivity of oil reserves equal to zero. Any movement of resources away from this equilibrium will imply an inefficiency.[7]

Furthermore, it is not al all clear that there is an inelastic supply of capital available to the economy, so that assigning this factor to a given sector of the economy implies taking it away from others. In an open economy, risk adjusted returns will tend to equal world interest rates. Projects that have positive net present values should be able to find capital in world markets.[8] Moreover, oil production requires very little labor. In Venezuela, the oil industry represents about 23 percent of total GDP but less than 1 percent of the labor force. Thus, competition for this factor will not have a significant aggregate impact. Hence, with capital in elastic supply and labor not very much in demand, it is hard to argue against a policy that tries to maximize the use of the third factor (oil) that has no alternative use.

The optimal growth path for the economy would be consistent with decentralized decision making, sector by sector, such that ex-post, industries will have different shares in investment, employment and growth, but these shares need not, and should not, come out of an ex-ante calculation performed by a social planner who thinks he knows more than the market.

It is important to note that most of the adjustment costs generated by oil income uncertainty have to do with the induced changes in expenditure, not with the income itself. In the terminology of Corden and Neary (1982) and Corden (1984), the "Dutch disease" can be broken down into two elements: the resource movement effect and the spending effect. The first one has to do with the fact that a rise in the relative price of a booming export industry will cause resources to move towards that industry. However, in the case of oil,

---

[7] Endogenous growth theory would argue that there may exist increasing returns to scale in other activities due to nonconvexities such that an increase in the level of activity today may imply a higher output level or growth rate in the future. However, to defend this position would require an argument in favor of some specificity of other activities that do not occur in oil related fields. Typical candidates such as learning-by-doing, innovation, and external effects may be just as applicable, if not more, to the oil industry itself.

[8] The fact that the Venezuelan government has been recently rationed in the international financial markets does not imply that British Petroleum, EXXON, or Royal Dutch Shell would find similar limitations raising capital.

labor movements will not be significant at the margin since capital could come from abroad. Thus, the resource movement effect is likely to be insignificant.

The spending effect has to do with the fact that as income grows, demand for nontraded goods goes up, increasing their relative price and moving resources out of nonoil tradeables. It is this latter effect that is relevant for Venezuela; however, it is dependent on a fiscal decision to spend, not on the decision to produce. Hence, the two aspects can be treated separately.

The point is that the solution to the optimal growth problem for an economy with oil reserves must deal separately with two distinct issues: first, how to extract the maximum income out of all its resources, including the non-diversifiable reserves; secondly, how to deal with the costs generated by the resulting uncertainty. Economic diversification as carried out in Venezuela has implied limits to the development of a highly profitable industry in order to finance sectors that are risk-return dominated. Such a resource move has been possible only through active government intervention: it goes against market forces, but it does not solve a market failure. The benefits of such a *dirigiste* approach remain to be seen.

In synthesis, economic diversification is not a solution to the problem of oil income uncertainty because:

- Oil reserves are not diversifiable.
- The international supply of capital is elastic.
- Labor demand in the oil industry is unimportant.
- The costs of uncertainty are related to spending, not income volatility, and this is a government decision.
- There is no market failure affecting resource allocation that would justify an active policy to limit the expansion of the oil industry.

Third Best: Optimal Saving as Self-insurance

If risk cannot be transferred by selling oil reserves, is not hedging viable given the insufficient term and liquidity offered by the markets, then the remaining option is some form of self-insurance. By saving resources in some periods of time, the government can cushion the need to cut spending in other periods, making overall public expenditures more secure, thus allowing a more stable evolution of aggregate demand and of the macroeconomic environment as a whole.

The question then is to define how much of the unstable revenue should be budgeted and spent in any given period, how much should be saved, and how it should all react to the stock of assets accumulated in this dynamic process and to news about oil prices. We will assume throughout that the spending commitment of the government is made before the actual realization of income is known.

By stabilizing spending, oil policy can be fixed so as to maximize expected revenue (disregarding its instability), and then fiscal policy will spend the resources so as to maximize utility, taking into account the costs of instability and uncertainty. The criteria that go into defining optimal saving rules will be developed in the next section.

Optimal Saving Rules

In this section we briefly review the literature on optimal saving rules in order to set the stage for our proposed model, which we will formulate in the following section. We start with a review of the standard approach to stabilization funds and then study the underlying assumptions regarding the stochastic process that generates income. We then study the optimal rules under alternative assumptions about the availability of credit. We indicate that under the standard assumptions, if the underlying process is nonstationary, there are no reasons to save, and optimal spending would simply follow income.

Stationary Processes and Liquidity Constraints: The Traditional Approach

Imagine a situation in which there is a rather clear idea of the long-run price of a commodity. Periods in which prices are above the long-run level are known to be temporary, as are periods in which the price is below. Standard optimal consumption models without liquidity constraints would indicate that spending should follow permanent income and that transitory disturbances should be either saved or dissaved, depending on their sign. This framework, originally proposed by Friedman (1957) has been reproduced in intertemporal optimizing models (see Blanchard and Fischer [1989, Ch. 2 and 6], Sargent [1987, Ch. 3], Basch and Engel [1991, Ch. 2]).

This approach has been the underlying model of most existing stabilization funds. These funds generally set explicitly or implicitly a projection of the long-run price of the commodity and set spending as a function of that price, with the difference being saving or dissaving.

If there are liquidity constraints, this spending rule will not be viable in certain scenarios, since it would call for borrowing beyond the amounts allowed by the assumed constraint. This calls for precautionary savings in order to protect the agent from the low utilities that would be derived from periods in which consumption could not be smoothed otherwise.

However, these results assume that the underlying process is stationary. If instead the process is assumed to be nonstationary, there is a drastic change in results. As explained by Basch and Engel (1991), a nonstationary process can be thought of as one in which shocks are perfectly correlated, making them all permanent. This means that the best predictor of the future price is some trend over the current price. Changes in today's prices will feed into changes in tomorrow's price expectations. In this context, no notion of permanent income as different from transitory income can be developed. As a consequence, any change in price will lead to a full reestimation of permanent income, calling for a proportional change in consumption and leaving no reason to save. Deaton (1989) further shows that this result is maintained even if there are liquidity constraints. This result is troublesome since it implies that if oil income is nonstationary, the model provides no rationale for the adoption of a stabilization fund.

What is the Nature of the Stochastic Process Followed by Oil Revenue?

Given the importance of the nature of the stochastic process in determining the optimal saving rule, we carried out an econometric analysis of the data on oil exports and prices. A detailed description of the tests performed is presented in the Appendix. We will describe the main results here.

- Venezuelan oil export earnings and relevant oil prices are nonstationary. In other words there is no evidence of a long run 'normal' level of oil prices. If, in the very long run, there is any reversion towards a mean level of income then the speed of reversion is extremely slow indeed.
- On quarterly data, there is no evidence of serial correlation (i.e., there is no capacity to predict changes in price [beyond a constant trend] given current information). There is only some mild evidence of first order serial correlation at very high frequencies (i.e., for monthly data on oil prices and exports).
- There is evidence that the log change in oil prices and exports have excess kurtosis (i.e., the probability of large changes in price is higher than would be the case if the distribution were normal). In other words, distributions of these variables are not normal because they have 'fat tails'.
- There is no evidence of an ARCH interpretation of this data (i.e., the volatility does not seem to be auto-correlated).
- The characteristics of oil prices and oil income fits the so-called jump diffusion process, in which a normal random walk or diffusion process coexists with a jump process in which there is a finite probability each period of a discontinuous jump in prices of random size.

The fact that oil income and prices follow nonstationary Martingale[9] type processes may seem counterintuitive. It is commonly believed that prices have a long-run trend and medium-term projections are useful and necessary for planning. Elaborate arguments based on different scenarios are used to out-guess the market. Moreover, without a long-run price trend, how can one distinguish between permanent and transitory shocks in order to decide on a saving rule?

Venezuela has a long experience in attempting to plan its economy as if the evolution of oil prices could be projected with some confidence. In fact, oil projections are made regularly for planning and budgetary purposes by the national petroleum company PDVSA and are revised by the Ministries of Energy and Finance. Since they affect major political decisions, these projections are the object of intense scrutiny and bickering between government agencies, political parties, and the press. Hence, they must obey a legitimacy constraint that usually implies adopting some sort of international standard: expectations must be consistent with the conventional wisdom in the world oil market. We will now present data produced for the medium-term development plans and for the yearly national budgets. The sixth medium-term National Plan covering the period 1981-1985 was presented in September 1981 while the seventh plan covering 1984-1988 was made public in November 1984.

Table 3.6 contrasts the projected oil exports of the sixth plan with the actual values. Notice that a stable increase was expected instead of the marked decline observed. The difference represents 40.4 percent of expected income in 1983 and 54.3 percent in 1985. Moreover, exports never returned to forecasted levels. Since all the resources available had been assigned by the plan, which also included some borrowing, the shortfall was bound to make fiscal policy unsustainable.

The Seventh National Plan was written after the dramatic forecasting error of its predecessor, which was severely criticized for the inadequacy of its planning techniques (Matus, 1985). Consequently, the government decided to allow for contingencies by presenting three scenarios of oil exports. Table 3.6 shows the data for the planning period 1985-1988 and compares it with actual developments. Again, we notice that real income was about 40 percent below the levels expected by the worst scenario. Furthermore, income never returned to the projected trend. Notice also that in every projection, exports are expected

---

[9]   A Markov process is one in which future states are a function of current variables only, independently of their previous evolution. A Martingale is a Markov process in which the best predictor of future prices is the current price. These processes will exhibit no long-run trend and will make all shocks permanent, since any price revision will affect fully expectations about future prices.

Table 3.6 Actual and Estimated Oil Exports
(in millions of US$)

	1981	1982	1983	1984	1985	1986	1987	1988
Actual exports	19,094	15,659	13,667	14,634	13,144	7,592	9,104	8,158
Sixth National Plan Projections								
Projected exports	18,273	20,466	22,922	25,672	28,753			
-% difference	4.5	−23.5	−40.4	−43.0	−54.3			
Seventh National Plan Projections								
High scenario					15,280	16,800	19,180	21,400
-% difference					−14.0	−54.8	−52.5	−61.9
Baseline scenario					14,800	15,740	17,360	19,300
-% difference					−11.2	−51.8	−47.6	−57.7
Low scenario					13,060	13,740	14,580	16,130
-% difference					0.6	−44.7	−37.6	−49.4

Source: Background Information to Budget Bill, various years; Central Office of Budget, Petroleum, and Other Statistical Data; Ministry of Energy and Mines, various publications; Sixth and Seventh National Plans of CORDIPLAN (1984); and the Central Bank of Venezuela.

to rise smoothly in value. This is consistent with Hotelling's rule,[10] since otherwise it would be profitable for suppliers with different expectations to change their desired level of output.

Table 3.7 shows yearly projections for Venezuelan oil exports. The data, presented in column 1, is taken from the yearly budget laws approved by Congress in the last quarter of each year. These numbers are also based on projections made by PDVSA and approved by the Ministry of Energy and by the Presidential Budget Office. They are used to estimate oil tax revenues that averaged around 60 percent of central government current income during this period. Column 2 shows the actual value of exports. Column 3 calculates the percentage difference between the first two columns. Column 4 computes the implied rate of growth between the actual value of exports of the present year and the predicted value for the next year. Column 5 indicates the difference between the actual rate of growth and the predicted rate of growth.

---

[10] According to Hotelling's rule, the expected change in price of an exhaustible resource should equal the interest rate. This can be understood as a no-arbitrage condition. If prices are expected to rise at a faster rate, producers would have incentives to leave oil underground.

Table 3.7 Estimated and Actual Oil Exports
(in millions of US$)

	Predicted exports	Actual exports	Diff. (%)	Predicted growth (%)	Growth error (%)
1978	19,737	8,535	−20.5		
1979	9,941	13,517	36.0	16.5	16.7
1980	13,482	17,959	33.2	−0.3	33.6
1981	20,189	18,863	−6.6	12.4	−16.9
1982	29,894	15,395	−26.3	10.8	−33.5
1983	16,013	13,714	−14.4	4.0	−17.7
1984	13,912	14,670	5.4	1.4	4.0
1985	14,824	12,820	−13.5	1.1	−14.4
1986	12,774	7,117	−44.3	−0.4	−44.1
1987	8,700	9,054	4.1	22.2	−14.9
1988	9,265	8,136	−12.2	2.3	−14.2
1989	8,877	9,862	11.1	9.1	1.8
	Average		−4.0	7.2	−9.0
	Standard Deviation		23.9	7.6	21.9

Source: Background Information to Budget Bill, various years; Central Office of Budget, Petroleum, and Other Statistical Data; Ministry of Energy and Mines, various publications.

As can be seen, predicted exports tend to be similar and on average somewhat higher than actual exports of the previous year. This is indicated by the positive average expected growth and by the low standard deviation for the series as a whole. Part of the deviations can be explained by the fact that the information available in the fourth quarter of the year may differ from the yearly average. This is particularly important for the two years where the predicted growth was highest (1979 and 1986). In 1979, the oil shock took place in September-October and thus affected estimates for the following year. In July 1986, OPEC reacted strongly to the sharp fall in prices so that by October prices were well above the low levels reached in May-July. Thus it appears as if each year, or, more specifically, each month of October becomes the basis of the following year's estimate. This is what you would expect if the underlying stochastic process were a nonstationary Martingale process instead of trend stationary.

Given that in the Martingale process all shocks are interpreted as permanent, the current price becomes the best estimate of future prices, thus leading to a full revision of expectations. If the process were trend stationary, today's price rise (above a certain level) would imply expectations of a decline in next year's price. Given this knowledge, part of the instability in the series would be predicted. However, this does not happen in Table 3.7. As indicated, the level and growth rate prediction errors of the series (columns 3 and 5) have similar standard deviations.

Hence, our finding that oil follows a Martingale process is consistent with the nature of short- and medium-term projections (smooth upward paths starting from the current level), with the failure of medium-term projections and with the actual behavior of political agents in the yearly budgetary exercises.

Moreover, the fact that oil income is nonstationary may explain why it has been so difficult to finance periods of price declines. Since all changes are perceived as permanent, a negative shock implies that given current spending, the government is insolvent, not just illiquid. Hence by attempting to borrow, it may signal an unwillingness to adjust spending, in spite of the fact that it is not expecting any revenues with which to pay back the debt.

Nonstationarity, Adjustment Costs, and Liquidity Constraints

According to the previous discussion, oil income seems to be nonstationary. This implies that current models would not justify any saving, even under liquidity constraints (Deaton 1989). However, we have noted earlier that changes in spending seem to have significant macroeconomic adjustment costs, an element that would justify some sort of consumption smoothing, even if income were nonstationary.

Moreover, the presence of liquidity constraints may limit such smoothing since it may call for borrowing in periods when credit is not available. An optimal rule would incorporate this problem ex ante, given the expected costs involved. Hence, the optimal spending rule relevant for Venezuela's oil income uncertainty should involve adjustment costs, liquidity constraints, and nonstationary processes. We will develop such a model in the next section.

Optimal Spending Out of Nonstationary Income with Liquidity Constraints and Adjustment Costs

In this section we present our main model. We assume that the government is trying to maximize a social utility or objective function that includes four terms. First, the level of public spending generates utility. However changes in the level of spending affect the economy, causing two types of losses. On the one hand, planned shifts in expenditure cause standard adjustment costs because of the movement of resources required to accommodate changes in demand. On the other hand, since the government faces a liquidity constraint, because of its inability to borrow enough when income falls, it will be forced to adjust spending from the planned levels to a lower restricted one. We refer to these as default costs. These budgetary cuts will be more costly to the economy than the standard adjustment costs since they usually fall arbitrarily on high and low priority items or are financed in very inefficient ways, such as defaults, devaluations, and inflation. Finally, resources unused at the end of the period may be spent in future periods, thus generating (discounted) utility.

By putting end-of-period reserves in the utility function, we can convert a formally intertemporal problem into a one-period model, in which the future utility generated by current savings is captured by this term. This approach has both advantages and disadvantages. The major advantage is that the problem has an explicit solution that can be written into law and used in comparative statics analyses. The alternative intertemporal model allows only numerical solutions as in Deaton (1989) and Basch and Engel (1991). The main disadvantage is that it assumes that end-of-period reserves affect utility in a straightforward (and as we shall see, linear) manner, while implicitly it would be variable in the intertemporal model. Since we are interested in spending rules that can be written into law so as to break the inefficiencies generated by collective choice and by the strategic interactions between government and households, we require an explicit solution. Hence, we shall follow this approach.

We assume that the government is risk neutral so that spending and reserves enter linearly in the utility function. Costs, however, are quadratic: the larger the adjustment, the more costly it becomes at the margin. In fact, quadratic adjustment costs imply linearly increasing marginal costs. These costs are also symmetric: it is equally costly to move resources from tradeables to non-tradeables in a boom as it is in a bust. However, default costs occur only in negative shocks.

Formally, we assume that the government maximizes spending and end-of-period reserves net of the two sorts of adjustment costs:

$$\max_{G_t} E\left\{G_t - L_t(G_t, G_{t-1}) - A_t(G_t, G_{t-1}, G_t^*) + \rho F_t\right\} \qquad (1)$$

$$L_t = \frac{\alpha}{2}\left(\frac{G_t}{(G_{t-1})} - 1\right)^2 G_t$$

$$A_t = \frac{\beta}{2}\left(\frac{G_t}{G_{(t-1)}} - \frac{G_t^*}{G_{t-1}}\right)^2 (G_t - G_t^*)$$

where:

G_t government spending in period t

L_t loss function due to standard costs

A_t loss function due to default cost

Z_t oil revenue in period t

G_t^* maximum spending allowed given the liquidity constraint

F_{t-1} level of resources in the stabilization fund at the beginning of the period

μ maximum fraction of resources in the fund that can be extracted in any given period

ρ discount rate on end of period reserves

α marginal standard adjustment cost with respect to percentage changes in G_t measured as a share of G_t

β marginal default cost with respect to percentage changes in G_t measured as a share of G_t.

Standard adjustment costs L_t depend on the change in spending, while the default costs A_t depend on the difference between planned spending G_t and actual restricted spending G_t^*. The government must fix next year's budget before it knows how much it will earn. The restriction it faces is determined by actual (yet unknown) oil income Z_t, by the interest on current reserve holdings F_{t-1} plus a fraction μ of those reserves that can be extracted in any given year to cover revenue shortfalls.

$$G_t \leq Z_t + (\mu + r)F_{t-1} = g_t^* \qquad (2)$$

To incorporate uncertainty we assume a relatively simple stochastic process. Oil income either stays constant or goes up or down by a fraction λ. These three events happen with probabilities $(1-\delta), \delta - 2$, and $\delta/2$, respectively. Hence,

$$Z_t = \begin{cases} Z_t^1 = Z_{t-1}(1-\lambda) & \text{w / prob } \delta/2 \\ Z_t^m = Z_{t-1} & \text{w / prob } (1-\delta) \\ Z_t^h = Z_{t-1}(1+\lambda) & \text{w / prob } \delta/2 \end{cases} \qquad (3)$$

In this process the expected value of Z_t, $E(Z_t) = Z_{t-1}$, while the variance is $\delta\lambda^2$ and the kurtosis equals $1/\delta$. The odd moments are all zero, since the distribution is symmetric. We will use these properties to estimate the two parameters of the process using Venezuelan data.

This stochastic process captures some important statistical features of oil prices. As shown in the Appendix, oil seems to follow a nonstationary

Martingale type process with odd moments not significantly different from zero and with a kurtosis too large to be explained by normal distributions. These characteristics can be reproduced by equation (3). Moreover, such a process is analytically tractable and will allow us to find closed-form solutions, something that is not possible for more complicated processes such as the jump-diffusion process estimated in the Appendix.[11]

Planned G_t must be smaller than available resources in the high income scenario. Otherwise, the government would be intending to default with probability 1, something that would never be optimal given that it will certainly be forced to adjust spending and in addition will have to pay default costs, a situation that it could avoid by having a smaller budget, while incurring in no other losses.

We will solve the model for the case in which G_t is greater than available resources in the low-income scenario, labeled G_t^1. However, optimal G_t could be smaller than G_t^1 if the resources are high relative to past spending as would occur after a major positive shock. We will study this case later on. Nevertheless, let us return to the case when $G_t > G_t^1$. In this case, there will be a "bust" or default with probability δ. Given this assumption, in the high- and middle-income scenarios, the government spends planned G_t and faces only standard adjustment costs. By contrast, in the low-income scenario, the government is constrained to spend only G^*_t, and faces both sorts of costs: the standard cost of moving from G_{t-1} to G_t^* and the default cost due to the cut in spending from planned G_t to actual G^*_t. In the low-income scenario the government will be spending the following restricted amount:

$$G_t^1 = Z_{t-1}(1-\lambda)+(\mu+r)F_{t-1} \tag{4}$$

We can define $g_t = G_t/G_{t-1}$ and $g_{t1} = G_{t1}/G_{t-1}$ and as the gross rate of growth of government spending. Given this, the solution to our constrained optimization problem provides the optimal spending rule g_t:

$$\bar{g}_t = \frac{2(2-\delta)\alpha+3\beta\delta g_t^1 + \sqrt{(2-\delta)(6+\alpha-6\rho)[(2-\delta)\alpha+\delta\beta]-\alpha\beta\delta(2-\delta)(3g_t^1-2)^2}}{3(2-\delta)\alpha+3\delta\beta} \tag{5}$$

Even though the formula looks quite intimidating, once the parameters are chosen it can be written in the following, much simpler form:

---

[11] In an intertemporal model, μ would be endogenously determined so as to maximize expected utility.

$$\overline{g}_t = a + b\,g_t^1 + c\sqrt{d - \left(3g_t^1 - 2\right)^2} \qquad (6)$$

This formula indicates how much should be budgeted for period t (next year), given the information available in period $t-1$. It does not depend on any long-run price expectation, and it includes an optimization of the different costs and benefits considered in the utility function. Spending will be asymmetric: it will react more to positive shocks than to negative shocks, because of the impact of default costs.

If income happens to be low, this spending commitment will not be affordable since $g_t > g_t^1$. However, the expected default costs they cause have already been weighed against the benefits of having a higher budget if income happens to be higher.

Let us now return to the case in which $g_t < g_t^1$. Here the probability of default is zero. We can study this case by setting $\beta = 0$, and we thus obtain the following simpler formula:

$$\overline{g}_{t,\beta=0} = \frac{2 + \sqrt{1 + 6(1-\rho)/\alpha}}{3} \qquad (7)$$

This equation indicates the maximum rate at which governing spending will grow. This formula does not depend on oil income, so that even if it became infinite, the government would not budget an amount greater than that indicated by the expression above since the costs of increasing spending any further would outweigh the benefits.[12] This means that optimal g_t, labelled $\hat{g}_t$ is given by:

$$g_t = \begin{cases} \overline{g}_t & \text{if } \overline{g}_t \leq \overline{g}_{t,\beta=0} \\ \overline{g}_{t,\beta=0} & \text{if } \overline{g}_t > \overline{g}_{t,\beta=0} \end{cases} \qquad (8)$$

Notice that if we assume away default costs (i.e., $\beta = 0$) and if standard adjustment costs are infinite, the spending rule would call for $g_t = 1$. No changes in spending would occur since they would be unaffordable. Moreover, if end-of-period reserves are considered worthless $(\rho = 0)$, then there is no incentive to keep reserves, and spending grows at its maximum rate. If, by contrast, end of period reserves generate the same utility as current spending

---

[12] This is related to our comment in the previous footnote. If g_t is less than g_t^1, then the determinant of equation (5) will be negative. The government will spend as if $\beta = 0$, since no default would occur and that will determine a maximum rate of growth of government spending.

$(\rho = 1)$, then spending would be constant since it would be pointless to incur any adjustment costs. This point helps to clear the meaning of ρ. Besides the standard interpretation of this parameter as a discount factor related to the rate of time preference, it also contains two other terms. First, it includes the net present value of the standard adjustment costs that will be caused in the future by trying to spend the accumulated funds. Second, it incorporates the saving in default costs that will not be required in the future given the higher level of reserves.

Suppose now that standard adjustment costs are zero. Then the rule can be simplified to obtain the following expression:

$$\overline{g}_{t,\beta=0} = g_t^1 \frac{\sqrt{(2-\delta)(1-\delta)}}{3\delta\beta} \tag{9}$$

Notice that if default costs were infinite, the government would always choose g_t^1, which is a level of spending that would never cause it to default.[13] Also if $\rho = 1$, the same result is obtained since the government would have no incentive to incur in default losses, for any finite value of β, given the utility of end of period reserves.

Parametrizing the Model

We must now find suitable parameters for the optimal spending model developed in the previous section. Some of these parameters are related to the underlying stochastic process of oil income. These will be derived from the econometric analysis presented in the Appendix. The remaining parameters will be chosen using Monte Carlo simulation methods.

Estimating the Parameters of the Stochastic Process

In the model presented above we assumed a trinomial distribution for the stochastic variable Z_t. However, as shown in the Appendix, actual numbers resemble more a random walk or a jump diffusion process in which the underlying distributions are more continuous. In theoretical models, working with these sorts of processes is difficult because it makes the probability of default a function of G_t. Hence, it has been common in the literature to use binomial or trinomial trees as approximations to models in which the stochastic

---

[13] Also, it would never choose a lower level since there are no standard adjustment costs.

Table 3.8.   Estimates of the Parameters of the Stochastic Process

	Real exports (BCV)		Nominal exports (IFS)		p^*		WTI
	71-90	80-90	71-90	80-90	71-90	80-90	82-90
Mean	0.04	-0.04	0.10	0.01	0.12	0.03	-0.04
Variance	0.12	0.09	0.12	0.08	0.14	0.06	0.08
Stand. Dev.	0.35	0.29	0.35	0.29	0.37	0.25	0.28
4 moment	0.07	0.02	0.05	0.03	0.17	0.02	0.02
Kurtosis	4.46	2.45	3.04	3.57	8.87	4.41	3.09
δ	0.22	0.41	0.33	0.28	0.11	0.23	0.32
λ	0.74	0.46	0.62	0.55	1.10	0.53	0.50

process is more complex. This approach, initiated by Cox, Ross, and Rubinstein (1979) has been shown to lead to similar results provided the expected value of the stochastic variable in the binomial tree and its variance are the same as that generated by a normal distribution (Hull, pp. 220-222).

Here we will follow a similar approach. Our process is characterized by two parameters: λ and δ. Moreover, the variance of the process is equal to $\delta\lambda^2$ while the kurtosis must equal $1/\delta$. Hence, these two moments fully identify the process. Since the model we developed will be used for yearly budgetary purposes, we require these moments to be measured in annual terms. However, it is not clear how parameters estimated for a monthly process can be converted to a yearly one: if there is a certain probability of a jump in any month, then there will be a probability of more than one jump per year. However, we are restricting the process to include only one jump per year. This implies that parameters cannot be readily transformed from one frequency to another. Hence, for the purpose of parameterizing our model we will use yearly data.

The data is presented in Table 3.8. We use four different time series. The first one uses the log difference of real oil exports, as published by the Central Bank of Venezuela. The rest are log differences of average annual values, calculated from monthly data published by International Financial Statistics. These include nominal exports and an implicit price, which we call P*, composed of the ratio of these exports and a quantum index and prices for West Texas Intermediate (WTI) crude oil.[14]

We notice that these data show standard deviations between 0.25 and 0.37,

---

[14] More information on the data is provided in the Appendix.

in which the higher numbers are obtained when the period of estimation includes the decade of the 1970s. For the decade of the 1980s, the estimated standard deviations are 0.29, 0.29, 0.25, and 0.28.

Kurtosis is in general greater than 3 (i.e., excessive by the standards of a normal distribution), except for the case of real exports in the 1980s. In the Appendix, excess kurtosis seems to be a robust feature of the monthly data, ranging between 4.9 and 8. Given these facts, we chose a standard deviation of 0.3 (i.e., close to most estimates of the 1980s, but slightly higher) and a kurtosis of 4. This leads us to the values of 0.25 for δ and 0.6 for λ. These numbers are within the range of those estimated in Table 3.8.

Determining the Other Parameters

To choose a particular set of parameters, it would be ideal to have independent econometric estimations of α and β. However, these variables are difficult to estimate. First, it is hard to separate them, since they involve adjustment costs that tend to occur simultaneously. Moreover, β may have a somewhat different interpretation than would appear from the formula. In real life, a rise in G_t increases both the likelihood, and the cost of a default is independent of the choice of G_t, given the discrete nature of our assumed stochastic process. Hence, to mimic reality we would need a higher β so as to compensate through higher default costs for the constancy of the probability of a bust, keeping thus a similar expected value.

However, an econometric measure was done to gauge the order of magnitude of α. Assume there is a relationship between the log differences of national nonoil income Y^* and government spending G of the following sort:

$$Y^* = bG - \alpha/2\, G^2 + c$$

Assume that there is a dynamic adjustment towards this relationship that follows a Koyck polynomial:

$$Y_t - Y_{t-1} = d\left(Y_* - Y_{t-1}\right)$$

Combining the two equations we obtain the following relationship:

$$Y = bdG - d\alpha/2G^2 + (1-d)Y_{t-1} + dc$$

Where α is the parameter we are after.

Estimating this equation using quarterly data for the period 1978/I-1984/IV we obtain the following equation:

$$Y = 0.0394G - 0.12985G^2 + 0.8277Y_{t-1} + 0.0041$$
$$\quad (1.23) \qquad (-1.65) \qquad (8.61) \qquad (0.45)$$

$$R^2 = 0.6785$$
$$N = 48$$
$$DW = 2.156$$
$$F = 30.95$$

$$\alpha = 2 * \frac{0.12985}{1 - 0.8277} = 1.5073$$

The equation shows that α is significantly different from zero and provides an estimate of α of 1.5 with a confidence interval between 0.4 and 5.2. This is obviously a very wide margin. Moreover, we must remember that these are just the adjustment costs as measured by a decline in the measured rate of growth of the economy, not in wasted spending or in other forms of disutility. So higher values of α seem plausible.

Given that we lack direct and reliable econometric estimates of α and β, we will follow an alternative route for their selection. Our purpose is to find the most effective stabilization at the lowest cost. Since the fund is a self-insurance device, lower cost means fewer average resources in the stabilization fund. Effective stabilization must meet two criteria. First, it should reduce the volatility in government spending. Second, it should avoid defaults or busts. These three criteria lead us to the following variables.

Σ: Stabilization coefficient. It measures the reduction in the standard deviation of percentage changes in $G_t(o_g)$ relative to that of Z_t:

$$\Sigma = \frac{\sigma_2 - \sigma_2}{\sigma_2}$$

Q: Average level of resources in the fund as percentage of Z_t.
B: Probability that the fund goes "bust" (i.e., number of times per century that the government has to adjust its budgeted spending downward due to insufficient resources).

This suggests a simulation approach to the effectiveness of the formula. Since these effectiveness criteria are path dependent, the appropriate technique is a Monte Carlo study.

We generated 10 100-year histories of oil income using the estimated variance of oil revenue and a pure random walk. With these constant histories, we varied the different remaining parameter of the model: α, β, ρ, and μ, allowing them to take different values, as shown in Table 3.9.

Table 3.9

Parameter	Minimum	Maximum	Step
α	2.0	8.0	0.500
β	10.0	32.0	2.000
μ	0.2	0.50	0.033
ρ	0.0	0.95	0.100

These tests represent 9,500 simulations per history for a total of 95,000 experiments. In each of the simulations we estimated Σ, Q, and B and averaged them out for all 10 histories. We thus obtained a set of 9,500 vectors in R^7 with coordinates (β, α, μ, ρ, Σ, Q, B).

Our object is to find a combination of parameters that maximize Σ as a "good" and Q and B as "bads". We then plotted them in the space Σ vs. q and Σ vs. B in order to find an efficient frontier that reflects the trade-offs between these variables.

From these frontiers we chose points with values of Q less than 100, 150, and 200 and with fewer than 21 busts. The sets of parameters that obtained the highest stabilization coefficients are given in the following three tables. Notice that as the amount of resources in the fund (Q) goes up, higher degrees of stabilization are achieved. This is a measure of the cost of self-insurance. Notice also that the busts do not go down significantly when Q is increased from 100 to 150, but they do fall in the following table.

Table 3.10a. Parameters with Maximum Σ, for Q < 100 and Bust < 21

β	α	μ	ρ	Σ	Bust	Q
24	2.0	0.20	0.85	0.52450	13.9	198.0
24	2.5	0.20	0.75	0.52407	17.1	195.3
32	3.0	0.20	0.75	0.52407	15.4	198.2
32	6.0	0.25	0.50	0.52736	17.5	198.9

For the purpose of further discussion we will use mostly the parameters in Table 3.10b, and for other purposes we will concentrate on the vector indicated in bold type. In particular, for this latter vector, the spending rule becomes:

Table 3.10b. Parameters with Maximum Σ, for Q < 150 and Bust < 21

β	α	μ	ρ	Σ	Bust	Q
24	3.5	0.30	0.50	0.45128	20.5	146.4
28	2.5	0.25	0.50	0.45122	20.6	138.4
28	3.0	0.25	0.50	0.46455	20.6	149.0
32	2.5	0.25	0.50	0.45190	18.2	136.6
32	3.0	0.25	0.50	0.36478	19.0	147.5

Table 3.10c. Parameters with Maximum Σ, for Q < 200 and Bust < 21

β	α	μ	ρ	Σ	Bust	Q
24	2.0	0.20	0.85	0.52450	13.9	198.0
24	2.5	0.20	0.75	0.52407	17.1	195.3
32	6.0	0.25	0.50	0.52729	15.4	198.2
32	6.0	0.25	0.50	0.52729	17.5	198.9

$$\overline{g}_t = 0.3368 + 0.4948 g_t^1 + 0.1667 \sqrt{3.7530 - \left(3 g_t^1 - 2\right)^2} \qquad (10)$$

where

$$g_t^1 = \frac{0.4 Z_{t-1} + 0.35 F_{t-1}}{G_{t-1}} \qquad (11)$$

and

$$\overline{g}_{t,\beta=0} = 1.1209.$$

Dynamic Characteristics of the Spending Rule

In this section we will analyze the stability and dynamic adjustment properties of the proposed formula. We first establish the existence and stability of a steady state and then analyze the path through which the formula reaches it.

The spending rule derived from our model exhibits a well-defined and stable steady state[15] with $g_t' = 1$ and Q equal to a constant Q^*.

---

[15] By steady state we mean a situation in which oil income is constant so that $Z_t = Z_{t-1}$.

To solve for the value of Q^* we note that in the steady state $g_t = 1$. Using this fact, we invert equation (6) to solve for g_t^1:

$$g_t^1 = \frac{b(1-a) + 6c^2 + c\sqrt{d(9c^2 + b^2) + (2b - 3(1-a))^2}}{b^2 + 9c^2} \tag{12}$$

Also, using equation (4) in the steady state[16] we can derive the following expression for Q^* as a function of g_t^1:

$$Q^* = \frac{g_t^1 - (1-\lambda)}{\mu + \rho} \tag{13}$$

These two expression can be used to solve for Q^* as a function of the parameters of the model. Table 3.11 shows the values of Q^* for the parameters in Table 3.10b. The steady-state fund level Q^* depends on δ, λ, β, ρ, and μ but not on α. This can be seen in the fact that vectors (b) and (c) as well as vectors (d) and (e) have the same Q^*. Also, it can be shown that Q^* increases with β and ρ and decreases with μ.

To show that this steady state is stable we will develop a relationship between Q_t and Q_{t-1} and show that it is a contraction mapping with a fixed point.[17] To do so, note that if $Z_t = Z_{t-1}$ there is no possibility of a bust. Hence, $F_t = F_{t-1} + Z_t$. Dividing this equation by G_{t-1} we obtain the following relationship between Q_t and Q_{t-1}:

$$Q_t = \frac{Q_{t-1} + Z_{t-1} - g_t}{g_t} \tag{14}$$

where lower case variables are equal to capital letter variables divided by G_{t-1}. Using equation (4) to substitute for g_t^1 in equation (6)[18] and substituting for g_t in equation (14) we obtain the desired function between Q_t and Q_{t-1}. This equation is plotted in Figure 3.5 for the parameter values of bold-face vector (a). Here we plot the functional relationship between the two variables and a 45° line. The latter is used to indicate the steady state point in which $Q_t = Q_{t-1}$.

---

[16] Here we use the fact that in the steady state $G_t = G_{t-1} = Z_t = G_{t-1}$.

[17] For a technical introduction to this technique see Stokey and Lucas (1989).

[18] Notice that:

$$g_t^1 = \left[(1-\lambda)Z_{t-1} + (\mu + r)F_{t-1} \right] / G_{t-1}$$

This can be rearranged as $g_t^1 = (1-\lambda)Z_{t-1} + (\mu + r)Q_{t-1}$, which gives a functional relationship between g_t^1 and Q_{t-1}

**Figure 3.3   The Fixed Point Q^* and the Constancy of g_t
at the Steady State**

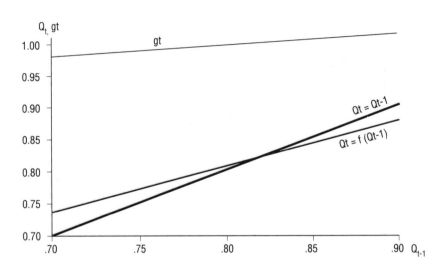

Since the functional relationship crosses the 45° line from above (i.e., with a slope less than 1) the point is stable. For the chosen values it equals 82.3. Notice that this value is less than the average $Q = 146.4$ estimated in the historical simulations. This is because of the asymmetric reaction of spending to shocks: when the level in the fund is low, spending is cut more than the increase in spending when the fund level is high: Hence, on average the economy will spend more time above Q^* than below it.

At the steady state, we can check that $g_t = 1$ by finding the value of g_t determined by Q_t and plugging it into equation (6) to determine g_t. We plot this equation in Figure 3.5 together with the functional relationship between Q_t and Q_{t-1} around the steady state. Notice that when Q_t reaches its steady state value Q^*, $g_t = 1$.

Hence, our rule has a unique and stable steady state characterized by a constant level of spending $(g_t = 1)$ and an equilibrium-fund level equal to Q^*.

Let us study now the dynamic adjustment to the steady state. In Figure 3.4 we simulate the convergence to a steady state in which $Z_t = 10,000$, starting from two different initial fund levels ($F_0 = 0$ and $10,000$). As shown, the path involves oscillations, an indication that the underlying system of difference equations has complex roots.

This behavior can be approximated by functions of the form $(\phi + 2\pi/\tau)$, where ϕ is the asymptotic envelope and τ is the frequency of the oscillations. A higher ϕ forces the economy to adjust more quickly to the steady state by

Figure 3.4   Dynamic Adjustment to the Steady State from Different Initial Fund Levels

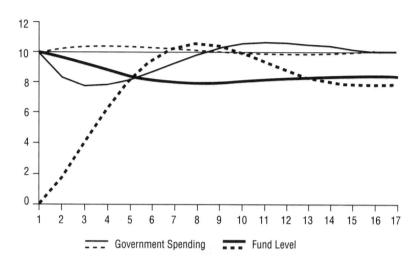

saving more quickly, thus causing the fund to be more stable but the economy more unstable. To measure this effect we calculate the saving rate during the first three years of operation of the fund, starting from $F_0 = 0$. These values are shown in Table 3.11. They vary from 20.9 percent to 26.7 percent and will reach 90 percent of the steady value in the fourth year.

For Venezuela, where oil represents 23 percent of GDP, such saving rates are obviously too large a real shock to the economy, representing between 4 percent and 6 percent of GDP. Moreover, they would be unacceptable since they are the consequence of the adoption of an institutional rule and not of any real change in the economy. Hence, to ease the adoption of the rule, it would be convenient to start the mechanism with an initial fund level higher than zero, that reduces saving requirements to socially tolerable levels.

Figure 3.5 shows the required saving rates starting from different initial fund levels. We can use this graph to choose the initial fund level and to discriminate between alternative parameter vectors that would be thought of as equivalent in terms of Σ, Q, and B. For example, if we restrict the saving rates to less than 10 percent, vector (a) requires an initial Q of only 40, while the other vectors require more than 55. We used this criterion to select vector (a).[19]

---

[19] We will discuss the problem of the initial fund level when we study the institutional aspects of the fund.

Figure 3.5   Initial Fund Levels and Required Saving Rates for the First Three Years

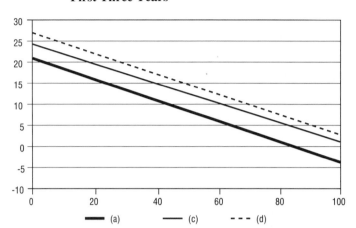

| | (a) | | (c) | - - - (d) |

The oscillary aspect of the adjustment path is studied by measuring its period τ and the magnitude of the first peak along the path towards the steady state starting with $F_0 = 0$ (see Table 3.11). A higher τ implies lower distortions to the economy caused by the dynamic properties of the spending rule. If $\tau \to \infty$ there will be no oscillations. In all parameter vectors considered in Table 10, the period is very similar and long enough (16 - 17 years) so as not to be of very much importance. We also measure the amount of overshooting in the fund level over the steady state value Q^* during the first peak of the adjustment path. These average between 5 percent and 8 percent of Q^*, not a large amount given the low initial level of the fund ($F_0 = 0$) with which we started the simulation.

Hence, the spending rule not only achieves a significant amount of stabilization but it also has adequate dynamic properties: it has a unique and stable steady state with a known equilibrium-fund level Q^*. It has a smooth convergence path with very long oscillations and predictable ex ante saving rates that can be used to generate criteria for the initial fund level.

Predictability, the Reduction in Instability and Uncertainty

Our spending rule, as parameterized and analyzed in the previous sections, generates significant reductions in instability, which averaged around 45 percent for Qs of 150. However, much of the remaining variability in spending is now predictable given the autocorrelated nature of the spending rule that determines G_t as a function of G_{t-1} and F_{t-1}. Thus, the reduction in uncertainty exceeds the reduction in instability.

Table 3.12. Variance Reduction

	DLZ_t	DLG_t	Reduc.
Variance	8.97%	2.14%	76.1%

To show this, we studied the predictability of future changes in spending, given current information. We used our spending rule with parameter vector (d) and applied it to one of our 100 year histories. The formula achieved a 76.1 percent reduction in the variance of log changes in G_t (called DLG_t),[20] as shown in Table 3.12.

To study the predictability of future changes in G_t we ran the regressions shown in Table 3.13. The first one attempts to predict the future value of DLZ_t, using known variables such as LG_{t-1}, LZ_{t-1} and LF_{t-1}. Since LZ_t is a random walk its log difference is white noise. Hence, government spending and the fund level have no predictive capacity, as can be seen from their insignificant coefficients. Of course, these results are just a consequence of the way we constructed Z_t. However, if government spending were to follow income, this would be the relevant equation in attempting (uselessly) to predict G_t. Hence, it serves as a benchmark with which to measure the reduction in uncertainty achieved by our spending rule.

The next three equations attempt to measure the predictability of DLG_t with one, two, and three years of anticipation, respectively.

In all these equations, LG_t, LZ_t, and LF_t are significantly correlated with future log changes in G_t and are able to account for 78.8 percent, 37.8 percent, and 16.1 percent of the variance in this variable, one, two, and three years ahead, respectively. Using these values, we can determine the amount of uncertainty that was reduced because of the fall in total variance and in the predictability of that variance. These calculations are performed in Table 3.14. Column 3 is the predictable variance and is calculated as the product of R^2 and of the variance of DLG_t, which is 2.14, as indicated in Table 3.12. The difference is the unexplained portion and is presented in Column 4. Column 5 shows the total percentage reduction in uncertainty as the sum of the reduction in variance and the predictability of the remaining variance. Column 6 indicates the share of the reduction explained by predictability.

In synthesis, our spending rule achieves an important reduction in the variance of government spending relative to that of oil revenues. However, not

---

[20] Logs of variables are indicated by a letter L preceding its name, while log differences have the letters DL as prefixes.

Table 3.13.   Regressions Between G_t, Z_t and F_t

$DLZ_t = -0.142$	$LZ_{t-1} = +0.052$	$LG_{t-1} = +0.0006$	$LF_{t-1} = +0.902$	$R^2 = 0.052$	
(-0.13)	(0.56)	(0.01)	(1.97)	$DW = 1.866$	
$DLG_t = 0.216$	$LZ_{t-1} = -0.629$	$LG_{t-1} = +0.1560$	$LF_{t-1} = -0.04$	$R^2 = 0.788$	
(7.71)	(-17.8)	(6.72)	(-0.42)	$DW = 2.099$	
$DLG_t = 0.116$	$LZ_{t-2} = -0.261$	$LG_{t-2} = +0.0740$	$LF_{t-2} = +0.262$	$R^2 = 0.378$	
(3.46)	(-7.46)	(1.87)	(1.50)	$DW = 1.780$	
$DLG_t = 0.108$	$LZ_{t-3} = -0.161$	$LG_{t-3} = +0.009$	$LF_{t-3} = +0.440$	$R^2 = 0.161$	
(1.94)	(-3.86)	(0.20)	(2.18)	$DW = 1.260$	

Table 3.14. Predictability and Uncertainty Reduction
(percentage)

Periods Ahead	R^2	Predictable Var(DLG_t)	Unpredictable Var(DLG_t)	Uncertainty Reduction	Due to Predictability
1	78.8	1.7	0.5	94.9	18.8
2	37.8	0.8	1.3	85.1	9.0
3	16.1	0.3	1.8	80.0	3.8

all of the remaining variance in DLG_t is noise, but a portion of it is systematic and can be predicted. Hence, part of the remaining instability is not uncertain but is known. Hence, agents will be able to anticipate it, thus reducing further its social cost.

Ex-post Simulation

It is interesting to ask the following question: what would have happened in Venezuela if the stabilization fund had been put in place, as designed here, in 1972. To find out we ran ex post simulations with historical oil exports and with an initial fund level equal to existing international reserves.

As shown in Figure 3.6, spending would have increased at the maximum rate allowed from 1974 until 1983. Figure 3.7 graphs the amount of resources held by the fund and compares it with the international reserves actually held by

**Figure 3.6   Ex-post Simulation of Oil Exports and
             Government Spending**

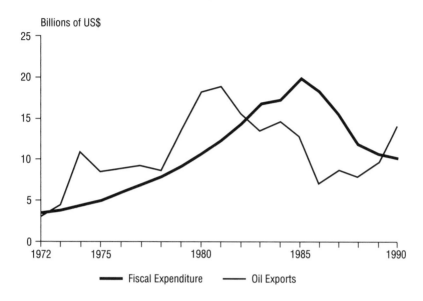

Fiscal Expenditure   Oil Exports

**Figure 3.7   Ex-post Simulation of Fund Level and Actual
             International Reserves**

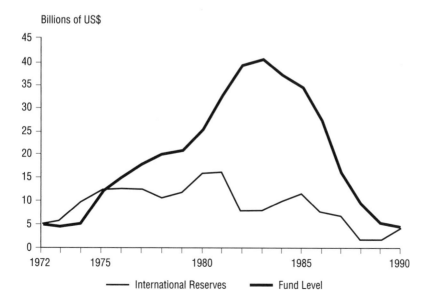

International Reserves   Fund Level

Venezuela during the period. As can be seen, the fund would have accumulated up to US$42 billion by 1983. These resources would have been used to cushion the decline in oil prices in the 1980s. Between 1983 and 1988, spending some US$35 billion above income and this gap was financed by drawing resources from the fund.

It is interesting to compare this path with the one actually followed by the country's international reserves. The amount of savings actually generated in Venezuela during the two positive shocks of the 1970s was significantly below the levels accumulated by the fund. This implied that when the negative shocks of the 1980s took place, there were insufficient resources to cushion them, forcing the government into several major balance of payments crises.

In looking at the past, one may be tempted to use hindsight in order to criticize actual policies. However, it is important to point out that our formula does not make use of any information that was not available at the time. Moreover, the parameters were chosen because of their stabilizing properties for general stochastic processes with characteristics similar to those of oil income but without taking into account its actual path in recent history.

Institutional Design

In this section we discuss some important institutional aspects of the Stabilization Fund such as its placement, its links to the budget and to the monetary authority, the nature of the assets it will hold, the provisions elative to the initial fund levels, and other matters.

Design Criteria

The following criteria must be considered in designing the stabilization mechanism:

- The fund must ease fiscal budgeting and execution. It must be compatible with the yearly fiscal process and should permit the approved budget to be carried out with a minimum of oil related revisions.
- The fund must deal simultaneously with the fiscal and balance of payments aspects of oil instability and uncertainty.
- The stabilization fund should not affect the oil industry. The problem at hand is one of stabilizing fiscal spending, not oil revenues. Hence, the fund should not create any new restrictions or distortions in the oil sector.
- The fund must stabilize the whole public sector and not just the central government. Many legal provisions force the central government to share

revenue with other institutions. The fund should also stabilize these transfers.
• The functioning of the fund must not depend on long-term oil income projections. There is little predictability in oil prices but projections can be maliciously used to draw excessive resources from the fund.

Basic Framework

The adoption of the stabilization mechanism requires a distinction between accrued and budgeted oil tax revenue. The oil industry should pay all its taxes into the stabilization fund according to existing laws: this is the accrued tax (our Z_t). No change in these laws is required. The only difference comes from the fact that taxes will be paid into the stabilization fund and not the General Treasury's accounts.

The government will draw resources from the fund according to the budgeted oil tax (our G_t). This figure should be calculated on a yearly basis at the moment of budget preparation. To calculate this number, the spending rule developed above should be used. It should use current accrued oil income (i.e., for $t-1$), current budgeted income, and current fund levels. There is no discretion in the estimation of next year's income in order to prevent the government from drawing down the resources in the fund through willful over-estimation. The formula already considers adjustment costs, the probability and cost of "busts" and the opportunity cost of holding resources idle in the fund.

Through the period of budget execution, money will go into the fund according to the real behavior of the oil market but will flow out of the fund according to the budgeted commitment. The fund is obliged to transfer the budgeted resources unless doing so would cause its level to drop to less than a fraction $1-\mu$ of the level observed at the beginning of the year. When such a level is reached, the fund should transfer a volume of revenue consistent with the minimum fund level for that year. This parameter was calculated so as to provide smoothing after a negative shock for several budget years and not just the first.

Positive shocks that occur within the period of budget execution cannot be used for the purpose of increasing that year's budgeted income. This is a welcome change that will end a pernicious game that currently affects the budgetary process. At present, spending ministries tend to increase their real budgets by underestimating actual commitments in those areas that cannot be reduced because of social, political, or legal reasons. This allows them to increase allocations for other, less sensitive programs, knowing that the government will be forced to approve additional appropriations during budget execution. In anticipation of this outcome, the Finance Ministry tends to underestimate fiscal revenue in order to have sufficient resources for these additional demands. This makes the strategy of the spending ministries optimal since resources will actually be available and will be distributed according to the squeaky-wheel rule: the wheel that squeaks the most, gets the grease. It also makes the Finance Ministry keep underestimating its revenue, in order to reduce tensions during budget execution. Knowing that resources are available, other agents pressure the ministries into demanding a larger budget. The system is thus trapped in an inefficient equilibrium.

By making explicit the amount to be transferred by the fund to the government, this double underestimation game cannot be sustained. The Finance Ministry can credibly precommit its revenue level and can stand firmer *vis à vis* the spending ministries. These will know that additional resources will not be available and will have less incentives to willfully underestimate spending.

Guidelines for the Management of Fund Resources

The resources held by the fund should be *invested abroad*, so as not to transmit oil instability to the domestic financial market. Assets should be invested in *safe and liquid securities* so as to be available to cover potential shortfalls between inflows and outflows. Since the fund has very irregular inflows but rather fixed outflows, it will have a very unstable level and should thus be very liquid. The fund is *not created for real fixed capital formation* but to smooth spending. Such expenditures represent budgetary decisions of the government, which should be made on the resources it has available for expenditure, not on those that are held by the fund.

Institutional Location

The fund should formally be owned by the central government. However, the law that creates it must limit the government's ability to use the fund's resources according to the spending rule derived above and used for the general fiscal budget. Moreover, the law should supersede other laws that obligate the government to transfer resources to other agencies and levels of government. In particular, the Venezuelan Constitution requires the government to transfer a fraction of its ordinary revenue to state and local governments. Other laws require it to make transfers equal to fixed proportions of its income to the Venezuelan Investment Fund, to the housing sector and to others agencies. These laws should be interpreted as relating to budgeted and not accrued oil income. The fund may be administered by the Central Bank but should ideally be managed by an autonomous agency in order not to interfere with monetary targets or be manipulated with monetary or exchange rate objectives.

Initial Fund Level and Transitory Provisions

The adoption of the stabilization fund poses the question of its initial endowment. As discussed above, if started with a very low initial level, the formula proposed will demand a very high ex ante saving rate until the fund reaches levels close to those of the steady state. This is unlikely to be tolerated. Moreover, such a real shock to the economy is likely to be damaging and inefficient.

The point is that if the fund is created to stabilize the economy, resources currently available for this purpose should be committed to the fund. In fact, the current level of international reserves in Venezuela is high by international standards,[21] in part because of the need to cushion oil uncertainty. A fraction of these reserves could be transferred to the fund, where they would serve more explicitly for this purpose. In particular, there is a sizeable amount of capital reserves that were constituted as an accounting counterpart to the valuation changes in foreign exchange holdings given the depreciation of the currency. The government could declare capital gain profits and transfer them in dollars to the stabilization fund. This would eliminate most of the excessive saving rate that the rule would otherwise impose in the first years of operation.

Furthermore, to ease the process of reserve accumulation by the fund, multilateral agencies could provide a contingent credit line, which would be considered as part of the fund level F_t for the purpose of calculating the budgeted oil income G_t, although no disbursements would actually be made unless these were required. Since the contingent facility will generate a more stable climate for the growth and the adjustment process it should be viewed as a worthwhile activity by these multilateral development agencies.

Stabilization Fund and Exchange Rate Regime

Oil is simultaneously an external and a fiscal income. Consequently, it affects simultaneously the balance of payments and the government accounts. These are two sides of the same coin and must be dealt with simultaneously. However, depending on the exchange regime, there may be coordination failures between one and the other.

---

[21] At the end of 1991, International Reserves held by the Central Bank amounted to more than one year of oil exports.

If there is a positive shock, our mechanism would call for a fiscal surplus and an accumulation of funds abroad (i.e., a balance of payments surplus). This happens automatically. The internal economy will be left mostly unaffected as resources would be sterilized. However, assume the following situation which resembles very much Venezuela's attempt to establish a contingency mechanism in 1990: the fund is defined only as a fiscal device and its resources are deposited at the Central Bank, without any clear link to the asset side of the bank's balance sheet. Suppose further that the country has a floating exchange regime so that it fixes exogenously its reserve target. In this case, there is no clear link between the fiscal and the balance of payments aspect of the stabilization fund and coordination failures will be reflected in unstable exchange and interest rates.

Suppose, for example, that there is a positive shock, that the government saves according to the stabilization rule but that the Central Bank does not explicitly adjust its reserve targets. Then there will be a nominal appreciation of the currency, as the Central Bank increases its supply of dollars to the market given its greater supply. Alternatively, suppose the Central Bank does adjust its reserve targets but the government fails to save the additional resources; in this case, the exchange rate would depreciate the interest rates.

Moreover, reserve targets can be managed on a daily basis while fiscal policy is decided annually. The possibility of coordination failures implies that it is very dangerous to attempt to fix reserve targets exogenously. Consequently, to be consistent with our stabilization fund, monetary policy should be based on predetermined exchange rates (fixed or crawling), and net reserve accumulation should be an endogenous macroeconomic outcome of (mostly) fiscal policy. If the Central Bank wants to protect its international reserves, it should make use of interest-rate not exchange-rate policy.

APPENDIX

THE NATURE OF THE STOCHASTIC PROCESS
FOLLOWED BY OIL INCOME

In this appendix, we consider a set of relevant questions regarding the nature of the statistical process generating oil income. The first part considers which data should be analyzed and presents some descriptive statistics. The second part performs some econometric tests and the third part presents the main conclusions of the analysis.

The Data

We study here the nature of the stochastic process generating oil income. There are two possible ways forward. Should we model income as such or should we instead model prices and then consider how income changes as a function of price? We actually followed both routes. In the first case, we use Venezuelan US-dollar exports, and in the second we consider oil prices separately.

Note that Venezuela exports many different varieties of oil, including crude and refined products. However, it is generally assumed that there are fairly constant long-run relationships between many of these prices such that, although in the short term important fluctuations in the relevant spreads between different grades may occur, in the longer term it is possible to consider a benchmark grade and then study spreads between that grade and other oil related products.

Here there is a question about which prices should be used. At least two possibilities exist. First, we could use an actual benchmark (average) price obtained by Venezuela, or we could use a market price for oil. It is to be imagined that the former would be some function of the latter. Again we followed both routes. For actual prices, we use Venezuelan oil-related exports in dollars and divide this by a quantity index. We used IMF International Financial Statistics monthly data for the period January 1972-June 1991. We refer to this price as P^*. For market prices we use West Texas Intermediate (WTI) nearby futures prices. Nearby futures are as close as it is possible to get to a truly market-determined spot price for oil. WTI was selected as a reasonably long series since data exists from 1982 onwards.[22]

---

[22] Data was obtained from DATASTREAM services through the Institute of Economics and Statistics, Oxford University, where Ricardo Hausmann was visiting in the spring and summer of 1991. All econometric tests were carried out on PC-GIVE.

Finally, the periodicity of the data must also be considered. WTI prices are available on a daily basis but actual export prices are available only on a monthly basis. The stabilization fund proposed would operate on a monthly or quarterly basis. We decided that we would consider both monthly and quarterly prices although we performed some additional tests on weekly WTI prices.

Descriptive Statistics

Here we present some descriptive statistics of the data series considered. First of all we present the first four moments of export values, prices, and market prices on monthly data. These statistics relate to the change in the log of the relevant variable. The reason for using this transformation is that if the variable is nonstationary, it is these moments that are constant whereas the moments applied to the levels will, by definition, be nonstationary. Also, the statistics are easily interpreted. As the log change is, essentially, the percentage change, the minimum and maximum are the minimum and maximum percentage change of the relevant variable and the standard deviation can be read as a percentage.

These descriptive statistics are of interest for a number of reasons. First of all, there is a high standard deviation attached to all of them between 10 percent to 14 percent on a monthly basis. As an annualized measure this is equal to 34 percent to 48 percent. Secondly, all of the variables have excess kurtosis, in other words the distributions have fat tails. This means that there is a large probability of wide price fluctuations, compared to what would be predicted if these jumps were drawn from a normal distribution. Each of the normality tests presented rejects normality for these variables. In actual fact, the normality test used takes into account both the excess kurtosis and the skewness but

Table 3.15a.   Analysis of DLP*
(change in the log)

Sample size	227
Mean	0.010004
Std. Devn.	0.140438
Skewness	−0.095595
Excess Kurtosis	1.621673
Minimum	−0.470644
Maximum	0.561156

CHI-SQUARED Test for NORMALITY on LP* :CHI^2(2) = 25.108

Table 3.15b.   Analysis of DLEXPORTS
(change in the log)

Sample size	227
Mean	0.008769
Std. Devn.	−0.143227
Skewness	−0.378342
Excess Kurtosis	1.980604
Minimum	−0.503783
Maximum	0.542279

CHI-SQUARED Test for NORMALITY on DLEXPORTS: CH2(2) = 42.331

Table 3.15c.   Analysis of DLWTI
(change in the log)

Sample size	227
Mean	−0.004482
Std. Devn.	0.101122
Skewness	−0.424218
Excess Kurtosis	5.263556
Minimum	−0.473085
Maximum	0.392287

CHI-SQUARED Test for NORMALITY on DLWTI : $CHI^2(2)$ = 131.465

each of the skewness measures is actually very small, and these variables are failing normality due to the excess kurtosis.

A second set of descriptive statistics is useful to determinate whether the series are stationary or not. Here, we present Durbin-Watson statistics, Dickey-Fuller, and Augmented Dickey-Fuller statistics for the log levels. Dickey-Fuller tests are obtained by regressing the change in the variable against the lagged level of the variable. They may be thought of in the following way. Consider a simple levels regression.

$$X_t = a + bX_{t-1} + d \tag{15}$$

where a and b are constants and d is an error term. If X is nonstationary, then b may be very close to unity. If this is the case, then d will have a non-constant distribution and the standard errors on a and b will not be easily interpretable. However, by subtracting X_{t-1} from each side, we obtain,

$$D(X_t) = a + (b-1)X_{t-1} = d \tag{16}$$

where $D(.)$ is the first difference of a variable. Now, if the coefficient on X_{t-1} is zero, then b must be close to 1 and X_t is nonstationary. However, d now has a constant distribution and the t-statistic on X_{t-1} provides a means of testing for nonstationarity. If the coefficient on X_{t-1} in equation (16) is less than 1, then we know that b must be less than 1 and hence X must be stationary. However, the standard errors on b, even in this regression, do not have the standard distribution. Hence, there is a special table for deciding if X is stationary or not. The test is on the t-statistic of the coefficient on X_{t-1} in equation (16) above.

The second test for nonstationarity is the Durbin-Watson test. Consider regression (15) above. The Durbin-Watson statistic is roughly given by the following equation,

$$DW = 2(1-r)$$

where r is the correlation coefficient between X_t and X_{t-1}. Note that if X is white noise, then r is zero. Hence DW is 2.0, and in this circumstance X is clearly stationary. As r approaches 1, the DW coefficient approaches zero. If r is equal to 1 then X is non-stationary. Hence a test can be constructed as to whether the DW statistic is significantly different to zero.

The results of these tests are given below for the period 2/82 to 12/90, in total 107 observations:

Table 3.16

	LP·	LEXPORTS	LWTI
Durbin-Watson statistics	.2862	.2355	.1092
Dickey-Fuller test	−2.779	−2.1835	−1.70403
Augmented Dickey Fuller test	−2.293	−1.8799	−2.38313
Durbin-Watson statistics on Log changes	2.3869	2.2392	1.3397

These tests all fail to establish stationarity of the log levels and indeed indicate that the log levels are integrated processes. The final Durbin-Watson statistics on the changes in logs indicate that they are integrated of order 1 or, roughly speaking, that first differencing yields a stationary series.

Econometric Tests

The conclusions from this set of tests are that:

- Oil revenues and oil prices are nonstationary processes and are integrated of order 1, written at I(i).
- On a monthly basis there is some evidence of serial correlation in the percentage change in oil income and in returns of the price series considered. However, on a quarterly basis there is no evidence of serial correlation.
- There is some evidence of excess kurtosis in the series and this is most marked in the WTI price (i.e., the market price variable).
- There is no evidence of ARCH effects in any of the variables considered.

Parameters of a Jump-diffusion Process

One potential process of interest for the purpose of modelling oil prices is the so-called jump-diffusion process. Briefly, this process is based on the idea that oil prices follow a diffusion (random walk) process but that infrequently there is a significant shock and oil prices jump. Then, oil prices reflect the mixture of two distributions, a normal diffusion distribution and a jump distribution. It fits the characteristics detailed above for quarterly WTI prices. For example that they are nonstationary, that oil price returns are nonserially correlated, and that oil price changes have excess kurtosis. The process may be written as:

$$\frac{dp}{p} = \lambda dt + \sigma dz + dq$$

where:

$$dq \begin{cases} O & \text{w / prob} = (1 - \delta) \\ Y & \text{w / prob} = \delta \end{cases}$$

where: $\text{Log } (Y) \text{ is } N(m, \lambda^2)$

There are five parameters to this process, γ, σ, m, δ, and λ. In theory, these can be estimated from the data. However, for a symmetric distribution it follows that m is zero and that the third and fifth moments are also zero. Thus, to identify the remaining four parameters, four nonzero moments are required from the data. This entails obtaining estimates of the first, second, fourth, and sixth moments from the data. However, it is often the case that the sixth moment, in particular, is not well-determined from the data.

Below, we present estimates of the first six moments of the returns in the WTI price, the price P^* and log changes in exports and associated standard errors for the monthly data:

Table 3.17a. Six Moments of Log WTI Price Changes

Moment	Value	Standard error	T-Statistic
1	−0.0044818	0.00956	−0.46905
2	0.0102150	0.00264	3.87205
3	−0.0007085	0.00115	−0.61598
4	0.0008769	0.00051	1.72366
5	−0.0001615	0.00024	−0.68158
6	0.0001474	0.00011	1.33931

Table 3.17b. Six Moments of Log P* Price Changes

Moment	Value	Standard error	T-Statistic
1	0.00193	0.01199	0.16129
2	0.01509	0.00233	6.46819
3	−0.00040	0.00078	−0.51557
4	0.00080	0.00023	3.48587
5	−0.00008	0.00008	−0.97215
6	0.00006	0.00003	2.45562

We know that the even moments must be positive but the odd moments could be zero, negative, or positive. The t-statistics on the odd moments show that they are all insignificantly different from zero. We can therefore conclude that the distributions are symmetric. The standard errors on the even moments indicate whether these are determined accurately by the data. The second moments and the fourth moments do appear to be reasonably accurately determined by the data but there may be some doubt about the sixth moment.

From these estimates we can infer the parameters of an appropriate jump-diffusion process. This is not really an estimation technique but rather one of "moment matching." See Powell (1989) for a true estimation technique based on the same approach. It turns out that for some of the estimates of the sixth moment above we find that either δ is greater than one, or at least one of the variances (σ or λ) is negative, neither of which can be possible. This also implies that the sixth moment has not been determined accurately by the above procedure. However, using the standard errors attached to the sixth moment estimate given above, we can deduce the likely range of values for the sixth moment.

Conclusions

The conclusion from this analysis are as follows:

- Oil prices relevant for Venezuela and Venezuelan oil export earnings are nonstationary. In other words, there is no evidence of a long run 'normal' level of oil export earnings. If, in the very long run, there is any reversion towards a mean level of income, then the speed of reversion is extremely slow indeed.
- There is no evidence of first order serial correlation on quarterly data for log changes in prices and exports. There is evidence for mild first order serial correlation for monthly data.
- There is evidence that log changes in oil prices and oil exports have excess kurtosis. In other words, the distributions of these variables have fat tails.
- There is no evidence of an ARCH interpretation of this data.
- The characteristics of oil prices and oil income fit the so-called jump diffusion process.
- To identify the parameters of the jump-diffusion distribution, estimates of the sixth moment are required, but unfortunately this does not appear to be accurately determined by the data.
- However, the three tables above do allow likely parameter values to be selected for use in any simulation exercise.

BIBLIOGRAPHY

Akerlof, G. 1970. The market for lemons. *Quarterly Journal of Economics* (August): 488-500.

Anderson, R.W., C.L. Gilbert, and A. Powell. 1989. *Securitization and Commodity Contingency in International Lending.* Discussion Paper No. 295. London: CEPR.

Anderson, R.W., and A. Powell. 1991. Market stabilization and structural adjustment in East European agriculture. In *International dimensions to structural adjustment: Implications for developing countries agriculture,* ed. A. Winters and I. Goldin. Paris: OECD.

Baptista, A. 1989. Tiempo de mengua: Los años finales de una estructura económica. In *Venezuela contemporánea 1974-1989,* ed. Cunill-Grau et al. Caracas: Fundación Mendoza.

Basch, M., and E. Engel. 1991 Stocks transitorios y mecanismos de estabilización: el caso chileno. CIEPLAN, Santiago. Mimeo

Bevan, D., P. Collier, and J. Gunning. 1991. Temporary trade shocks: An international comparison. Manuscript for publication. Oxford: The World Bank.

Bhagwati, J. 1982. Directly unproductive profit seeking (DUP) activities. *Journal of Political Economy 90* (no. 5).

Black, F. 1976. The pricing of commodity contracts. *Journal of Financial Economics* (no. 3): 167-79.

Black, F., and N. Scholes. 1973. The pricing of options and corporate liabilities. *Journal of Political Economy 81:* 637-59.

Bray, M. 1990. Rational expectations, information and asset markets. In *The economics of missing markets, information and games,* ed. F. Hahn, 243-77. Oxford: Oxford University Press. 243-77.

Brennan, G., and J. Buchanan. 1985. *The reason of rules: Constitutional political economy.* Cambridge: Cambridge University Press.

Brock, P. 1991. Copper price shocks and macroeconomic behavior in Chile. In *Temporary trade shocks: An international comparison.* See Bevan, Collier, Gunning 1991.

Calvo, G. 1981. Devaluation: Level vs. rates. *Journal of International Economics* 11: 165-72.

Corden, W.M. 1984. Booming sector and Dutch disease economics: Survey and consolidation. *Oxford Economic Papers* (no. 36):359-380.

Corden, W.M., and P. Neary. 1982. Booming sector and de-industrialization in a small open economy. *The Economic Journal* (December): 823-848.

Corden, W.M., 1988. *Macroeconomic adjustment in developing countries.* IMF Working Paper Series 88/13. Washington, DC: International Monetary Fund.

Deaton, A. 1989. *Saving and liquidity constraints.* NBER Working Paper No. 3196 (December). Cambridge, MA: National Bureau of Economic Research.

Deaton, A., and G. Laroque. 1989. *On the behaviour of commodity prices.* Discussion Paper No. 145. Princeton: Woodrow Wilson School.

Dornbusch, R., and A. Giovannini. 1990. Monetary policy in the open economy. In *Handbook of monetary economics,* Vol. II, eds. B.M. Friedman and F.H. Hahn, Chapter 23, 1232-303. Amsterdam: North-Holland.

Duffie, D. 1988. *Security markets: Stochastic models*. San Diego: Academic Press.

Fama, E., and M. Jensen. 1983. Agency problems and residual claims. *Journal of Law and Economics* (June): 327-49.

Gelb, A., *et al.* 1989. *Oil windfalls: Blessing or curse?* Oxford: Oxford University Press.

Gibson, R., and E. Schwartz. 1990. The pricing of crude oil futures contracts. Manuscript. Anderson Graduate School of Management, University of California, Los Angeles.

Gilbert, C.L. 1990. Domestic price stabilization for LDCs. Queen Mary and Westfield College, London. Mimeo.

Hansen, P., and T. J. Sargent. 1989. Recursive linear models of dynamic economies. Manuscript. University of Chicago.

Hausmann, R., 1990a. *Shocks externos y ajuste macroeconómico*. Caracas: Ediciones Banco Central de Venezuela.

————. 1990b. Venezuela. In *Latin American adjustment: How much has happened?* ed. J. Williamson, 224-44. Washington: Institute of International Economics.

————. 1990c. Adoption, management and abandonment of multiple exchange rate regimes with import controls: The case of Venezuela. Paper presented at the World Bank Workshop on Multiple Exchange Rates, 1-3 November.

————. 1991a. The big bang approach to macro balance in Venezuela: Why so sudden? Why so painful? Washington, DC: Economic Development Institute, The World Bank.

————. 1991b. Dealing with negative oil shocks: The Venezuelan experience in the 1980s. In *Temporary trade shocks: An international comparison*. See Bevan, Collier, and Gunning 1991.

Hausmann, R., and A. Powell. 1990. El fondo de estabilización macroeconómica: Lineamientos generales. Final report, CORDIPLAN Project, World Bank.

Hausmann, R., A. Powell, and R. Rigobón. 1991. Fiscal policy under revenue uncertainty. IESA, Caracas. Mimeo.

Holmstrom, B., and R. Myerson. 1983. Efficient and durable decision rules with incomplete information. *Econométrica* 51: 1799-1820.

Hull, J. 1989. *Options, futures and other derivative securities*. 2d. ed. Englewood Cliffs, N.J.: Prentice-Hall.

Knudsen, A., and R. Nash. 1990. Domestic price stabilization schemes in developing countries. *Economic Development and Cultural Change* 38 (no. 3): 539-556.

Kouri, P.J.K. 1976. The exchange rate and the balance of payments in the short run and in the long run: A monetary approach. S*candinavian Journal of Economics* 78: 280-304.

Kreps, D.M. 1990a. *A course in microeconomic theory*. Princeton, N.J.: Princeton University Press.

————. 1990b. *Game theory and economic modelling*. Oxford: Clarendon Press.

Krueger, A. 1973. The political economy of the rent seeking society. *American Economic Review* 64 (no. 3): 481-87.

Kydland, F., and E. Prescott. 1977. Rules rather than discretion: The inconsistency of optimal plans. *Journal of Political Economy* 85 (no. 3): 473-92.

Lal, D., and H. Myint, eds. 1990. *The political economy of poverty, equity and growth: A comparative study.* Washington, DC: The World Bank.

Lucas, R. E. 1987. *Models of the business cycle.* Oxford: B. Blackwell.

Meller, P. 1990. Chile. In *Latin American adjustment: How much has happened?*, ed. J. Williamson, 54-84. Washington: Institute of International Economics.

Mirrlees, J. A. 1988. Optimal commodity price intervention. Nuffield College, Oxford. Mimeo.

Mueller, D. 1988 *Public choice II.* Cambridge: Cambridge University Press.

Murphy, K., A. Shleifer, and R. Vishny. 1988. *Industrialization and the big push.* NBER Working Paper No. 2078. Cambridge, MA: National Bureau of Economic Research.

————. 1989. Income distribution, market size and industrialization. *Quarterly Journal of Economics* 104: 537-64.

Newberry, D., and J. Stiglitz. 1981. *The theory of commodity price stabilization: A study in the economics of risk.* Oxford: Clarendon Press and Oxford University Press.

Nickel, S. 1985. Error correction, partial adjustment and all that. *Oxford Review of Economics and Statistics* (September).

Obstfeld, M. 1981. Macroeconomic policy, exchange rate dynamics, and optimal asset accumulation. *Journal of Political Economy* 89: 1142-61.

Palma, P. 1985. 1974-1983: Una década de contrastes en la economía venezolana. Cuaderno No. 11, segunda edición, noviembre. Caracas: Academia Nacional de Ciencias Económicas.

Pazos, F. 1979. Efectos de un aumento súbito en los ingresos externos: la economía venezolana en el quinquenio 1974-1978. Banco Central de Venezuela. Mimeo.

Pindyck, R.S. 1991. Irreversibility, uncertainty, and investment. *Journal of Economic Literature* 29 (no. 3, September):1110-48.

Powell, A. 1989. A general method of moments for estimating the parameters of stochastic processes for asset prices: An application to the jump-diffusion process of oil futures. Applied Economics Discussion Paper Series No. 76. Oxford: Institute of Economics and Statistics.

————. 1990a. Options to alleviate the costs of uncertainty and instability: A case study of Zambia. Manuscript, Nuffield College, Oxford.

————. 1990b. The cost of commodity price uncertainty. Manuscript, Nuffield College, Oxford University.

Priovolos, T., and R.C. Duncan, eds. 1991. *Commodity risk management and finance.* Oxford and New York: Oxford University Press for the World Bank.

Rodríguez, M. 1987a. La estrategia del crecimiento económico para Venezuela. Cuaderno No. 19. Caracas: Academia Nacional de Ciencias Económicas.

————. 1987b. Consequences of capital flight for Latin American debtor countries. In *Capital flight and third world debt*, eds. D.R. Lessard and J. Williamson, 129-144. Washington, DC: Washington Institute for International Economics.

Ross, S. 1973. The economic theory of agency: The principal's problem. *American Economic Review* 63: 134-9.

Sargent, T. 1987. *Dynamic Macroeconomic Theory.* Cambridge, MA: Harvard University Press.

Sen, A. K. 1987. Social choice. In *The new Palgrave: A dictionary of economics*, eds. J. Eatwell, M. Milgate, and P. Newman. New York: Stockton Press.

Stiglitz, J. 1974. Incentives and risk sharing in sharecropping. *Review of Economic Studies* 41 (April): 219-55.

————. 1987. Principals and agents. In *The new Palgrave: A dictionary of economics*. See Sen 1987.

————. 1988. Futures markets and risk: A general equilibrium approach. In *Managing futures markets*, ed. D. Streit, 75-106. Oxford: B. Blackwell.

Stokey, N., R.E. Lucas, and E.C. Prescott. 1989. *Recursive methods in economic dynamics*. Cambridge, MA: Harvard University Press.

Tollison, R.D., and G.L. Tullock. 1980. *Towards a theory of the rent-seeking society*. Co: Texas A&M University Press.

Tullock, G.L. 1987. Public choice. In *The new Palgrave: A dictionary of economics*, vol. 3, 1041. See Sen 1987.

CHAPTER FOUR

TEMPORARY EXTERNAL SHOCKS AND STABILIZATION POLICIES FOR BOLIVIA*

Juan Antonio Morales
Justo Espejo
Gonzalo Chávez

Introduction

From 1950 to 1990, exports of three primary commodities—tin, zinc, and natural gas—have constituted an average of 65 percent of the value of Bolivian exports. Given the significance of tin, zinc, and natural gas exports, it is not surprising that their prices are very important determinants of the terms of trade of the country and hence, of national income, foreign exchange inflows, and fiscal revenues. The prices of these three commodities are highly volatile, and their fluctuations have major repercussions on the national economy. At the end of the last decade, the contribution of these three commodities to total exports and to public sector accounts fell considerably; however, current available information indicates that this decline is not permanent. This situation justifies the concentration of the analysis on these commodities.

The main objective of this study is to ultimately propose mechanisms to stabilize national income and consumption in the face of price fluctuations of the three commodities. Stabilizing the earnings of producers for a given real exchange rate, stabilizing the real exchange rate itself, and stabilizing government spending are intermediate objectives to the main objective of stabilizing national income and consumption. The discussion should also be framed within the context of the transition that Bolivia is currently undergoing, including the profound changes in the structure of property and public

---

* The authors are grateful for the efficient collaboration of Gilka La Torre, and José Luis Evia. They also wish to thank Miguel Basch, Eduardo Engel, Montague J. Lord, and Patricio Meller for helpful comments.

enterprises and the concurrent reduction in their role. When the exporting sector is predominantly private in nature, external shocks affect the public sector rather indirectly, through taxation.

Both the external and domestic shocks to the Bolivian economy during the 1970-1990 period have been strong. Separating the effects of export price fluctuations on the national economy from other shocks is a difficult task that will frequently depend on questionable hypotheses.

Bolivia has been and continues to be a participant in several international price stabilization schemes involving regulatory stocks or production quotas. The country has a long tradition in this respect; Bolivian producers, however, have been virtually absent from the financial hedging markets. Nevertheless, it can be expected that with the strong expansion of private sector participation in the production and export of minerals and hydrocarbons, there will be a more intensive use of these markets.

In addition, Bolivia has no national macroeconomic stabilization fund similar to Chile's Copper Stabilization Fund (FEC). It must be noted from the outset that the nature of ownership in the sector that exports primary commodities has an influence on how the macroeconomic stabilization fund is defined; thus, the FEC (as well as the proposals for its reform) could not be replicated in Bolivia unless it were to undergo substantial modifications.

To our knowledge, no other studies have explored the effects of external sector instability on Bolivia's macroeconomy. However, it is important to note the recommendation of the Musgrave Mission on Fiscal Reform (Musgrave and Desormeaux, 1976; Musgrave 1981), which proposed the creation of a macroeconomic stabilization fund when export prices were booming in the 1970s.

A good introduction to the analysis is the differentiation of temporary shocks from permanent ones. The viability of certain stabilization instruments depends on this distinction. Identifying the process that generates the fluctuations is not easy and is specific to each export market. While the treatment of tin and zinc may be similar, natural gas must be handled rather differently, because international trade in natural gas is heavily marked by bilateralism. Moreover, Bolivia suffered a negative price shock very recently when the gas contract with Argentina expired: the danger that the shock will become permanent lends its own peculiarities to the analysis. The March 1992 agreement extending gas sales for nearly another two years contains a price that is far more unfavorable than the one that had prevailed until then.

The literature contains a large number of articles devoted to the problems stemming from price instability. Until a few years ago, instability was measured by deviations from a trend defined in an *ad hoc* manner. The study of price fluctuations in all their complexity is a relatively recent phenomenon. Our work attempts to complete what is known in this respect for tin, zinc, and natural gas.

The main results of the study are the following. First, tin prices, in real terms, with annual data and in logarithms, have a stationary trend. Although the process that generates this phenomenon is stationary, shocks are, nevertheless, highly persistent. For shorter-term prices (quarterly and monthly), the tests applied favor the hypothesis of a nonstationary process. The results for real prices of zinc are similar to those of tin; however, the shocks with annual data are much less persistent. Natural gas prices, whatever the periodicity of the data, appear to follow a non-stationary process, as do oil prices. Although natural gas prices have been frequently pegged to oil prices, the two series do not appear to be co-integrated. Second, the impact of the fluctuations produces significant sacrifices in income. Instability in the three commodities could be as high as 0.7 percent of GDP per annum. Third, the stabilization strategy should cover a broad spectrum of measures, some macroeconomic and others more specific. Among the latter type is the possibility of gaining access to the international hedging markets and of establishing a macroeconomic stabilization fund (MSF) when prices improve. Establishing an MSF does not yet appear to be opportune; in the meantime, the management of international reserves is crucial. The 1988-91 rule indexing the price of natural gas to the price of oil appears to have had major stabilizing effects. This rule, with some modifications, should be included in the new contracts to which Bolivia is about to agree.

This study is organized in the following manner. Section 1 reviews the significance of tin, zinc, and natural gas in exports and in public sector revenues. Section 2 discusses the highly important transformations in the nature—public or private—of commodities-sector investments that have taken place since the second half of the last decade. Section 3 presents some estimates of the costs of external instability and reviews the significance of the negative tin and natural gas shocks that took place during the second half of the 1980s. Section 4 is devoted to an examination of the stochastic processes that generate international prices. Section 5 discusses the specific stabilization mechanisms, grouped around three main topics: the hedging markets, the rules for price formation in bilateral natural gas transactions, and the establishment of a macroeconomic stabilization fund.

The Importance of the Primary Sector

Contribution to Exports of Goods

Until 1965, more or less, tin exports constituted 70 percent of total exports of goods (Table 4.1). Since 1965, this mineral has been declining in importance, and Bolivian exports of the commodity fell sharply after its price crashed on the London Metal Exchange in October 1985.

Table 4.1 Share of Tin, Zinc, and Natural Gas in Total Exports of Goods, 1930-1990
(percentages)

	Tin	Zinc	Natural gas	Total
Annual averages				
1930-39	70.1	3.5	–	73.5
1940-49	69.9	2.7	–	72.7
1950-59	60.9	5.5	–	66.5
1960-69	62.8	2.4	–	65.2
1970-79	43.1	6.3	6.4	55.7
1980-89	24.3	6.1	40.4	70.9
Period 1980-1990				
1980	36.5	3.5	21.3	61.3
1981	34.5	4.1	33.8	72.4
1982	31.0	4.3	42.5	77.8
1983	25.4	4.1	46.3	75.8
1984	31.7	4.8	48.0	84.5
1985	27.8	4.4	55.4	87.5
1986	16.3	4.4	51.5	72.2
1987	12.1	5.8	43.6	61.5
1988	12.8	10.0	35.8	58.6
1989	15.4	16.1	26.0	57.5
1990	11.2	15.8	24.3	51.3

Source: Based on data from the External Sector Bulletins and the Statistical Bulletins of the Central Bank of Bolivia.

While production has recovered in the past two years, its outlook is still uncertain. In contrast to tin, zinc has been gaining considerable importance. Exports of this commodity have grown substantially since 1988, making zinc the Bolivian mineral with the highest value as a percentage of exports during the past three years.

Bolivia has an eight percent share of the world production of tin, while its share of world zinc production is under one percent, even after three years of strong output growth. Tin exports consist of concentrates and refined metals, while those of zinc are entirely of concentrates.

Gas exports have been directed exclusively toward Argentina. They began in 1972, under the terms of a 20-year contract. The value of sales to Argentina from 1972 to 1992 has been decisively influenced by price fluctuations stemming from particularly difficult bilateral negotiations.

In March 1992, the contract was extended for an additional year and a half. This extension, part of an Energy Complementation Agreement, set the price of natural gas at almost 50 percent below the prevailing price before that date. The volume of sales remains constant.[1]

On average, tin, zinc, and natural gas constituted 64 percent of the annual value of Bolivia's (legal) exports from 1950 to 1990. In the 15 years before the crisis of 1985, these three products accounted for 64.2 percent of total exports. From 1986 to 1990, this proportion fell only slightly to 60.2 percent, but there was a rather substantial change in its composition, with zinc and natural gas replacing tin. Given the weight of these exports, it is not surprising that their prices are critical determinants of the terms of trade.

Despite the importance of these three commodities, their contribution to total foreign exchange availability, as measured by the foreign exchange balance in the Central Bank, has been surprisingly small since 1985. It should be noted that the capital account of the balance of payments also affects the foreign exchange balance. Moreover, the foreign exchange balance indicates the movements of reserves on a cash flow, rather than earned income basis. For this reason, Argentina's frequent situation of arrears from 1985 to 1989 led to an understatement of the importance of natural gas in the foreign exchange balance.

Although the contributions of mining and natural gas to the foreign exchange balance have been shrinking, their marginal contribution continues to be important, particularly because they provide convertible currency crucial to satisfying the expanding private sector demand for imports.

The Contribution of Fiscal Revenues

Public sector accounts are probably the main mechanism for transmitting export price fluctuations to the domestic economy. Shocks directly affect public enterprises that are exporters and, indirectly but no less significantly, the government in general.

Foreign sales (before taxes and transfers) of the Corporación Minera de Bolivia (COMIBOL), and its affiliate since August 1985, Empresa Nacional de Fundiciones (ENAF), accounted for over six percent of GDP in the early 1980s (Table 4.2). With the domestic economic crisis of 1982-1985 and the subsequent international crisis, these sales fell in 1988 to as low as 1.4 percent of GDP. Since then, there has been some recovery, but foreign sales remain sluggish. In foreign sales (as a percentage of GDP), Yacimientos Petrolíferos

---

[1] As a manner of compensation for the sharp reduction in the price, Argentina is granting Bolivia a 10-year interest-free loan in the amount of US$110 million, with a 4-year grace period. From 1996 forward, the amortization payments from this loan will be employed in the construction of works of binational interest, using Argentine goods and services.

Fiscales Bolivianos (YPFB) also suffered a drop in the second half of the 1980s; however, it was neither as steady nor as pronounced as that of COMIBOL.

Table 4.2 Foreign Sales of the Main Public Enterprises 1981-1990

	COMIBOL + ENAF	YPFB	Total public enterprises
A. As percentage of PNB			
1981	6.0	5.1	12.3
1982	7.9	6.9	16.3
1983	5.6	5.3	11.7
1984	4.2	6.6	11.7
1985	2.6	5.2	8.8
1986	n.a.	n.a.	n.a.
1987	5.2	4.9	6.0
1988	1.4	4.9	7.5
1989	2.2	2.7	5.2
1990[p]	2.1	4.3	8.2
B. As percentage of total sales			
1981	69	55	51
1982	70	73	62
1983	95	71	63
1984	96	84	76
1985	95	54	50
1986	n.a.	n.a.	n.a.
1987	91	39	39
1988	86	38	41
1989	79	25	32
1990[p]	95	34	41

Source: Author's calculations, based on unpublished data from the Economic Policy Analysis Unit (UDAPE), Ministry of Planning.
Notes: COMIBOL: Corporación Minera de Bolivia.
           ENAF: Empresa Nacional de Fundiciones.
           YPFB: Yacimientos Petrolíferos Fiscales Bolivianos.
[p]: Preliminary.
n.a.: Not available.

The tax revenues of the National Treasury (NT) present a similar picture. NT accounts are closely linked with central government accounts and have the

Table 4.3 Annual Tax Revenues of the General Treasury of the Nation, 1970-1990
(percentage of GDP)

	Taxes on Mining			Taxes on Hydrocarbons			Other Taxes on External Trade	Domestic Taxes	Total
	State Royalties	Private Royalties	Total	Exports	Domestic Production & Consum.	Total			
	(1)	(2)	(3)	(4)	(5)	(6)	(7)	(8)	(9)
1970	0.0	1.4	1.4	0.0	0.0	0.0	3.8	3.4	8.7
1971	0.4	0.0	0.4	0.0	0.4	0.4	3.2	4.1	8.1
1972	0.8	0.0	0.8	0.3	0.4	0.7	2.8	3.5	7.7
1973	1.4	0.2	1.7	1.0	0.9	1.8	2.5	3.3	9.3
1974	1.7	1.2	2.9	1.0	1.9	2.9	3.1	2.7	11.7
1975	0.6	0.4	1.0	1.3	1.6	2.9	4.3	3.3	11.5
1976	1.1	0.4	1.5	1.4	1.9	3.3	3.3	4.0	12.1
1977	1.4	0.6	1.9	1.1	1.2	2.2	3.4	4.2	11.7
1978	1.5	0.5	2.0	0.8	1.0	1.8	3.3	4.1	11.2
1979	1.6	0.7	2.3	0.0	0.1	0.1	2.9	3.8	9.1
1980	1.1	0.5	1.5	0.7	0.9	1.5	2.8	3.8	9.6
1981	0.4	0.2	0.6	0.8	2.0	2.8	2.7	3.1	9.2
1982	0.4	0.1	0.4	0.4	0.8	1.2	1.2	2.0	4.8
1983	0.0	0.1	0.1	0.1	0.2	0.3	0.6	1.6	2.7
1984	0.5	0.2	0.7	0.0	0.3	0.3	0.9	0.7	2.6
1985	0.0	0.2	0.2	1.9	2.8	4.7	0.9	0.9	6.6
1986	0.0	0.0	0.0	1.2	4.6	5.8	1.1	2.4	9.4
1987	0.0	0.1	0.1	1.1	4.6	6.1	1.6	3.2	10.9
1988	0.0	0.1	0.1	2.1	4.7	6.7	1.3	3.6	11.7
1989	0.1	0.0	0.1	1.3	5.0	6.4	1.1	3.7	11.3
1990p	0.0	0.1	0.1	2.3	8.5	10.8	1.4	3.1	15.4

Source: Author's calculations, based on data from the Ministry of Planning, Economic Policy Analysis Unit (UDAPE)

p: Preliminary.

greatest impact on real variables (public investment), as well as on monetary aggregates (and other nominal values). Enterprises from the mining, and above all, hydrocarbon sectors also pay royalties to the regional development corporations (RDCs) of the departments in which they operate. These levies are not included in NT revenues.

With the crisis of 1982-1985 and the subsequent economic policy reforms—including the highly important tax reform law of 1986 (Law 843)—there has been a significant change in the structure of NT revenues. If the 1970s are compared with later years, a declining role for taxes in foreign trade (the sum of columns [3], [4], and [7] in Table 4.3) can be seen. Their share in the total tax revenues of the NT has likewise decreased, with domestic taxes currently more important. This structural change has a major macroeconomic stabilization effect—a point to which we shall return.

In the third column of Table 4.3, it can be seen that taxes from the mining sector, which once accounted for 2.9 percent of GDP, virtually disappeared during the 1980s, and by 1990 represented barely 0.1 percent of GDP.[2] Taxes on natural gas exports constituted around 1.5 percent of GDP after 1985, a slightly higher percentage than before.

The substantial decrease in mining taxes can be explained first by the effects of hyperinflation during the first half of the decade, which caused a general drop in tax revenues; second by the fall in the price of tin (and other minerals) since the last quarter of 1985; and third by the nature of royalty-based mining taxation. This last point will be examined in more detail further on.

The Growing Importance of the Private Sector

Tin and Zinc

From the nationalization of the large mining companies from 1952 until 1985, COMIBOL dominated tin production and exports. From 1952 to 1958, this enterprise gained control of 80 percent of production. Between 1959 and 1985, its control stabilized at roughly two-thirds of production. The remainder of tin production was distributed among private mining companies, classified under Bolivian law as mid-sized mining (with just over 20 percent of production), small mining, and cooperatives.

The drop in the price of tin in 1985, together with a major effort to stabilize inflation, led to a serious crisis in COMIBOL. Both the volume of its output

---

[2]   Unfortunately, there is no disaggregated data on taxes from tin and zinc.

Table 4.4 Annual Production of Tin by Sectors, 1952-1990
(in TMF and percentages)

Average	COMIBOL	%	Medium mining	%	Small mining	%	Others	%	Total
1952-1960	21,579	79.9	2,333	8.6	2,552	9.5	532	2.0	26,995
1961-1970	16,044	62.5	4,592	17.9	3,421	13.3	1,617	6.3	25,674
1971-1980	19,676	65.5	6,431	21.4	3,127	10.4	815	2.7	30,048
1981-1990	9,415	49.4	3,897	20.4	3,326	17.4	2,424	12.7	19,061
1971-1985	18,305	65.6	6,073	21.8	2,971	10.6	554	2.0	27,903
1986-1990	3,267	22.5	3,438	16.8	3,991	27.5	4,814	33.2	14,510
1990	6,068	34.2	1,876	10.6	2,105	11.9	7,687	43.3	17,736

Source: Annual Reports of the "Asociación Nacional de Mineros Medianos" (National Association of Mid-sized Mining Companies). From 1974 on, Statistical Bulletins of the Ministry of Mining and Metallurgy.
Note: COMIBOL - Corporación Minera de Bolivia.

and its share in total production were dramatically reduced in the three succeeding years.[3] The crisis of 1985 affected not only COMIBOL but mid-sized enterprises as well (Table 4.4). Only small enterprises and cooperatives maintained or even increased their levels of production, with highly labor-intensive technologies and very small-scale operations.

This "informalization" of production is today one of the most salient characteristics of the Bolivian tin industry.

Since 1989, exports of private mining companies have become more important than those of state mining operations—but with zinc (followed by gold), instead of tin, accounting for the largest share. From 1985 to 1990, private production of zinc almost tripled, and its share in the output for this period was nearly 80 percent (Table 4.5).

The information available from the investment plans of private companies suggests a strong expansion in output in the coming years. The private sector will continue to expand within its own concessions, as well as in association with COMIBOL in joint ventures.[4] It should be added that, after the state Mining Bank closed its doors in 1991, the marketing of concentrates from private enterprises has been entirely in the hands of private agents who work with a very broad spectrum of companies, in terms of the scale of their operations.

Natural Gas

The outlook for private investment in hydrocarbons is similar to that for mining. YPFB is authorized to enter into operations contracts, contracts of association, and joint ventures involving Bolivian and foreign capital. The export of natural gas is reserved to YPFB, but it is legal to market the product with the participation of private contractors.

From 1977 to late 1991, YPFB entered into 14 operations contracts with private Bolivian and foreign enterprises, as well as one for enhanced recovery, and two joint contracts for operations and enhanced recovery. The land area involved in the contracts with private oil companies covered 146,000 km²— that is, a sizable 13 percent of the nation's territory. At present, the production and export of natural gas is largely in the hands of YPFB, but exports by private enterprises are growing more rapidly (Table 4.6).

---

[3] A very thorough description of COMIBOL's crisis, its origins, and its impact can be found in CEMYD (1990).

[4] Joint ventures constitute one of the most important reforms in the update of the Mining Code in 1990.

Table 4.5 Annual Production of Zinc by Sectors, 1961-1990
(in TMF and percentages)

Average	COMIBOL	%	Med-Sized mining	%	Small mining	%	Others	%	Total
1961-1970	4,472	28.8	2,412	15.5	2,398	15.4	6,251	40.2	15,532
1971-1980	34,698	68.6	12,614	25.0	1,483	2.9	1,750	3.5	50,545
1981-1990	16,170	31.5	31,976	62.3	2,514	4.9	704	1.4	51,364
1988-1990	17,276	23.0	52,314	69.6	4,392	5.8	1,132	1.5	75,114
1990	24,773	26.4	63,695	67.9	2,287	2.4	3,093	3.3	93,173

Source: Annual Reports of the Asociación Nacional de Mineros Medianos (National Association of Mid-sized Mining Companies). From 1974 on, Statistical Bulletins of the Ministry of Mining and Metallurgy.
Note: Corporación Minera de Bolivia.

Table 4.6 Natural Gas Exports
(millions of cubic ft.)

Year	YPFB	%	Contractors	%	Total
1972	35,800	100.0	–	–	35,800
1973	55,415	100.0	–	–	55,415
1974	54,593	100.0	–	–	54,593
1975	54,974	100.0	–	–	54,974
1976	55,498	100.0	–	–	55,498
1977	57,887	100.0	–	–	57,887
1978	47,275	84.4	8,733	15.6	56,008
1979	42,328	69.4	18,642	30.6	60,970
1980	44,673	62.0	27,359	37.9	72,032
1981	44,805	57.8	32,737	42.2	77,542
1982	51,525	63.5	29,591	36.5	81,116
1983	53,773	68.4	24,879	31.6	78,652
1984	55,519	71.1	22,546	28.9	78,065
1985	53,582	68.5	24,673	31.5	78,255
1986	48,747	62.4	29,410	37.6	78,157
1987	49,072	65.5	25,807	34.5	74,879
1988	53,919	68.5	24,782	31.5	78,701
1989	44,398	56.9	33,639	43.1	78,037
1990	42,815	55.0	34,986	44.9	77,801

Source: Yacimientos Petrolíferos Fiscales Bolivianos, Statistics Division.

Greater participation by private investment in natural gas depends on the opening of external markets. Bolivia has the possibility of entering into contracts with buyers from Argentina, as well as from Brazil and Chile. Under a stipulation of the Energy Complementation Agreement of March 1992, from 1994 to the year 2002, Bolivian natural gas will have free and unrestricted access to Argentina's market. Talks are also under way with Brazil and Chile. Negotiations with Brazil are particularly advanced.

It is important to note that the three countries mentioned above are also producers of natural gas, and Bolivia will have to compete with them in their own and neighboring territories.

Taxation

From the standpoint of macroeconomic equilibria, it is important not only that the levels of production and exports be higher, but also that additional stable fiscal revenues be generated. In view of the anticipated expansion in private investment, it will be important to avoid what happened from 1985 to 1990, when, due to shortcomings in the legislation, the Bolivian government had to make greater fiscal sacrifices than would otherwise have been necessary.

Bolivian mining taxation traditionally has been based on the royalties system. The tax base of the royalty is presumed profits. This is determined by the official quotation, less the presumed cost and the operational expenditures per unit, multiplied by the volumes exported. International prices determine the official quotation. An aliquot (53 percent for tin and 20 percent for zinc) is applied to presumed profits.

The presumed cost is calculated by type of mineral, regardless of the situation of each individual mining company. This mode of taxation ignores the basic fact that average costs are determined essentially by the quality of the mineral deposit and that they therefore differ from mine to mine. If the presumed cost is set by the costs of the marginal mines, as is often the case, a drop in the international price produces a greater tax loss than if profits comprised the tax base. If the international price falls, the mining companies and the government share the losses, but the government assumes a greater proportion of them. In other words, with the royalty system and high price fluctuations, the income risk to the government is greater than it would be with a tax on profits.

The royalty system clearly penalizes the government beyond expectations when international prices are low. However, does the system attract private investment? The answer is no, because of the inherent problems of uncertainty. In fact, there are no credible parameters in the system to enable investors to reasonably estimate their future earnings flows, and thus make decisions. Furthermore, the government may at any time change the presumed cost, a possibility that generates a good deal of uncertainty.[5]

Fortunately, the new mining law of 1991 corrects this shortcoming, establishing a new tax regime comprised of: (1) a tax of 30 percent on net profits; and (2) an advance payment of the profit tax, in the amount of 2.5 percent, on the value of sales (net of operational expenditures).[6]

Until the promulgation of the hydrocarbons law of 1990, enterprises of this sector, like the mining companies, were subject to royalty payments. YPFB was (and is) obliged to pay royalties directly. Private companies with contracts to operate (more properly, to share production) with YPFB, do so indirectly. The gas produced by the contractor is turned over to YPFB in its entirety. The

---

[5] In the 1970s, mid-sized private enterprises strongly opposed the royalty system.

[6] The new regime applies to all mining enterprises that start up activities after the promulgation of this law. Existing companies that add new concessions after 1991 to those already registered are incorporated into this new tax regime. The remainder of the existing mining enterprises will be incorporated by 1999; in the meantime, they are subject to the royalty system, in no case paying less than 2.5 percent of the value of their net sales.

contractor has the right to a payment from the enterprise equal to a percentage negotiated in each contract. Moreover, YPFB retains the volumes of gas necessary to cover the tax and royalty payments that the contractor must make (31 percent on his earnings on the value of production at the wellhead).

Note that under the system that prevailed up to 1990, royalties, in contrast to mining taxes, are true taxes on production, and the government shares equally the losses generated by price drops. For contracts signed after the approval of the new law, a 40 percent tax on net profits is levied. Contractors are still obliged to pay the 31 percent corresponding to royalties and taxes, but these payments are credited toward the tax on net profits. If the amount of this tax is less than the royalties paid, the contractor records the difference as a loss, which can be credited toward the taxes on future operations.

The Cost of Variability in Primary Sector Earnings

Domestic Mechanisms for Transmitting External Fluctuations

It is worthwhile to recall the channels through which fluctuations in export earnings affect income and consumption. Shocks have an immediate impact in the form of modifications in disposable income (increases when the shock is positive and decreases when negative). Moreover, if the shock stems from improvements (or deteriorations) in the terms of trade, there will be a transfer of income from (or to) the country. With rigid domestic prices and external credit constraints, shocks also have a direct impact on the capacity to import, which will generate losses in GDP and not just in disposable income. This is one of the more direct effects.

Changes in consumption do not directly follow the external shocks and will depend on the alterations in permanent income that they produce. These, in turn, will depend on whether the shocks are perceived as permanent or transitory. Even if no changes in consumption take place, or such changes are of little significance, there will, in any case, be modifications in the savings rate, which would give rise to an effect resulting from the intertemporal distribution of the shock's impact. Instability and, above all, uncertainty about the prices themselves will also affect investment decisions.

The other channel through which fluctuations in export earnings (and not just the trend) affect the level of economic activity and of inflation is changes in relative prices, especially in the real exchange rate. The effect of positive shocks on the price of nontradeable goods versus that of tradeable goods has given rise to the literature on the "Dutch disease" (Corden, 1984) and its extension in the theory of construction booms (Bevan *et al.*, 1989). One very important lesson of these studies is that it is the general economic policy framework that, *in the final analysis*, determines the impact of positive external shocks on the economy.

Negative external shocks can generate exchange rate crises that, to be resolved, require rapid depreciations in real terms, which normally implies a drop in real wages.[7] Resistance to cutting real wages can set the economy on an inflationary path. Once again, it is the general economic context that will define the inflationary impact of an external shock.

Finally, the destabilization of public expenditures caused by exogenous shocks can prove very costly. Moreover, as the literature stresses, the costs of positive and negative shocks are not symmetrical. In particular, interruptions in the flow of funds for irreversible investment projects already under way can generate adjustment costs that are especially high.

Estimating Risk Premiums

To determine the cost of risk, we shall use the expressions derived by Newbery and Stiglitz (1981). Let θ be the annual risk premium that the representative consumer is willing to pay to have an assured income instead of an uncertain one dependent on transitory shocks. The premium is approximately equal to $1/2\,RV^2C^*$, where C^* is the expected consumption, R the coefficient of relative risk aversion, and V the coefficient of variation (CV) of income. In what follows, we shall assume that all earnings are consumed. With this simplifying hypothesis, the expression $RV^2/2$ measures the risk premium as a percentage of income (for which, moreover, we shall use GDP as a proxy). We shall also assume in what follows that all variations in exports are attributable to variations in prices. This assumption is, perhaps, too strong and could be excluded without much difficulty.

Let a_i be the share of exports i in GDP and $CV_i(i=1,2,3)$ the CV of the real price of i. Subscript one indicates tin; two, zinc; and three, natural gas. It can be shown without much difficulty that V^2 is equal to the quadratic formula $V^2 = x'Qx$, with $x' = [a_1CV_1a_2CV_2a_3CV_3]$ and Q a positive, defined, symmetrical 3x3 matrix of simple price correlations.

The estimations in section four give us the following CVs for prices: tin, 0.561; zinc, 0.181; and natural gas 0.577. Furthermore, the following correlations are obtained with real annual data (18 observations): between natural gas and tin, 0.122; between natural gas and zinc, –0.425; and between tin and zinc, 0.069. If we assume that the shares of tin, zinc, and natural gas exports in the 1980 GDP are representative of the average share, the corresponding a_i

---

[7]   In this statement, we can see an analogy with what happened as a result of the external debt crisis in Latin America in the early 1980s.

values will be: 0.123 for tin, 0.012 for zinc, and 0.072 for natural gas. Inserting these values in the above formula, we obtain $V^2 = 0.007$. If it is assumed that $R = 2$, which is usual in this type of study, the annual risk premium will be equal to 0.7 percent of GDP. Over a long period of time, and discounting at a real interest rate of 10 percent, the country would be transferring 7 percent of its GDP (in terms of present value) in the form of a risk premium.

The above result should be interpreted with caution, because it may over-estimate the magnitude of the transfer.[8] However, if we were to add the effects of fluctuations in output, the annual cost of risk would increase.

The Impact of Negative Shocks on Tin and Natural Gas, 1985-1989

Employing a different perspective from that of the section above, which emphasized the costs of instability, it is worth noting the costs of the negative price shocks that occurred from 1986 to 1989, in terms of 1985 GDP. The losses were substantial—some 2.9 percent of 1985 GDP, on average, during that period. Cumulative losses for the period, in present values with a discount rate of 10 percent, would be equal to nearly 10 percent of 1985 GDP.

Despite these losses, the economy adapted to the new situation in a more or less orderly fashion, and it was possible to maintain the anti-inflationary program. A detailed explanation of the adaptation process can be found in Morales (1992).

The Nature of the Stochastic Processes of the Prices of Primary Goods

Identifying the stochastic processes that generate prices is central to the design of stabilization mechanisms. This analysis will use annual series of real prices for tin, zinc, and natural gas. For tin and zinc, three price series have been considered—those of London and New York and the statistics employed domestically for tax purposes, which fall under the heading of official prices. Unfortunately, these series refer to different time periods. Natural gas prices are taken from YPFB. Appendix A provides a more detailed description of data sources.

A key point of the analysis concerns the persistence of shocks. For this, the quotient of variances proposed by Cochrane (1988) is used, and also random walk tests.

---

[8]   See, in this regard, the inventory of constraints that Kletzer et al. (1990) impose on the use of the cost measurement that we have employed.

The quotient of variances determined by (1) makes it possible to judge the relative importance of permanent versus temporary fluctuations:

$$V = (1/k)\,\mathrm{var}\big(y(t) - y(t-k)\big)\big/\mathrm{var}\big(y(t) - y(t-1)\big).$$ (1)

In the above formula $y(t)$ represents the natural log of the price under consideration and k the number of periods in our ad hoc definition of the long term. For convenience, k is the size of the "window." Note that the numerator contains the variance of the average growth rate (expressed in log differences) in k periods, while the denominator shows the variance of the growth rate from period to period.

The quotient of variances V indicates: (1) the closer it is to zero, the greater the importance of transitory shocks; (2) the higher it is, the greater the importance of permanent changes. Coefficient V lends itself to an even more interesting interpretation; that is, it is equal to one if prices follow a random walk process, and only if it is significantly less than one can it be concluded that the process is stationary. A random walk process means that all shocks are permanent. The results of the random walk tests in Tables 4.7 to 4.9 have been obtained with annual price data (in real terms) in logarithms.

It is worthwhile to rapidly review the main elements of the random walk tests.[9] To do this, let us first consider the following model with positive autocorrelation:

$$y = \alpha y_{-1} + u \qquad 0 < \alpha \le 1$$ (2)

with the us distributed independently, with zero mean and common variance σ^2. In the extreme case of $\alpha = 1$, we have a random walk process. The random walk hypothesis for the model in (2) can be reformulated as a unit root hypothesis, rewriting the equation as:

$$\Delta y = \phi y_{-1} + u$$ (2')

with $\phi = \alpha - 1$, the null hypothesis of unit root is $H0: \phi = 0$, while that of the autoregression implies that $\phi < 0$. A convenient statistic for this test is the Augmented Dickey-Fuller (ADF) statistic.

To model (2) can be added a deterministic trend DT in the form of $\beta_0 + \beta_1(t - T/2)$, such that $y = DT + \alpha_{y-1} + u'$, with u' having properties like those of u. With this particular DT we have a random walk model with a constant (or "direction") and a trend. (For a model without a trend, it is enough

---

9   See Campbell and Perron (1991) and the references in that work for a presentation of the random walk process and the more general case of unit roots.

to put $\beta_1 = 0$). The ADF test can also be calculated for the model with a deterministic trend.

The results of the ADF test, like those of the other unit root tests, should be interpreted with caution. Their low power is well known—that is, the probability is low that the tests will reject the unit root null hypothesis when the alternative hypotheses of an autoregressive process is true.

Finally, measurements of symmetry and kurtosis for the various prices and their logarithms have been calculated in order to judge deviations with respect to a normal distribution of the stochastic processes that generate these series. It may be recalled that the symmetry is zero and the kurtosis is three for a normal distribution.[10] Normality has also been tested with the statistic proposed by Jarque-Bera (1981) for large samples. This statistic, under the null hypothesis for normality, has a distribution Chi^2 with two degrees of freedom.

The deviations from normality may explain the rather abrupt changes observed in some prices (and in their logarithms), despite the persistence of the shocks. The lognormality of the prices is a hypothesis that will be required for some of the stabilization mechanisms discussed in section five. In that context, it is worthwhile to identify the presence of deviations from normality.

Tin Prices

The strong fluctuations in the price of tin can be seen in Figure 4.1. For the subperiod 1900-1980, a rising trend can be observed; however, when the entire period from 1900-1989 is considered, the trend disappears. Moreover, the CVs confirm the magnitude of the price fluctuations (Table 4.7). Similarly, the high CVs for the annual growth rates of tin prices (measured by the differences in their logarithms) again highlight the volatility of the prices.

The quotients of the variances suggest that permanent shocks are more important than temporary shocks. As the windows lengthen, the quotient falls, though not very rapidly. The rather slow decline in the quotient of the variances indicates that the shocks are highly persistent.

The results of the unit root test are not uniform and depend on which of the different price series (which refer to different periods) was employed.

With the London price series, at the 1-percent level of significance, the random walk hypothesis is rejected in the model without a constant or a trend; in the other two cases it cannot be rejected. With the price series for the United States, at the 10-percent level of significance, the random walk hypothesis is

---

[10] Our value for the kurtosis of a normal distribution may differ from that of other works, where three is subtracted from the value that we obtain. In that case, the kurtosis corresponding to a normal distribution is zero.

Figure 4.1 Tin prices (USA), in Real Terms, 1980 base
(US$ cents per pound sterling)

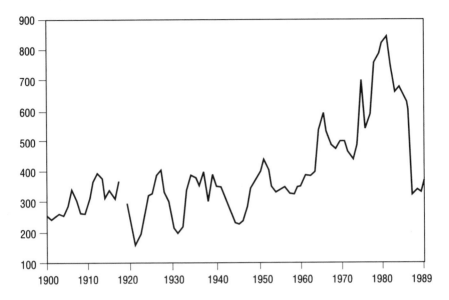

Source: See Appendix A.

rejected for the model with a constant, and at the 5-percent level of significance, for the model with a constant and a trend. Only with the series of official
data can the hypothesis not be rejected for any of the models.

The random walk hypothesis is an extreme hypothesis. What is important
to point out is that even when it is rejected, the series shows that there is a high
degree of persistence among the shocks and that reversion to the trend is slow.[11]
Note that for the series of logarithms for the New York prices, in real terms,
from 1900 to 1989, the coefficient of autoregression of the first order $AR(1)$
is 0.88, and that of the second order $AR(2)$, 0.74.

Finally, it must be pointed out that the conclusions regarding the nonstationary property of the series depend on the periodicity of the observations.
The tests carried out with quarterly and monthly data (both nominal and real)

---

[11] Campbell and Perron (1991: 157) and Cochrane (1991) point out that for finite samples, a
stationary process can be arbitrarily approximated by a unit root process and vice versa. For
example, note that with a value of $\alpha = 0.999$ in equation (2), a stationary process very
similar to a random walk process is obtained. There is a quasi-equivalence in the observations.

Table 4.7 Annual Prices of Tin, in Real Terms, 1900-1989

	New York	London[a]	Official[b]
Coefficients of Variation			
- of prices	0.38	0.31	0.56
- of growth rates for prices[c]	34. 61	25,92[d]	21.21
Symmetry	1.25	0.28	−0.06
Kurtosis	4.13	2.34	2.34
Jarque-Bera normality test	27.33	0.87	1.41
Probability	0.00	0.65	0.49
Quotient of variances test			
With windows of:			
- 10 years	0.49	0.26	0.62
- 20 years	0.27	—	0.26
- 40 years	0.11	—	0.16
Prices in logarithms			
Symmetry	0.37	−0.38	−1.24
Kurtosis	2.98	2.55	3.14
Jarque-Bera normality test	1.86	0.91	19.43
Probability	0.39	0.63	0.00
Unit root tests			
Without constant or trend	0.13	−0.39	0.24
Augmented Dickey-Fuller Statistic			
MacKinnon critical values			
1%	−2.59	−2.66	−2.59
5%	−1.94	−1.95	−1.94
10%	−1.62	−1.62	−1.62
With constant	−2.86	−1.38	−1.50
Augmented Dickey-Fuller Statistic			
MacKinnon critical values			
1%	−3.51	−3.71	−3.52
5%	−2.89	−2.98	−2.90
10%	−2.58	−2.63	−2.59
With constant and trend	−3.91	−1.36	−1.57
Augmented Dickey-Fuller Statistic			
MacKinnon critical values			
1%	−4.06	−4.36	−4.09
5%	−3.46	−3.59	−3.47
10%	−3.16	−3.23	−3.16

Source: Calculations based on data from the IISEC-UCB. MacKinnon critical values, MicroTSP 7.0

a. Prices available for 1962-1985.
b. Official prices in Bolivia, 1915-1989.
c. Growth rates expressed as a difference in logarithms.
d. In absolute value.

Figure 4.2   Annual Zinc Prices (USA), in Real Terms, 1980 base
(US$ cents per pound sterling)

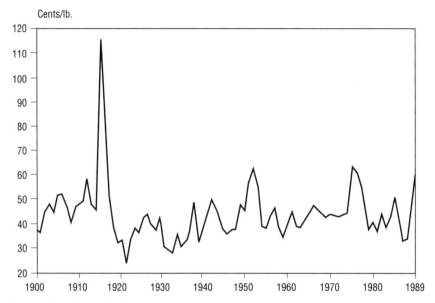

Source: See Appendix A.

do not show that the random walk hypothesis can be rejected in any of the cases.[12]

The measurements of symmetry and kurtosis for the annual prices suggest difficulties with the hypothesis of normality of the series. Notwithstanding the observed values, the Jarque-Bera test with annual data, in real terms, for London and official statistics, does not permit the hypothesis of normality to be rejected when a 5-percent level of significance is employed.

Likewise, normality for real prices in logarithms cannot be rejected when using the series for London and the United States. This poses the problem of selecting between a normal distribution and a lognormal distribution for the process that generates the prices.

Zinc Prices

Figure 4.2 shows strong fluctuations in the real price of zinc. As in the case of tin, abrupt changes are observed, but there are no excessively salient peaks

---

[12] These tests, as well as those for zinc, can be obtained from the authors.

Table 4.8 Annual prices of Zinc, in Real Terms, 1900-1989

	New York	London [a]	Official [b]
Coefficients of Variation			
- of prices	0.27	0.35	0.18
- of growth rates of prices[c]	34.73	9.84	34.81
Symmetry	2.95	2.51	0.82
Kurtosis	16.78	9.27	2.86
Jarque-Bera normality test	816.55	75.19	4.52
Probability	0.00	0.00	0.10
Quotient of variances test			
With windows of			
- 10 years	0.21	0.07	0.14
- 20 years	0.30	—	0.07
- 40 years	0.16	—	—
Prices in Logarithms			
Symmetry	1.08	1.68	0.48
Kurtosis	6.89	5.89	2.57
Jarque-Bera normality test	71.44	22.87	1.85
Probability	0.00	0.00	0.40
Unit root tests			
Without constant and trend	0.06	0.11	0.41
Augmented Dickey-Fuller Statistic			
MacKinnon critical values			
1%	−2.59	−2.66	−2.63
5%	−1.94	−1.95	−1.95
10%	−1.62	−1.62	−1.62
With constant	−4.78	−3.07	4.18
Augmented Dickey-Fuller Statistic			
MacKinnon critical values			
1%	−3.51	−3.71	−3.62
5%	−2.89	−2.98	−2.94
10%	−2.58	−2.63	−2.61
With constant and trend	−4.75	−3.08	4.08
Augmented Dickey-Fuller Statistic			
MacKinnon critical values			
1%	−4.06	4.36	4.22
5%	−3.46	−3.59	−3.53
10%	−3.16	−3.23	−3.20

Source: Calculations based on data from IISEC-UCB. MacKinnon critical values, MicroTSP, 7.0

a. Available prices for 1962-1989.
b. Official prices in Bolivia for 1950-1989.
c. Growth rates expressed as a difference in logarithms.

after 1920. The CVs of zinc prices are somewhat lower than in the case of tin. The CV for the growth rates is similar to that of the U.S. price of tin, but significantly lower for the London price. Based on this last information, it can be concluded that zinc prices are less volatile than tin prices.

The quotients of the variances for the price of zinc are relatively low, which would indicate relatively short durations for the shocks. The random walk tests with annual price data in logarithms, with the U.S. and official data series, cause us to reject the hypothesis when the test includes a constant, and a constant and a trend, at the level of 1 percent (Table 4.8). With the London data, the hypothesis is rejected in the model with a constant, at the level of 5 percent. These are robust results, which make the random walk hypothesis difficult to sustain. As a complement to this conclusion, note that for the series of logarithms for the real New York prices from 1900 to 1989, the coefficient of autoregression of the first order $AR(1)$ is 0.63 and that of the second order $AR(2)$ is 0.27. The trend for zinc prices appears to change directions much faster than that for tin prices.

It should be pointed out, however, that the above conclusions change with quarterly and monthly series, and thus, the random walk hypothesis cannot be rejected with this type of data.

The calculations of bias and kurtosis make it very difficult to accept the normality of the series. For all series, the kurtosis is over three. The Jarque-Bera test leads to a rejection of the hypothesis of normality for the prices and also for their logarithms, except in the case of the official price series.

Price Formation for Natural Gas

It is difficult to speak of an international market for natural gas in the strict sense of the term. What we are dealing with is actually a series of potentially regional and juxtaposed markets that tend to influence one another, but may follow operational logics that are rather different. Once a contract is signed and the investment made, a bilateral monopolistic relationship is established between the contracting parties.

The high investment levels and irreversibility implied in the sale of natural gas generate a high degree of rigidity in the delivery clauses. A common feature of such contracts is the "take or pay" clause. Under this stipulation, the buyer is obliged to purchase the volume established in the agreement for the duration of the contract, whether or not the importer takes it or consumes it. In other words, the importer is obliged to pay for the amount of gas contracted, even if it is not consumed. The rigidity of delivery may conflict with the buyer's demand profile, giving rise to major fluctuations in both price and earnings for the exporter.

After the first oil crisis in 1973, it became customary in contracts to set the price, using the price of competitive fuel in the market of the importing country as the point of reference. Thus, it is an attempt to reproduce events in the international energy market—especially the oil market—in bilateral trade. This reproduction, however, may be neither immediate nor complete.

The contract for the sale of gas to Argentina from 1972 to 1992 had a large number of the general characteristics mentioned in the above discussion. The initial contract and subsequent agreements were based on the "take or pay" principle, with a certain flexibility in its application. The first contract established a price but did not provide mechanisms for its readjustment. After the first oil crisis in 1975, a semiannual price review clause was introduced, although an agreement was not reached that would make it automatic. It was not until 1987 that a rule for indexing prices was established.

The indexing mechanism, with a partial price adjustment, was in effect from 1988 to 1991. With this mechanism, natural gas prices were indexed (every quarter) to the price of petroleum derivatives (fuel oil) and that of transportation, based on the formula:

$$Pt = 0.30P(t-1) + 0.70P*(t-1) \tag{3}$$

where Pt = price of residual gas (US$/MBTU) at the contractual point of delivery, and $P*t$ = the average price of a basket of fuels sold in Buenos Aires.[13]

In the March 1992 negotiations with Argentina, this indexing rule was eliminated, which meant a significant change of regime. The international reference point for the negotiations provided by the price for oil has been lost (or at least, its impact has been attenuated), and it has been replaced by whatever may result from the negotiations between the private distributor that will replace Gas del Estado and the Argentine suppliers. This has accentuated the bilateralism.

Price Trajectory in Contracts for Sales of Natural Gas to Argentina

From the annual real data in Figure 4.3 can be seen both the rising trend in the real prices of Bolivian natural gas exports to Argentina from 1972 to 1985 and its dramatic fall from 1986 to 1989. It should be added that, starting in 1984,

---

[13] To be more precise, P^* is a basket of fuels affected by a multiplying factor K, which initially served only to link the price resulting from the formula with the last price, before the formula was applied. K, however, has become an object of negotiation. A discussion of the modifications to K is beyond the scope of this work.

Figure 4.3 Annual Gas Prices, in Real Terms, 1980 base

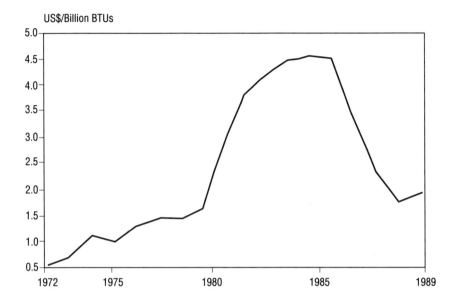

Figure 4.4 Nominal and Effective Price of Natural Gas

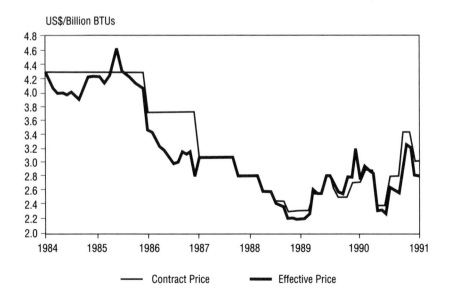

Argentina began to make 50 percent of its payments in goods and services; this percentage later decreased. If the payment in goods and services is corrected for the change in Argentina's real exchange rate in relation to the last quarter in which payments were made in convertible currency, the prices actually paid for natural gas are substantially lower and much more variable than the nominal prices up to 1987 (Figure 4.4).[14]

Fluctuations in real prices (without correction for the payment in goods and services), as measured by their *CV*s, do not appear to have been very important (Table 4.9). The *CV*s of the growth rates of real prices (as measured by their differences in logarithms) are high, however.

The quotients of variances systematically show values of greater than one. However, the limited number of observations and the short length of the windows can reduce the validity of any conclusions based on this information. We shall provisionally conclude that permanent shocks are more important than transitory ones. Random walk tests also support this assertion.

The coefficient of symmetry of the prices is relatively far from zero. The coefficient of kurtosis of the prices is lower that what would be obtained if prices were generated by a normal distribution. This means that small deviations from the average price have been more frequent than the deviations that would have occurred under a normal distribution. Put another, more intuitive way, while there are large deviations from the mean that determine the magnitude of the variance, they have been relatively infrequent. This is not surprising, in view of how the nominal prices (which are the contract prices) are negotiated. Nominal price jumps (strong but infrequent) also give rise to strong but equally infrequent changes in real prices, while the small, more numerous price changes result from the effect of the price deflator. It must be noted that, despite the values encountered for symmetry and kurtosis, the Jarque-Bera test cannot make us reject the hypothesis of normality at the 5-percent level of significance. Nor can we reject the hypothesis at the 5-percent level that the logs of the prices have a normal distribution.

Price Convergence for Natural Gas and Oil

The underlying principle of the bilateral negotiations from 1972 to 1991 has been that price movements of gas should follow those of oil. In line with this assertion, Figure 4.5 appears to signal a convergent trajectory for the prices of

---

[14] For a more complete view of the price trajectory, prices would have to be corrected for the effects of Argentina's payments arrears. To obtain the effective price, the (nominal) price of the contract paid in arrears should be discounted by a factor $(1 + i)$, where i is the interest rate per period.

Table 4.9 Annual Gas Prices, in Real Terms, 1972-1990

Coefficient of Variation	
- of prices	0.60
- of the growth rate of prices[a]	3.48
Symmetry	0.43
Kurtosis	1.58
Jarque-Bera normality test	2.06
Probability	0.36
Quotient of variances test	
With windows of	
- 4 years	2.10
- 5 years	1.88
Prices in Logarithms	
Symmetry	-0.23
Kurtosis	1.92
Jarque-Bera normality test	1.03
Probability	0.60
Unit root tests	
Without constant or trend	-0.73
Augmented Dickey-Fuller Statistic	
MacKinnon critical values	
1%	-2.73
5%	-1.96
10%	-1.63
With constant	
Augmented Dickey-Fuller Statistic	-1.83
MacKinnon critical values	
1%	-3.92
5%	-3.07
10%	-2.67
With constant and trend	-1.05
Augmented Dickey-Fuller Statistic	
MacKinnon critical values	
1%	-4.67
5%	-3.73
10%	-3.31

Source: Calculations based on data from IISEC-UCB. MacKinnon critical values, MicroTSP 7.0

a. Growth rates expressed as a difference in logarithms

these two commodities. For a formal verification of the long-term convergence of these prices, Engel-Granger cointegration techniques have been used.

Oil prices, like those of natural gas, appear to follow a nonstationary process (Hausmann *et al.*, 1991). Assuming these prices are $I(1)$, a test was carried out to determine whether the residuals of the regression of natural gas prices on oil prices were stationary. These tests were run with annual, quarterly, and monthly series. Only series up to 1987 were considered, since in the following year, an explicit rule indexing natural gas prices to a basket of fuels went into effect. The inclusion of the observations for 1988-1990 could have biased the results in favor of the cointegration hypothesis.

The hypothesis that the residuals are not stationary cannot be rejected based on the tests (Table 4.10). Thus, the two price series are not cointegrated.

To complete the analysis of price convergence, we have traced the dynamic trend of the structural model coefficients that link the variations in the price of gas sold to Argentina with changes in the price of oil. To do so, we have employed the Kalman filters technique, with quarterly data from 1972 to 1987.

Figure 4.5   Indices of Annual Prices of Oil and Natural Gas Base 1980 = 1

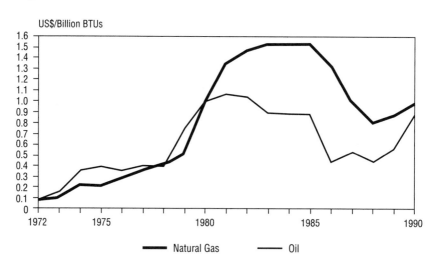

Graph 4.6 (panels A and B) shows the Kalman filters for the constant and the elasticity of the model $Pg = \alpha + \beta Pc$, where Pg = the log of the price of natural gas and Pc = the log of the price of oil, both in nominal terms. The recursive estimation of α is relatively constant until 1986, when it jumps. A similar estimation of β produces a more unstable trend, with values that gradually approach 80 percent up to around 1986 and decrease to about 50 percent thereafter. For comparative purposes, the graphs also include the least squares estimators of α and β. It can be seen that estimations using Kalman filters for α and β move out of the intervals defined by the least squares estimations ±2 standard deviations.

Table 4.10 Cointegration Tests for Natural Gas and Oil Prices
(1972-1987)

Series	Cointegration vector		Dickey-Fuller t Statistic	MacKinnon critical values		
	Natural gas	Oil		1%	5%	10%
Annual 1972-1987						
Nominal	1	-0.1306	-1.03	-4.81	-3.81	-3.37
Real	1	-0.1238	-1.09			
In logarithms						
Nominal	1	-1.2340	-1.12			
Real	1	-1.0859	-0.72			
Quarterly 1972.11 - 1987.1V						
Nominal	1	-0.1346	-1.65	-4.08	-3.44	-3.11
Real	1	-0.1102	-1.44			
In logarithms						
Nominal	1	-1.2163	-2.37			
Real	1	-1.0221	-1.79			
Monthly 1972.04 - 1987.12						
Nominal	1	-0.1353	-1.57	-3.96	-3.37	-3.07
Real	1	-0.1116	-1.29			
In logarithms						
Nominal	1	-1.2270	-1.82			
Real	1	-1.0352	-1.41			

Sources: Calculations based on data from IISEC-UCB. MacKinnon Critical values, MicroTSP, 7.0.

**Figure 4.6A   Kalman Filters, Equation for the Price of Gas
vs. the Price of Oil, 1972-1987**
(nominal quarterly prices in logarithms)

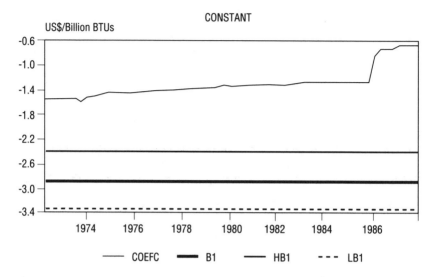

**Figure 4.6B Kalman Filters, Equation for the Price of Gas
vs. the Price of Oil, 1982-1987**
(nominal quarterly prices in logarithms)

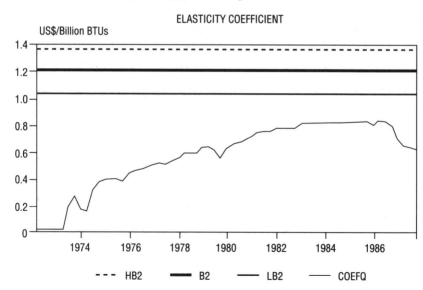

Stabilization Policies

General Stabilization Policies

One line of argument pursued throughout this essay is that, in the context of a private exporting sector that is more important than its public counterpart, and where several primary commodities of similar importance are involved, the entire range of economic policy mechanisms should be examined to stabilize earnings and consumption in the face of external shocks. In particular, the management of the capital account of the balance of payments, the external debt, and the tax structure are complements to the more specific instruments for stabilizing external income and at the same time, are more important. Import policy is also very important, but we can reasonably assume (for reasons other than those discussed in this document) that it will not vary to a large extent in the face of shocks from export earnings. The present openness of the current account should be considered permanent.

One of the most significant results of the study by Bevan *et al.* (1989) is that openness in the capital account is crucial for boosting the gains in permanent income in the event of a positive export price shock. Their argument is plausible, in terms of the distribution of investment over time, which points to the desirability of keeping earnings temporarily out of the country. Implicit in that recommendation is the stabilization of the real exchange rate.

This argument can be extended to the case of price decreases. These decreases produce an *increment* in the marginal efficiency of investment in the nontraditional tradeable goods sectors (in Bolivia's case, primarily agriculture for export), in terms of both tradeable and nontradeable goods. The loss of both external assets and external capital flows can provide the necessary financing for these investments and enable the reallocation of resources.

There has been no control of the exchange rate since late 1985, constraints on movements of private sector capital are few, and the tax burden on them is light. This exchange-rate and capital-account regime is in line with the recommendation that broad openness to international movement of funds be maintained.

Rapid changes in the net international reserves (NIR) of the Central Bank have major effects on the short-term real exchange (and inflation) rate. Stabilizing the NIR is necessary, but not sufficient, to stabilize the real exchange rate. This is especially true in light of the growing "dollarization" of the Bolivian economy, which makes the *changes* in the NIR very imperfect indicators of both what is going on in the monetary sphere and of the short-term effects of these changes on the real exchange rate. The stabilization of the NIRs under a fixed-exchange-rate regime will normally depend on monetary policy and the management of the fiscal deficit.

In theory, the 1986 tax reform, which attempts to establish a broad-based tax structure that mainly taxes consumption, dampens the effects on government revenues of fluctuations induced by external shocks. However, shortcomings in mining tax legislation increase the income risk to the government. It is hoped the new law, whose implications have been discussed previously, will correct this situation.

Hedging Markets for Tin and Zinc

Tin and zinc concentrates have several marketing channels organized in the form of a pyramid: Bolivian marketers, international marketers, and foundry enterprises. Refined ore is generally marketed through international concerns and, only rarely, directly to consumers. Transactions by Bolivian producers and marketers with international marketers and foundry enterprises involve the physical product and not paper. It should be recalled that in the international financial markets, tin and zinc operations are generally cash transactions (on the spot and forward markets). Hedging with futures is rare, although from 1978 to 1985 some significant tin transactions were recorded, more on the part of marketers and foundry enterprises than mining companies.[15] In the case of zinc, hedging operations in the financial markets are smaller and have been used only recently.

Marketing Bolivian minerals through "positions" like forwards and futures is not a frequent occurrence. Amassing stocks for speculative purposes is also rare nowadays. Before 1985, some large enterprises, like COMIBOL, the Banco Minero de Bolivia (BMB), and relatively large national marketing companies of a certain size, employed forwards contracts with rather unfavorable results. Private, mid-sized companies also held stocks for speculative purposes in anticipation of modifications in economic policy—especially devaluations in the exchange rate—rather than variations in international prices.[16]

Tin and zinc contracts between large Bolivian mining companies and international marketers are frequently long-term. They include a deferred delivery clause with respect to the date of signature of the contract, but the final liquidation by the marketer to the producer is made at the spot price a few weeks (usually three) after receipt of the mineral at the port stipulated in the contract. The marketer grants a loan (or a cash advance) to the mining company when

---

[15] One notable exception is that of Malaysia, which has done so on its own since 1978, through the Malaysia Mining Corporation and the KPS (Ntamungiro, 1988).

[16] In 1991, after a long interruption, some small futures operations between Bolivian tin marketing companies and foreign marketers were reinstituted.

the contract is signed—a very attractive feature for producers with very limited access to international credit.

This form of marketing partially amortizes the market instability, as the volume risk and the risk to the producer of holding involuntary inventories disappears. The price risk, however, remains. Fluctuating operational expenditures for handling the mineral, and the associated penalties, add an income risk for the producer. These contracts could easily be converted to forwards contracts if a price were preestablished at which the operation would be liquidated on delivery of the mineral. It should be noted that foreign foundries and marketers allow the Bolivian seller to fix the price of the mineral on specific dates during the life of the contract. Nevertheless, exporters prefer not to hedge (or not to speculate) with these facilities.

Bolivian tin marketers that acquire the output of small producers carry out back-to-back operations that consist of supplying themselves with the mineral of these producers, in amounts similar to those that they are almost simultaneously delivering to the foreign foundries and marketers, and under similar conditions. The spot price is employed in these transactions. With tin, a mineral with a high value per unit of weight, stockpiling large inventories to make its transport economically feasible is unnecessary. This obviously facilitates the back-to-back operations.

The situation for zinc is very different. It requires the stockpiling of much larger inventories, and, moreover, exports have to be moved by railroad—a far less flexible mode of transportation than the trucks used for tin. Because of this, and the fact that Bolivian zinc output is small in relation to world output, producers may discover an advantage in hedging with forward and (even more interesting) with futures and options. (For tin, large-scale Bolivian operations in the hedging markets could affect spot prices and future prices, with results contrary to those anticipated).

With the back-to-back procedure, national marketers almost totally minimize the price risk by transferring it entirely to the mining producer. As a rule, they do not adopt any hedging mechanisms for their mineral supply. The justification for this is that mining, especially tin mining, is becoming increasingly informal, consisting of a multitude of small-scale producers. Bolivian marketers are also numerous. Under these circumstances, it is difficult to foster stable relationships. In the long term, with the emergence of larger producers and improvements in international market conditions, there will be sufficient incentives to build lasting relationships with suppliers. By sharing coverage with producers, marketers will be able to count on a much more reliable supply.

Marketers also hedge against any potential short-term price risk with two mechanisms: (1) the establishment of favorable margins for the marketer between the international sale price and the purchase price from the producer;

and (2) the establishment of small reserve or contingency funds. Such funds are not very common.

The nonuse of financial markets by producers to hedge against risk has a number of explanations; most important among them is the lack of capital or access to credit needed to meet the margin requirements for the clearinghouses. The second is the fact that this type of operation normally is carried out with refined metals of a homogeneous quality. Bolivian enterprises (with the exception of ENAF) produce only concentrates. Finally, in the case of state enterprises, there is fear among the management of being held legally accountable in the event of an operation that incurs a loss.

Recognizing the problems of access to credit, Powell (1991:74) notes that options provide a greater degree of flexibility than futures. An option is a contract that, through the payment of a premium, grants the buyer the right to buy (or sell) the good (or asset) in question, at a given price (called the striking price) at a given time. The seller, for his part, acquires the obligation to deliver (or acquire) the good (or asset) in question. There are two types of options: options to buy (calls) and options to sell (puts).[17]

The simplest option strategy to cover producers would be to purchase a put option. The purchase of the put, however, can be costly. Powell suggests circumventing this problem for the producer by having him sell a call option simultaneously with the purchase of the put. If the put and the call are written on identical quantities but with different strike prices, such that the values of the put and the call are equal, the resulting combination has a zero cost, with complete insurance for the striking price of the put but a limit on the striking price of the call. The problem with this strategy is that the striking price of the call may not be attractive to the producer when prices are high. As an alternative, Powell suggests that the two options have the same striking price but be written on different quantities, such that their values offset one another.

Stabilizing Earnings Fluctuations from Natural Gas Exports

Hedging with Indexation of Natural Gas Prices

Natural gas contracts place much more emphasis on sales volumes than on prices; price volatility in this type of contract can therefore be highly significant. Hence, the importance of rules for price formation. In bilateral trade, the

---

[17] The options market has been receiving increasing attention. For a basic introduction to the subject in Spanish, see Alonso (1986).

price will have to move within a band that takes the following conditions into account: (1) a minimum price that covers the costs of operation incurred by the producer (including transportation) and the cost of capital; (2) a price ceiling that must be competitive with the cost of substitute fuels at the site of consumption.

Readjustments of natural gas prices should be indexed to variations in the prices of other energy sources—respecting, however, the principle that the levels must be kept within the boundaries defined by (1) and (2). In other words, the boundaries of the band should cause prices to rebound internally.

The indexation formula (3) in the gas contract with Argentina from 1988 to 1991, had the dual merit of not isolating contract prices from the international reference prices and of stabilizing fluctuations. The stabilization properties of formula (3) are analyzed formally in Appendix B. In that appendix, it is demonstrated that if P^*, the weighted price of the fuels, is such that the deviations from their mean are purely random (that is, "white noise"), then the partial adjustment formula produces a P with a lower variance than that of P^*. Even if P^* follows a first order autoregressive process, with a positive coefficient of autoregression, but strictly less than one, P is less volatile than P^*. If P^* follows a random walk process, the indexation formula will only reproduce the instability of P^* in the long term. However, even in this case the price of gas will be known with certainty in the following quarter. More relevant yet, for a *finite* number of periods in advance, the variance in the price of gas will be smaller than that produced by a random walk process. The difference in the variances shrinks, however, as the number of periods increases. At the limit, the two variances are infinite.

Preventing Natural Gas Shocks from Becoming Permanent and the Financing of Investment

The nature of the market for natural gas and the context of the March 1992 renegotiation with Argentina do not rule out expectations that the serious deterioration in earnings from this export will persist. To forestall a permanent shock, Bolivia is searching for new markets for its gas, while continuing sales to Argentina. We have already noted the advanced state of negotiations with Brazil to reach the Brazilian border and, eventually, supply São Paulo.

The emergence of large-scale projects for sales to Brazil will depend on: (1) the certification of Bolivia's natural gas reserves; (2) agreement on the volumes to be sold, probably under the "take or pay" system; (3) the length of the contract; (4) the establishment of rules for price formation; and (5) financing.

The discussion of conditions (1) to (3) is beyond the scope of this essay. For condition (4), the contracting parties could agree to an indexation rule similar to the one in effect with Argentina from 1988 to 1991, which we described in the previous section.

Financing is a very delicate issue. One of several possibilities would be the following. In combination with private capital, Bolivia's YPFB and Brazil's PETROBRAS (or one of its subsidiaries) would create a multinational company, organized as a private corporation, for the sale of gas to Brazil.[18] The official international credit agencies, with whom negotiations have been under way, would finance a major portion of the investments of this corporation.[19] The remaining fraction of the investment would be financed with contributions from state and private stockholders and by floating bond issues on the private capital markets.

The bonds could take the form of "natural gas bonds,"[20] endowed with the following characteristics: (1) they would be expressed in volumes of gas and promise the holder of the instrument the monetary equivalent of a fixed quantity of gas, valued at the price in effect at the end of the month; and (2) they would be zero coupon bonds. The bond issue could be implemented through an international bank with long-term expiration dates not to exceed 20 years. Ideally, these instruments would be tradeable on the secondary markets (that is, they would be "securitized").

The buyer of the gas bond would be faced with two types of risk: (1) the voluntary failure to pay on the part of the issuer of the bonds; and (2) the involuntary failure to pay, arising from default or delay on the part of the importer of the natural gas. One way of circumventing the above risks is to have the seller and the buyer commit themselves in the launching of the gas bonds and in the provision of collateral guarantees.

There are several ways to provide security for the buyers of gas bonds. One is to create fiduciary accounts in a bank acceptable to creditors within the international financial system. The eventual buyer of Bolivian gas would make his payments in convertible currency to the fiduciary accounts of the creditors. This payment instruction would form part of the contracts for the sale of gas, as an obligation of the buyer. The bank would turn the income over to YPFB, once the service on the bonds had been paid.

An equivalent to the gas bonds would be put bonds (in this regard, see Kletzer *et al.*, 1990, and Basch and Engel, 1991). These bonds would be pure bonds— that is, they would not depend on the price of the natural gas—and they would

---

[18] The establishment of the company as a private corporation is important to protect bond holders from the problems of sovereign risk.

[19] Negotiations are under way with the World Bank, the Inter-American Development Bank, the Andean Development Corporation, and the Export-Import Bank of Japan.

[20] The Banque Paribas has granted a loan pegged to the price of gas to the Trade and Development Corporation of New Orleans. The resemblance to gas bonds is evident.

be accompanied by the purchase of a put option on a fixed volume of natural gas.[21] In other words, the multinational corporation would issue a bond and the holder of the bond would simultaneously sell it as a put option. The obvious difficulty with this transaction is the financing of the put.

Another possibility is for the multinational corporation to issue bonds with two simultaneous options, the purchase of a put and the sale of a call, in a "collar" that has the additional advantage to creditors of providing them with an opportunity to share in the benefits of potential price increases (Basch and Engel, 1991). In this financial transaction, there are three possible outcomes:

- If the price of gas at maturity is lower than the strike price of the put, the multinational corporation exercises its option. The seller of the put acquires the volume contracted at the strike price and eventually collects from the Brazilian importer, if another party, thereby incurring a loss.
- If the price of gas at maturity is higher than the strike price of the call, the seller of the option pays the multinational corporation the volume contracted at that price, thereby realizing a profit.
- If the price of natural gas at maturity is higher than the strike price of the put and lower than that of the call, both options expire without being exercised. The bond continues to pay its monthly service.

The Macroeconomic Stabilization Fund

The configuration of Bolivian exports lends specific characteristics to the MSF. With this in mind, we have devised an MSF on two levels. On the first level, which we shall call MSF1, we would have a mechanism for stabilizing the earnings of the state enterprises, COMIBOL and YPFB, with regard to price fluctuations. On the second level, the MSF2 would have as its objective the smoothing of fluctuations in spending by the government (the central government and regional development corporations, RDCs).

An important point of departure for the discussion of MSF1 is whether three stabilization funds should be considered—one per commodity—or a single combined fund for the three commodities. We incline toward a single fund, but with the major proviso that the rules for intervention that govern accumulation (or spending) in the MSF1 be defined separately for each product.

The MSF1 has the dual objective of: (1) helping to stabilize the tax revenues of the NT; and (2) stabilizing the earnings of each mineral producer.[22] If the

---

[21] Kletzer et al. (1990) and Basch and Engel (1991) determine the strike price of the put, which establishes the equivalence with the commodity bond.

[22] Two enterprises, COMIBOL and YPFB, whose administrations are completely independent

criterion for stabilization is minimizing the coefficients of variation, we have the following results. Generally speaking, minimizing the CV of the sum of the earnings of the three primary goods and hence, the revenues of the NT, does not mean that the CV for each product and enterprise will be minimized. Nor does minimizing the CV for each of the earnings separately imply that the sum of the earnings will be minimized.

Only when the price correlations are not negative does minimizing the CV of the sum of the earnings imply that each of the CVs of its components will be minimized and vice versa. However, when all the correlations are not negative, the argument in favor of a single multiproduct fund instead of separate funds for each product disappears, a point that will be examined more thoroughly further on.

This work's recommendation of a single MSF1, but with separate intervention rules for each commodity, has its specific justification in the Bolivian situation, on the one hand, and in administrative convenience, on the other. The specific justification comes from observing the price correlations. Here, the only negative correlation encountered is between natural gas and zinc (-0.425), whose weight, moreover, is not very significant, because of the (still) low share of zinc revenues in the total revenues of the three products. There is a basis for supposing that stabilization by product implies the stabilization of total earnings. The justification of administrative convenience stems from the ease and transparency of operations when the rules are separate. In other words, the administrative difficulty of distributing the cost of the stabilization interventions among the enterprises that contribute to the MSF1 is circumvented.

From section four follows that we cannot discard the possibility that the annual prices of tin and zinc, in real terms (in logarithms), follow a stationary trend process, although their reversion to the trend may be slow. Furthermore, the indexation formula for natural gas has an "information content" that makes the uncertainty not very great for periods that are not too far distant. (The nominal price of gas is known with certainty one quarter in advance). There would be no justification for an MSF1 were these characteristics absent. Nevertheless, if the frequency is quarterly and monthly, the high volatility of tin and zinc prices demands characteristics specific to the MSF1.

A multiproduct fund will often, but not always, reduce the variance in the income of the MSF1 compared to a strategy of funds by commodity. This, in turn, should contribute to lowering the probability that the MSF1 will collapse because the funds are exhausted. In the case of the three products in question,

---

of one another, produce the three primary commodities. YPFB specializes totally in hydrocarbons. COMIBOL, on the other hand, is a holding company for other enterprises. COMIBOL enterprises that are tin producers are generally not the same ones that produce zinc.

there is the presumption, supported in the results with real data, that a reduction in the variance occurs with the multiproduct fund.

Assuming that 37 percent of the income of the MSF1 is derived from tin, 7.7 percent from zinc, and 55.3 percent from natural gas—figures that correspond to the historical averages of the 1980-1989 share of each commodity in a basket of the three goods—the standard deviation from the joint income would be 1.414. This value should be compared with 1.937 for tin, 0.079 for zinc, and 1.354 for natural gas.

Contributions to the MSF1 would come from the extraordinary income derived from the *foreign sales* of COMIBOL and YPFB (including those from joint ventures). If an *unanticipated* drop in the resources of these enterprises occurs, COMIBOL and YPFB could resort to the MSF1. Both enterprises can withdraw an amount equal to their contributions to the fund, minus their contributions for insurance against the fund's collapse. The MSF1 would neither manage stocks nor become involved in commercial transactions with metals or natural gas, and COMIBOL and YPFB would have to turn over (or receive) the appropriate amounts in foreign exchange. Contributions and other payments would be calculated on the basis of the methodology defined below.

The price bands for intervention by the MSF1 shall be defined separately for tin, zinc, and natural gas. The MSF1 would save when the price of a given product is above the upper threshold of the band and spend when it is below. Let F_t be the level accumulated in the MSF1 up to period t. The accumulation up to the following period will follow the rule:

$$F_{t+1} = (1+i)F_t + \sum \max\left(p_{i,t+1} - U_{it}, 0\right)x_i - \sum \max\left(L_{it} - p_{i,t+1}, 0\right)x_i \quad (4)$$

where $P_i(i = 1,2,3)$ is the price of the good i, U_i the upper threshold price of the band, L_i the lower threshold price of the band, and x_i the export volumes subject to price risk. The sum indicated in the equation covers 1 to 3. The saving (spending) rules of the MSF1 are independent of the level of resources already accumulated.

It should be noted that $z_i = E_t \max\left(L_{it} - P_{i,t+1}, 0\right)$—with E_t the operator of expected value at time t—is the premium of a put option for product i, with a strike price L_{it} and expiration at $t+1$.[23] This observation suggests that equation (4) can be completed with a hedging term. The premium of the hedge would be paid in period $t+1$ and determined by $S_{t+1} = \sum z_{it}x_{it}$. Equation (4), then, would be corrected to finally yield $F'_{t+1} = F_{t+1} + S_{t+1}$.

It should be noted that the system described is analogous to the purchase by

---

[23] Under the condition of profits equal to zero. Likewise, $E_t\max(P_{i,t+1} - U_{it}, 0)$ is the premium of a call option.

COMIBOL and YPFB of a put option to hedge against extraordinary drops in their export income. The price of the put is calculated based on the well-known Black-Scholes (1973) formula. Just as important, the writing of the put can be interpreted as a hedge that protects, in expected values, against the exhaustion of the MSF1. This does not mean that the MSF1 could not arrive at that situation; however, it could *very temporarily* break its constraint of non-negativity by simply not disbursing the agreed upon sums. The hedge would protect against more long-lasting situations of this type.[24]

The proposed scheme is for the initial stages, when the fund is being established. In the future, a correction will have to be made to the incentive that exists for administrators to set U_i too low, which would turn the MSF1 into an unintended tax mechanism. To prevent this, the formula S could be modified to $S_{t+1} = \sum z_{it} x_{it}$, with $z_i = E_t \max\left(L_{it} - P_{i,t+1}, 0\right) - E_t \max\left(P_{i,t+1} - U_{it}, 0\right)$. That is, the MSF1 would have to purchase call options from COMIBOL and YPFB with strike prices of U_i, for the same delivery volumes x_{it}.

Estimated annual exports of COMIBOL's tin and zinc production and YPFB's natural gas production, divided by four, would define the volumes of each MSF1 operation. Thus, for example, if estimates indicate that COMIBOL will produce 8,000 tons of tin next year, each MSF1 transaction will be on a volume of 2,000 tons. Thus, 2,000 times the value of the put will be COMIBOL's payment to the MSF1 for insurance.

MSF1 interventions will take place and the boundaries of the band will be reviewed quarterly. The intervention prices of the band will be set as a linear combination *around* a trend price and the last market price of the product, thus addressing the dual nature of fluctuations. More precisely, if P^*_{it} is the trend price for i, b_i the discrepancy allowed with respect to this trend price, and P_{it} the market price, the intervention prices will be defined by:

$$U_{it} = \mu\left(P^*_{it} + b_i\right) + (1-\mu)P_{it} \qquad 0 < \mu < 1 \tag{5a}$$

$$L_{it} = \mu\left(P^*_{it} - b_i\right) + (1-\mu)P_{it}. \tag{5b}$$

The trend price P^*_{it} could initially be based on historical values; e.g., by computing the average spot price of the six previous years on the London (or other appropriate) market, with prior adjustment for the U.S. Manufacturing Unit Values (MUV) or the Wholesale Price Index (WPI). The b_i's could be:

---

[24] The MSF1 should pay interest on these involuntary loans. In the simulations run, there are times when the MSF1 becomes negative, but this is corrected rapidly.

- US$.25 per refined pound of tin;
- US$.05 per pound of zinc;
- US$.25 per thousand cubic feet of natural gas.

The above data are entirely tentative. Furthermore, the selection of μ is crucial and will depend on initial fund operations.

The MSF2 would consist of the following contributions:

- All of the royalties and taxes owed by YPFB and COMIBOL to the National Treasury (NT) and to the RDCs, calculated on the basis of their actual earnings. If market prices fall within the band of the MSF1, the companies will pay taxes based on these prices. If the MSF1 has to compensate, the enterprises that receive the tax compensation will pay taxes based on the strike price of the put. Contributions to the MSF1 would be tax-exempt; in that case, the companies would be taxed up to the strike price of their call option.
- All royalties and taxes owed by the private sector to the NT and to the RDCs.
- Any interest yielded by the balances in the MSF2.

Before moving on to more specific aspects of the administration of the MSF2, the following is worth noting:

- All stabilization mechanisms outside the MSF2 would be used before the funds enter it. In particular, the mechanisms of the MSF1 would be employed. However, this does not rule out the possibility that the revenues for the MSF2 are not stationary. In particular, the possibility of collecting taxes from the private sector would remain.
- We repeat that compensation by the MSF1 to COMIBOL and YPFB for drops in their actual earnings would not be exempt from taxes. The taxes would have to be paid with the aliquots paid by their normal revenues.
- The private sector could dispose freely of its income, once its tax obligations had been met. Except for the existing taxes established in current law, it would not be obliged to contribute either to the MSF1 or the MSF2.

The use of the MSFs' resources would be defined annually, when the National Budget is approved.[25] The government (including the RDCs) would budget its expenditures, taking into account both current revenues (plus the net disbursements of the external debt) and the level of resources accumulated in the MSF2. However, to the degree that current revenues contain information

---

[25] In the recommendations that follow, we take our inspiration from Deaton (1991) and Basch and Engel (1991).

on future revenues, the marginal propensity to spend should be adjusted in the direction indicated by these revenues. Expenditures should also be adjusted in current operations when there is little uncertainty in future price predictions. A threshold can be defined for when saving in the MSF2 should commence in order to determine an optimal spending trajectory for the government.

The MSFs should be very liquid, and all savings should be invested in foreign assets. These would be held in fiduciary accounts in the Central Bank of Bolivia; however, it must be underscored that they would not form part of the country's international foreign exchange reserves, at least as they are conventionally understood.

The MSFs cannot go into operation until the prices of tin, zinc, and natural gas improve with respect to their current values, which are substantially below their historical levels. It should be noted that postponing the startup of the MSFs until revenues from the three natural resources reach a certain level is consistent with the optimal consumption program of Deaton (1991). Before arriving at that threshold, there is no place for saving in the MSF. Nevertheless, to cushion the fall in the price of natural gas in 1992, the government should temporarily resort to a greater accumulation of international reserves in the Central Bank.

Final Comments

This report began with a review of the significance of tin, zinc, and natural gas in Bolivia's total exports and in its public sector accounts. The major changes that occurred in the 1980s were noted, and it was concluded that the current situation does not appear to be stable, especially in light of the expected increase in the contribution of the so-called "new mining" (which includes zinc) to foreign exchange generation and fiscal revenues.

This was followed by a detailed analysis of price formation for the three primary commodities. The results for tin are comparable to those in other market studies of this metal and for similar markets. We believe that we have arrived at a good characterization of the stochastic process that generates prices, although it is still inadequate for resolving the problems of forecasting. Zinc has been studied far less in the literature, but our analyses enable us to draw conclusions similar to those for tin.

The situation is completely different in the case of natural gas. The end of the contract with Argentina and its renewal for a few more months leaves many questions open. It should be underscored that as a result of the increasing bilateralism in the new contract, the links with international reference prices and many of the possibilities for analyzing the fluctuations have been lost. The problems have shifted to the sphere of political economy, in which the mechanisms for oversight and ensuring that contracts are met occupy a central place. This is a new field that merits more study.

Among the macroeconomic stabilization measures, it appears essential to maintain a high degree of openness to the movements of private capital and a broad base for taxing consumption. The application of the tax reforms in the new legislation to the mining and hydrocarbon sectors is also central. The question remains as to whether or not it would be appropriate to speed up the implementation of the mining tax provisions currently scheduled for 1999.

With the ever-growing participation of the private sector in the export of minerals and hydrocarbons, the search for instruments to enable producers to share the risks has become much more important than in the past. The possibilities of benefitting in the financial hedging markets remain small, although the use of options should be more systematically considered. Improvements in the contracts to market the commodities, and a more frequent use of the forward markets can be anticipated in the short term.

Among the self-insurance mechanisms, we propose the creation of an MSF in the medium term, which would derive from close coordination between two funds—the first to stabilize the earnings of YPFB and COMIBOL, and the second to stabilize the expenditures of the central government and the regional development corporations. The design problems of an MSF for stabilizing the fluctuations of more than one commodity are substantially more complex than for a single one. Furthermore, we have emphasized that these funds could not commence operations right away, given the current persistence of low prices for tin and natural gas.

Specifics are still lacking as to how these funds would operate; these will have to be addressed in future works. These specifics are related to: (1) the initial sums in the funds; and (2) the conditions to prevent the funds from collapsing or overaccumulating. The analytical solutions to these problems are difficult, but numerical methods could help. However, the lack of an operational fund with which to contrast the results may impede substantive progress with numerical methods.

BIBLIOGRAPHY

Alonso, J. 1986. Una introducción a los mercados de opciones. *Información comercial española* 663:161-167.

Arrau, P., and S. Claessens. 1992. *Commodity stabilization fund.* WPS 835. Washington, DC: The World Bank, Department of International Economics.

Banco Central de Bolivia. 1990. *Boletín del Sector Externo* (no. 4, December). La Paz: Banco Central de Bolivia.

—————. 1991. *Boletín Estadístico* (no. 269, March). La Paz: Banco Central de Bolivia.

The World Bank. 1988. Commodity Trade and Price Trends, 1987-88 edition. Washington DC: The World Bank.

Basch, M., and E. Engel. 1991. Shocks transitorios y mecanismos de estabilización. Paper presented at seminar, Network of IDB Centers, July, at CIEPLAN, Santiago.

Bevan, D., P. Collier, and J. Gunning. 1989. The theory of construction booms: The new macroeconomics of external shocks. Oxford University. Mimeo.

Brennan, M.J. 1991. The price of convenience and the valuation of commodity contingent claims. In *Stochastic models and option values*, comps. D. Lund and B. Øksendal, 33-71. Amsterdam: North Holland.

Campbell, J., and P. Perron. 1991. Pitfalls and opportunities: What macroeconomists should know about unit roots? In *NBER Macroeconomics Annual 1991*, 141-201. Cambridge, MA: MIT Press.

Centro de Estudios Minería y Desarrollo (CEMYD). 1990. *Desempeño y colapso de la minería nacionalizada en Bolivia.* La Paz: CEMYD.

Cochrane, J.H. 1988. How big is the random walk in GNP?, *Journal of Political Economy* 96:893-920.

—————. 1991. Comment. In *NBER Macroeconomic Annual 1991.* 201-210. See Campbell and Perron 1991.

Corden, W.M. 1984. Booming sector and Dutch disease economics: Survey and consolidation. *Oxford Economic Papers* 36:359-380.

Deaton, A. 1991. Saving and liquidity constraints. *Econométrica* 59:1221-1248.

Deaton, A., and G. Laroque. 1992. On the behavior of commodity prices. *The Review of Economic Studies* 59:1-23.

Grilli, E., and M.C. Yang. 1988. Primary commodity prices, manufactured good prices, and the terms of trade of developing countries: What the long run shows? *The World Bank Economic Review* 2:1-47.

Hausmann, R., A. Powell, and R. Rigobón. 1992. Facing oil income uncertainty in Venezuela: An optimal spending rule with liquidity constraints and adjustment costs. Caracas: IESA.

Jarque, C.M., and A.K. Bera. 1981. *An efficient large sample test for normality of observations and regression residuals.* Working Papers in Economics and Econometrics N°49. Canberra: Australian National University.

Kletzer, K.M., D.M. Newbery, and B.D. Wright. 1990. *Alternative instruments for smoothing the consumption of primary commodity exporters.* WPS 558 (December). Washington DC: The World Bank, Department of International Economics.

Ministerio de Planeamiento de Bolivia. 1991. *Estadísticas económicas de Bolivia* (no. 2, June). Unidad de análisis política económica, UDAPE. La Paz: Ministerio de Planeamiento de Bolivia.

Morales, J.A. 1992. *Bolivia's tin and natural gas crises of 1985-1989.* Documento de Trabajo No. 04/92 (May). La Paz: Instituto de Investigaciones Socioeconómicas, Universidad Católica Boliviana.

Musgrave, P., and J. Desormeaux. 1976. *Stabilization and development with fluctuating export earnings.* Staff Paper N°3. La Paz: The Musgrave Mission on Fiscal Reform in Bolivia.

Musgrave, R. 1981. *Fiscal reform in Bolivia.* Cambridge: Harvard Law School.

Newbery, D.M., and J.E. Stiglitz. 1981. *The theory of commodity price stabilization: A study in the economics of risk.* Oxford: Oxford University Press.

Ntamatungiro, J. 1988. *Stabilisation des recettes d'exportation: Stock regulateur, contrats à terme et options.* Paris: Económica.

Passeto, R. 1987. Acuerdos para abastecimiento institucional. Seminar on Natural Gas, Montevideo, Uruguay. Mimeo.

Powell, A. 1991. Options to alleviate the costs of uncertainty and stability: A case study of Zambia. In *Commodity, futures, and financial markets*, comp. Louis Philips. Dordrecht: Kluwer Academic Publishers.

The World Bank. 1988. *Commodity Trade and Price Trends.* 1987-88 edition. Washington DC: The World Bank.

APPENDIX A

SOURCES OF PRICE DATA

The price data for tin and zinc used in this work are taken from three sources: (1) LME publications; (2) tin prices in the United States, from the *Engineering and Mining Journal,* and zinc prices, from Prime Western Zinc, East St. Louis. These data also appear in *Metal Statistics* (Frankfurt am Main); (3) data for both metals from Bolivia's Ministry of Mining and Metallurgy, which appear under the heading Official Prices. Natural gas prices are from YPFB, and oil prices from the data bank of the Institute for Socioeconomic Investigations of the Universidad Católica Boliviana, which has been developed with data from the International Monetary Fund, *Estadísticas Financieras Internacionales,* and *Platt's OILGRAM Price Reports.*

It should be pointed out that price indices for tin and zinc, derived from the three sources above, may differ occasionally because of the different areas of specialization of the London and New York markets, and because the "official price" is used for tax purposes and for the sale of foreign exchange.

Annual real prices have been obtained by deflating the nominal prices by the Index of Manufacturing Unit Values (MUV), developed by the World Bank (see Grilli and Yang [1988] and updates). The deflator for quarterly and monthly prices is the U.S. Wholesale Price Index.

APPENDIX B

STOCHASTIC PROPERTIES OF THE FORMULAS FOR INDEXING THE PRICE OF NATURAL GAS

Assume the indexation rule determined by (1), which is a simplified version of the formula used since 1987 for sales of natural gas to Argentina, with an adequate selection of units:

$$p = \mu p_{-1} + (1 - \mu)v \qquad 0 < \mu < 1, \tag{1}$$

where p = the price of gas and v = the price of oil (more precisely, the basket of fuels). Note that if μ were zero, p would follow exactly the trajectory of the oil price.

If p follows (1), it can be represented as a moving average of the v s. The magnitude of the stabilization, then, will depend on the stochastic process that v follows. Let us first consider the simplest case:

$$v = \bar{v} + u, \tag{2}$$

where $\bar{v}$ is the mean and the u s are independent and identically distributed, with a zero mean and a variance σ^2. It can be easily shown that the mean and the stationary state variance are:

$$\bar{p} = \bar{v} \tag{3a}$$

$$Var(p) = \left((1 - \mu)/(1 + \mu)\right)\sigma^2 < \sigma^2 \tag{3b}$$

The higher μ, the lower the variance of the price of gas. Observe, however, that while in the long term $\bar{p} = \bar{v}$ for any $0 < \mu < 1$, the time path of p will depend on μ and the initial value of p. The coefficient μ comes from the outcome of the bilateral negotiation; it will depend on the time preference rates and the time that the stabilization takes place. There generally will be a trade-off between stability and the desired trajectory of earnings.

The model for price determination (2) is too simple. A more realistic model would be:

$$v = \rho v - 1 + \alpha + u \qquad 0 < \rho < 1, \tag{4}$$

with the u s independent and identically distributed, with a zero mean and a variance σ^2. α is a parameter of displacement. Note that the mean and the stationary state variance of v are respectively, $\alpha/(1-\rho)$ and $Var(v) = \sigma^2/(1-\rho^2)$. $Var(v)$ increases with ρ.

Inserting (4) in (1) we obtain:

$$p = (\rho + \mu)p_{-1} - \mu\rho_{-2} + (1-\mu)(\alpha + \mu). \tag{5}$$

It can easily be shown that the mean of the stationary state of p in (5) is:

$$\bar{p} = \alpha/(1-\rho) \tag{6}$$

and that the variance of the stationary state, assuming that $\rho \neq \mu$ is equal to:

$$Var(p) = \sigma^2\left[(1-\mu)^2/(\rho-\mu)^2\right]\left[\rho^2/(1-\rho^2) + \mu^2/(1-\mu^2) - 2\mu\rho/(1-\mu\rho)\right] \tag{7}$$

or even

$$Var(p) = \sigma^2/(1-\rho^2)\left[(1+\mu\rho)/(1+\mu)\right]/\left[(1-\mu\rho)/(1-\mu)\right] \tag{8}$$

Since the numerator in brackets in (8) is less than one and the denominator in brackets is greater than one, it follows that $Var(p) < \sigma^2/(1-\rho^2)$. As in the simple model, the closer μ is to one, the lower $Var(p)$. The difference between $Var(p)$ and $\rho^2/(1-\rho^2)$ tends to disappear the closer ρ moves to one, for any μ value. Note that a low μ and a high ρ would imply the inadequacy of the indexation rule for stabilizing revenues from gas sales. In this case, the price of gas would be almost as variable as that of oil (or the fuels that make up the indexation basket).

What would happen if $\rho = 1$ in equation (4)? In that case, we would have a random walk model. Inserting $\rho = 1$ in equation (5), we note immediately that (5) is nonstationary, but that the first difference is stationary. Even in this case, for a finite number of periods, the variance of P (conditional to the latest known values of p and v) will be lower than that of v if equation (1) is followed.

CHAPTER FIVE

NEW FINANCIAL INSTRUMENTS: AN INTRODUCTION TO FUTURES AND OPTIONS*

Rodrigo Valdés

Introduction

The development of the international financial markets has meant an increasing number of more global and technical transactions, as well as a constantly growing number of financial instruments. Enterprises, moreover, have been linked closely to these processes. As Paúl (1990) points out, companies find themselves in an era of targeting, where specialization reigns and it is possible to avoid risks and business in which they lack comparative advantage through a variety of financial instruments. Avoiding risk through the use of financial instruments is customarily known as hedging, which attempts to make the outcome of business and projects independent of the movements of exogenous variables.

Latin America has been no stranger to these processes of financial innovation. Since August 1990, for example, a futures market in dollars has been operating within the Santiago Commodity Exchange, and in April 1991 futures contracts on stock indices commenced operations. In January 1991, the Chilean government, through the National Oil Enterprise (ENAP), acquired instruments similar to oil call options in the international markets to hedge against the risk posed by the Persian Gulf War. This aroused a heated political debate, primarily because of a lack of knowledge about this type of instrument. Private enterprises often acquire an assortment of financial instruments abroad to avoid being harmed financially by variations in currency parities and interest

* This chapter is a revised version of a work published previously in the *Serie Docente* No.4 by CIEPLAN. The author is grateful for the valuable comments of Miguel Basch, Andrea Butelmann, Dante Contreras, J. Cortés, and José Luis Mardones in a preliminary version. Any errors that remain, of course, are the author's responsibility.

rates. State enterprises also are using these kinds of instruments. For instance, Chile's National Mining Enterprise (ENAMI) usually hedges against the risks posed by price swings upon the stocks of copper that it holds by buying and selling futures. Finally, at the macroeconomic level, there are many ways of combining financial instruments to reduce variability in a country's income pattern. For example, external debt payments could be tied to foreign earnings, specifically to those of raw materials, through the change of the ordinary debt for commodity bonds.

In the developed world, futures and options contracts have been growing in importance. The higher volatility of commodity prices as well as that of currencies and interest rates increasingly has spurred the various market participants to employ these instruments to protect themselves against the risks in which they are involved. According to Rubinstein (1987), on June 30, 1986 (an ordinary day of trading), the value of the shares sold and listed on the New York Stock Exchange was US$6.4 billion. The value of options transactions on stock indices and equities on that day, in terms of the value of the claimed shares, was US$12.9 billion. The value of futures contracts on those same instruments, in terms of delivery obligations, was US$8.1 billion.

Despite the importance of this, a high degree of misinformation prevails among economists and the general public regarding the nature of each instrument and how it operates. A kind of dichotomy thus has developed between finance and economics, particularly among macroeconomists. The objectives of this chapter are to present a brief review of how these "new" instruments operate, provide some real-life examples, and offer some thoughts and viewpoints about the instruments acquired by ENAP, both to reinforce the concepts presented in this work and to evaluate the policy implemented. Specifically, the first four sections describe how futures and options contracts operate and present some methods for valuing them. The fifth discusses the terminology used to label some types of contracts, presents a couple of concrete examples, and reviews some ways of combining different instruments that may prove useful for Latin American exporting countries. Finally, the sixth section offers some thoughts on the options acquired by ENAP.

Futures Contracts

A futures contract (henceforth, a future) is a purchase agreement in which the seller contracts to deliver a specific commodity to the buyer on a specific date at a predetermined price. The price agreed upon is known as the future price; the date of delivery as the future date; and the commodity as the underlying asset.

There are also forward contracts, which are the equivalents of futures under the terms just described. However, several differences between the two make futures considerably more liquid. First, futures are highly standardized compared to forwards. Forwards are designed according to the requirements of the agent. With futures, in contrast, quantity and quality of the underlying asset, as well as the delivery date, are predetermined.[1]

Second, futures are traded on specialized exchanges whose proprietors are the brokers who actually do the trading. The mechanism is similar to the one for stocks: if a buyer needs to acquire a future, he resorts to a broker who will buy the instrument on the exchange. In contrast, forwards are not offered in competitive bidding, and the participants are mainly banks that trade currencies. Thus, it is difficult for an individual to break into the forwards market, for he would have to find a counterpart in search of a precisely inverse position. In the case of futures, the opposite occurs, owing to the standardization of the contracts and the physical proximity of the interested parties in a common place. Even more importantly, these futures characteristics allow positions to be closed—meaning, terminating a contract—easily, without the obligation to wait until the contract reaches maturity. In the case of a forward, it is harder to find an agent who possesses an exactly equal inverse contract and wishes to close his position, or who wishes to open a position that is exactly the same as the one that a holder desires to close.

A third difference is the existence of the clearing corporation (clearinghouse) for futures. This is a specialized agency that depersonalizes transactions by interposing itself between the parties to the contract and ensuring that they honor it. Thus, a futures buyer pays the clearing corporation for his purchase and not the seller directly. The seller receives the payment from the clearing corporation, thus reducing the level of risk associated with these transactions. It should be noted that in the future market it is not customary for the seller to deliver the underlying stock when the contract expires. Instead a sum of money equal to the loss or gain involved in the contract is turned over, which permits participation by speculators and avoids transportation costs.

A fourth difference is the periodicity with which the losses and gains derived from holding a contract are realized. In forwards they are realized on the date of delivery, whereas the holders of futures realize them on a daily basis through the clearing corporation (margin calls), reducing or augmenting the guarantee or margin deposited at the outset to cover the risk of defaulting on the contract. The size of the loss or gain is calculated as the difference between the futures price set in the contract and the current futures price. Thus, if an agent holds a contract to buy wheat at \$X and the future price of similar contracts falls to \$Y on a given day, he must pay \$X-Y to the clearing corporation, adding this

---

[1] For example, dollar futures traded on the Santiago Commodity Exchange are contracted for US\$10,000 each with delivery dates in odd-numbered months.

amount to the initial margin. If the price falls again to $Z the next day, he must pay $Y-Z. When an agent is selling, precisely the opposite occurs. The importance of acknowledging losses and gains on a daily basis is what permits guarantees to be substantially lower, since price swings increase considerably as the time span increases.[2] Lower guarantees, in turn, facilitate the widespread use of such contracts and endow the system with liquidity.

Finally, a fifth difference is that some futures markets have a rule that imposes a maximum daily limit on price variations, implemented by suspending trading when the price hits the predetermined maximum. The rationale behind this type of operation is that it discourages agents from defaulting on contracts.[3]

Determining the Futures Price and Valuing a Futures Contract

Theories that attempt to explain futures prices can be divided into two sets. The first considers those in which future prices are linked to the anticipated spot price for the date of delivery.[4] Among these, three are worth mentioning: the theory that considers the future price to be equal to the expected spot price; the insurance theory, which centers on excess supply or demand for hedging; and the theory derived from the capital assets pricing model (CAPM). The second set of theories considers the future price as a function of spot price at the time the contract is signed. Within this group, the most important theory—which is dealt with in the present article—is based on the premise that there are no possibilities of arbitrage in the markets.

Arbitrage can be defined as an investment strategy with a positive yield, on absence of risk, and no net investment on the part of the executor. In other words, it is the opportunity offered by the market to make sure profits without investing. In a developed market, with rational players who maximize benefits, these opportunities rarely present themselves, and when they do, they inevitably disappear, because the various players try to appropriate them for themselves.[5]

It is important to assume a lack of opportunity for arbitrage when seeking

---

[2] It is enough to consider that if prices are assumed to follow a random walk process, the standard deviation of the prediction error for t periods ahead can be written as $\sqrt{t}*\sigma_\varepsilon$ with constant σ_ε.

[3] For a more complete explanation and other alternatives to this practice, see Farren and Silva (1988).

[4] Especially valid for futures of nonfinancial goods.

[5] For a formal description and its implications in financial theory, see Dybvig and Ross (1987).

to explain how a futures price is determined, because it permits the use of the Value Additivity Theorem. This theorem establishes that the price of an asset whose yields are linear combinations of the yields of other assets should be determined by the same linear combinations of the prices of these other assets.[6] Expressed in formal terms:

If R_a and R_b are the yields of the two instruments A and B, whose prices are P_a and P_b, and there is a portfolio F whose yield is defined by :

$$R_f = (X * R_a) + (Y * R_b), \tag{1}$$

then the price of F will necessarily be

$$P_f = (X * P_a) + (Y * P_b). \tag{2}$$

The strength of this theorem in valuing financial instruments is easy to understand: if the characteristics of an instrument can be replicated from a combination of other instruments, it will be easy to determine the value of the former if the values of the latter are known. Moreover, if an instrument can be replicated, arbitragers will necessarily take it upon themselves to ensure that the instrument replicated will provide a return identical to that of the original. In the case of futures, it would be enough to identify the transactions that permit future purchases (sales) at a predetermined price. Specifically, it would be possible to buy today and pay the financial and storage costs of the underlying asset.[7] Thus, in this case, the futures price should be determined by the spot price, plus the interest rate, plus the storage cost, since any difference between these two values would move arbitragers to sell (buy) a future, incur debt (deposit), and buy and store (sell) on the spot market.

Formalizing the problem[8] and assuming that there are no storage costs, it can be stated that the value of a contract that permits the purchase of a unit of the underlying stock on the date of delivery (T) corresponds to:[9]

$$P_T = S_T - F_{T,a} \tag{3}$$

---

[6]   For a proof of this theorem and some interesting applications, see Varian (1987).

[7]   The convenience yield (business opportunity derived from possession of the asset) will be dealt with once the problem has been formalized.

[8]   In line with Rubinstein (1987).

[9]   In the case where the future allows for the sale of underlying stock, the valuation process is precisely the opposite. It is assumed that there is no base risk—that is, that the futures price for deliveries on a given day is the same as the spot price on that day. To be rigorous, the two prices could be different if the commodity is delivered in different places, depending on the particular market.

with P_T as the value of the contract, S_T as the spot price at date T, $F_{T,a}$ as the futures price agreed to at $t = a$, and with T as the date of delivery.

This contract at t can be defined through the value operator at t, V_t; thus, (3) is expressed using the Value Additivity Theorem as:

$$V_t(P_T) = V_t(S_T - F_{T,a}) = V_t(S_T) - V_t(F_{T,a}). \tag{4}$$

The expression $V_t(F_{T,a})$ can be considered equal to $F_{T,a}/(1+r)$, with r the risk-free interest rate corresponding to the period between t and T. Moreover, if the price of the underlying stock is assumed to follow a random walk (i.e., the best price prediction is the current price), and no actual events take place that cause it to change (e.g., the payment of stock dividends in the case proposed by Rubinstein (1987)), $V_t(S_T)$ will be equal to S_t; thus, the value of a future at t with delivery at T and signed at $t = a$ will correspond to:

$$V_t(P_T) = S_t - (F_{T,a})/(1+r). \tag{5}$$

To determine the future price set in a contract signed on a given date a, it should be noted that in future contracts no transfer of funds takes place between agents at the time of signature. That is, the value of contract $V_a(P_T)$ is zero; therefore, using (5), it can be written that:

$$F_{T,a} = S_a * (1+r). \tag{6}$$

It should be noted, however, that the above derivation assumes that the spot price contains all the information necessary to predict the future spot price and presupposes the absence of storage costs. If these assumptions are withdrawn, and CA is defined as the storage costs and CY as the convenience yield (i.e., the business opportunities derived from possession of the underlying asset),[10] the future price can be determined, as previously mentioned, by designing an optimal arbitrage strategy. When the future price is high, this strategy would consist of selling futures of the asset and buying it on the spot market, with the necessary financing provided by a loan to be repaid on the date of delivery. Within the cash flow of the transaction, earnings (in current value on signing the contract) can be expressed as:

---

[10] These opportunities arise from the possibility that the existing stocks will go down and the price will rise, and from the commodity's usefulness as a raw material, which allows the continuity of some productive processes to be maintained. Analytically, this possibility could be viewed as a dividend paid by the asset.

$$B_a + CY^{11} + \left(F_{T,a}\right)\big/(1+r) \qquad (7)$$

with B_a the loan obtained on date a and $\left(F_{T+a}\right)\big/(1+r)$ the present value of the agreed future price .

The outlays of the transaction can thus be expressed as:

$$B_a + S_a + CA, \qquad (8)$$

with repayment of the loan B_a in money of period a, (i.e., $B_a*(1+r)/(1+r)$ and S_a as the spot price in a. Furthermore, $B_a = S_a .^{12}$

A high futures price implies that (7) is greater than (8), and therefore, the transaction results in a positive surplus. Arbitragers thus will continue to carry on this transaction until (7) and (8) are equal (by increasing S_a or decreasing $F_{T,a}$). Consequently, if the arbitragers are efficient enough, the futures price at any given moment should be equal to:

$$F_{T,a} = \left(S_a + CA - CY\right) * (1+r). \qquad (9)$$

Finally, the intrinsic value of a future at moment t (between the dates of signature a and delivery T) that permits the purchase of the underlying asset is nothing but the anticipated loss or gain of the contract. This can be represented by:

$$P_t = Qf * \left(F_{T,t} - F_{T,a}\right)\big/(1+r) \qquad (10)$$

with the relevant risk-free interest rate r between t and T, and Qf as the amount of the asset stipulated in the contract.

In the case where the future is sold, the value of the contract will be determined by the inverse of (10)—that is,

$$Qf * \left(F_{T,a} - F_{T,t}\right)\big/(1+r).$$

Options Contracts

An option contract (henceforth, option) is a contract that permits the purchase (sale) of a certain amount of an underlying asset at a given price on a

---

[11] This assumes that the business opportunities present themselves before the delivery date. If they do not, then they will be outlays.

[12] Another outlay corresponding to the financial cost of maintaining a margin of guarantee in the clearing house could be added.

predetermined date. The contract does not require the transaction to be realized, but simply gives the holder of the option the possibility of executing it. The other party to the contract, on the other hand, is under obligation to realize the transaction should the holder so require. Thus, options place a ceiling on losses but not on gains, as do futures. An option will therefore be valued *per se*, since the holder always will expect a return that is non negative.

The option market employs a specific nomenclature. Options can be to buy or sell an asset. In the first case, they are termed calls and in the second, puts. The price at which the option permits the purchase (sale) of the underlying asset is known as the strike price, and the act of using it is called exercising the option; the date on which it can be exercised is the maturity or expiration date; and finally, the price that the buyer pays the issuer of an option is the premium. In addition, there are two types of options, American and European. The first may be executed at any time up to the expiration date, while the second, only on the expiration date.

The holder of an option exercise sell it only if this is profitable. Thus, in the case of a call, the option will be exercised only if the strike price is below the spot price. In the case of a put, the reverse is true; it is exercised if the strike is above the spot price. In any case, if the option is not exercised, there will exist *ex post* a loss for the option's holder equivalent to the premium paid initially. In more formal terms, a European option will yield *ex post* (in money valued at maturity):

- $C_t * (1+r) + \left(Max\{S_T - K, 0\} \right)$ in the case of a call; and

- $P_t * (1+r) + \left(Max\{K - S_T, 0\} \right)$ in the case of a put, with C_t and P_t the premium paid for the option, S_T the spot price at T, K the strike price, T the expiration date, and r the risk-free interest rate for the period t to T.

For the same reasons, the price of an option at maturity can be expressed as:

$$C_T = Max\{S_T - K, O\} \tag{11}$$

in the case of a call, and

$$P_T = Max\{K - S_T, O\} \tag{12}$$

in the case of a put.

From (11) and (12), and using the premise of no opportunities for arbitrage, an interesting conclusion can be drawn about the price relationship between an American and a European option on assets that do not pay dividends during the period to maturity. Following Varian (1987), it can be stated that the price of a European call option at any moment t should satisfy the following inequality:

$$C_T > Max\{S_t - K*B_t, O\} \tag{13}$$

where B_t is the price of a bond that yields \$1 on the date of expiration.[13]

Inequality (13) is satisfied since there is a possibility of buying the asset on the spot market and incurring debt in the amount of $K*B_t$ (i.e., selling K bonds). The cost of this portfolio at t will be $S_t - K*B_t$, and at maturity it will be valued at $S_t - K$. Because opportunities for arbitrage do not exist, and since at T the option may be worth the maximum between $S_T - K$ and 0, at time t, the European option should be worth at least the value of the portfolio—that is, $S_t - K*B_t$. Furthermore, since an American option should be worth at least the same as a European, inequality (13) also is satisfied. Finally, based on this, if at any moment t, the price of an American option on an asset that pays no dividends, is at least $S_t - K*B_t$, with $B_t < 1$, it will always be better to sell the option on the market than to exercise it, since in this latter case only $S_T - K$ is obtained. Hence, the price of an American option should always be equal to that of a European option, since it will never be sold before the expiration date.[14]

Another interesting outcome that can be obtained from (11) and (12) is the price relationship between a call and a put. Following Rubinstein (1987), (11) can be expressed as:

$$Max\{S_T - K, O\} = Max\{K - S_T, O\} + S_T - K \tag{14}$$

Applying the operator V_t implicit in the Value Additivity Theorem described earlier, since the components of (14) are related linearly, it can be stated that:

$$V_t(Max\{S_T - K, O\}) = V_t(Max\{K - S_T, O\}) + V_t(S_T) - V_t(K). \tag{15}$$

It should be noted that the left side of (15) corresponds precisely to the price of a call option at moment t, while the first component of the right side corresponds to that of a put. If it is assumed, as in the case of futures, that the best predictor of the future spot price in the presence of arbitrage is the current spot price and that $V_t(K)$ corresponds to $K/(1+r)$, with r as the interest rate

---

[13] If it is assumed that B < 1, the existence of positive interest rates is implicitly assumed.
[14] For a formal proof, see Varian (1987).

for the period t to T, the relationship between the price of a call and that of a put with identical characteristics can be obtained:

$$C_t = P_t + S_t - K/(1+r)$$ (16)

Assuming that we are dealing with assets that pay no dividends while the option matures, and since a deterministic relationship among the different types of options (European, American, put, and call) can be constructed with known variables at the time of the valuation, it will be enough to know how to determine the price of one type of option in order to know how to estimate the price of all.

Valuing a Call Option

Before presenting a formal derivation on how to value a call option, it is worthwhile to analyze intuitively how the price of a call is affected by changes in the different variables pertaining to the problem. Specifically, it is worth asking how the call premium would change in the face of variations in the strike price, the term to maturity, the spot price of the underlying asset, the variance of these prices, the interest rate, and if the underlying asset pays dividends, the change in the anticipated future price of the underlying asset, and whether the option is of the European or American type.

First, if two call options are identical except for the strike price, the premium paid for the one with the lower price will be higher. To understand this outcome, it is enough to observe the yield equation of a call. Clearly, the higher the strike price, the lower the yield, and thus, the price of the instrument (*ceteris paribus*) also will be lower.

Secondly, the longer the maturity, the higher the premium. The reasoning behind this is, the more time that passes between the issue of the option and its expiration date, the higher the probability that the change in the price will be greater and, therefore, the gains from exercising the option will be higher.

Third, the spot price of the underlying asset has a positive effect on the premium of a call. For example, suppose that a call is bought at a given time and sold immediately thereafter, but in the interim, the spot price of the underlying asset rises. Since the holder of the option now has greater possibilities of gain, because the strike price is the same and the spot price higher, the sale value clearly will be higher than the initial purchase value.

Fourth, the more the price of the underlying asset varies, the higher the option's premium. The explanation for this again lies in the possibilities for gain to be had by the option holder. That is, the greater the variance of the prices—and since losses are always limited given the possibility to refrain from exercising the option—the higher the potential for gain, and thus, the higher the premium of the option.

Fifth, it can be readily observed that the higher the interest rate is, the higher an option's premium. The logic of this lies in the fact that higher interest rates lower the present value of the strike price. Thus, as established in the first outcome, the price of the option will be higher.

Finally, for an asset that pays dividends between the date of issue and that of maturity, the higher the expected future spot price is, the higher the premium. Higher anticipated future prices may be associated with lower dividends, and since the holder of an option has no claim on these, he will prefer an option on assets that pay lower dividends (*ceteris paribus*). Moreover, an option of the American type will be worth more if it pays dividends. Since American options can be exercised at any time, the dividends paid can eventually be captured by the holder of the option if the option is exercised. For European options, in contrast, no such possibility exists; therefore, the value of an option will generally be considered lower if the underlying asset pays dividends prior to the expiration date.

Unfortunately, to formally determine the value of a call, the Value Additivity Theorem cannot be directly applied. Given the lack of a linear relationship between the yield of an option and that of a pool of other instruments, replication of the former and, hence, valuation by arbitrage, becomes impossible. In other words, no combination of instruments acquired on a given date can replicate what an option does. Nevertheless, so-called dynamic arbitrage strategies do exist that manage to create a substitute instrument for a call. These strategies are based on the purchase (sale) and maintenance of the asset as well as on the replication of futures. The basic difference, however, is that these strategies are dynamic in that they require continuous changes in the portfolio to replicate the option, whereas with futures, it is enough to open a single unvarying position until the contract matures.

The most important derivation in valuing options, which uses the premise of no arbitrage, is the 1973 model by Black and Scholes for European calls on assets that pay no dividends. However, several earlier works exist that determined the value of an option on the basis of other assumptions. Among these should be noted those of Bachelier (1900), Kruizenga (1956), Kassouf (1969), Sprenkle (1961), Boness (1964), and Samuelson (1965).[15]

Within the context of dynamic arbitrage strategies just described there are at least two ways to approach the problem of valuing a call on an asset that pays no dividends. The first, which will not be derived in the present chapter, is the solution by Black and Scholes, which is based on the assumption that the

---

[15] See Ingersoll (1987).

probable distribution of prices, corresponds to a log-normal and that investors know the variances of the prices.[16] The most important characteristic of this derivation is that the price of the option is finally determined in the end by only five factors: the strike price, the interest rate, the spot price of the underlying asset, the variance of this price, and the term to maturity.

A second, more intuitive way of explaining the price of a European call is presented in Cox, Ross, and Rubinstein (1979), based on the ideas of William Sharpe. Basically, this derivation maintains the principle of dynamic arbitrage that is behind the Black and Scholes model and can be considered a solution in discrete time of this very same model. For simplification, it assumes that the period of the option can be divided into small subperiods of equal length. In each of these subperiods it is assumed that the prices of the underlying asset can move only toward two new prices, which are known to the investors, although the probability of each price occurring is not known. Therefore, if the spot price at t is equal to S, at $t+1$ it may be hS or kS. In addition, a portfolio is considered in which a given quantity X of the underlying asset is purchased and a call issued, it can be determined that the value of this portfolio at t corresponds to:

$$X*St - C_t(S_t), \qquad (17)$$

where $C_t(S)$ is the value of a call at t that depends on the spot price at t S_t. At $t+1$ the portfolio will be valued at:

$$X*hS_t - C_{t+1}(hS_t), \text{ or } X*kS_t - C_{t+1}(kS_t) \qquad (18)$$

If X is selected such that both values of (18) are equal, then:

$$X = \left[C_{t+1}(hS_t) - C_{t+1}(kS_t)\right] / \left[(h-k)*S_t\right], \qquad (19)$$

---

[16] Black and Scholes solution for a call (that ignores dividends) is expressed as:

$$C_t = S_t * N\left\{\ln(S/K) + (r + 1/2\sigma^2)\tau / \sigma\sqrt{\tau}\right\}$$

$$-e^{-rt} * K * N\left\{(\ln(S/K) - (r + 1/2\sigma^2)\tau / \sigma\sqrt{\tau})\right\}$$

with:

$\tau = T - t$,

σ^2 = the variance of the log of the prices of the asset,

r = the continuous compound interest rate, and

$N\{\ \}$ = the cumulative standard normal distribution function.

so that the value of the portfolio at $t+1$ will be equivalent to:

$$\left[k*C_{t+1}(hS_t)-h*C_{t+1}(kS_t)\right]/[h-k].$$ (20)

If it is assumed that the opportunities for arbitrage are exhausted, the present value of (20) at t will be equivalent to (17), which corresponds precisely to the value of the portfolio at t. Defining r as the risk-free interest rate of the subperiod t to $t+1$ and applying some algebra, it can be stated that:

$$C_t(S_t)=[1/(1+r)]*\left[\{(1+r-k)/(h-k)\}*C_{t+1}(hS_t)+\right.$$ (21)

$$\left.\left[\{(h-1-r)/(h-k)\}*C_{t+1}(kS_t)\right].\right.$$

Since h and k are assumed to be known by the players, (21) yields an exact ratio between the price of a call at t and its two possible prices at $t+1$. In addition, since at maturity the option will be valued at $Max\{S_T-K,O\}$, then (21) can be used to obtain the price of a call at $T-1$. In the same way, the price at $T-2$ can be obtained, and by recursively solving the tree of possible prices, it can be written that:

$$C_t(S_t)=(1+r)^{-(T-t)*}\sum_{i=1}^{T-t}\frac{(T-t)!}{i!(T-t-i)!}*q^i*(1-q)^{T-t-i}*$$ (22)

$$\left(S*h^i*K^{T-t-i}-k\right)$$

where $q=(1+r-k)/(h-k)$ and i = the lesser whole number, such that $S_th^iK^{T-t-i}\geq K$

The solution for valuing an option that yields (22) differs from that of Black and Scholes in its assumptions about price movements. As established earlier, that model assumes that prices are distributed as a log-normal whose variance is known to the players, while (22) assumes a binomial distribution, where what is known are the two values that the price can take. In any case, behind both models is the assumption of dynamic arbitrage, since the only way to arbitrage will be to continuously change the portfolio, as presented in (19). Thus, spot price movements will determine the holdings of different amounts of the underlying asset. Finally, it should be pointed out that these derivations are backed by a series of strong assumptions. While later developments have shown that the models are rather robust when these assumptions are relaxed, they are worth keeping in mind. They are: the absence of transaction costs, taxes, and constraints on short-selling (i.e., incurring debt in financial instruments or physical assets); the presence of a constant risk-free interest rate; an underlying asset that pays no dividends; a market in continuous operation; and a European-type option.

Examples, Terminology, and Relevant Applications

For a better understanding of how options and futures function, it is useful to present some real-life examples and certain terminology used in the financial world for some types of contracts. It is also relevant to explore some useful applications in the case of Chile.

COPPER FUTURE, The Commodity Exchange, New York

- Size of the contract : 15,000 lbs.
- Quotation : US$ cents per lb.
- Liquidation : Physical delivery
- Grade deliverable : Electrolytic cathode copper (class 2). If they are bars of electrolytic copper, a premium of 1.5 cents per pound is charged and if the copper is refined by smelting, the premium is 1/8 of a cent. All copper for delivery should conform to the size, form, and chemical composition stipulated by the American Society of Testing Materials.
- Delivery dates : Notice of delivery is provided between the last business day of the month prior to the delivery month and the next to the last business day of the delivery month at the option of the seller.
- Final transaction : Two business days before the last day of the delivery month.
- Price changes : The minimum price change is registered in US$ in multiples of five one hundredths of a cent, which is equivalent to US$12.50 for a total contract.
- Daily limit : None.

The number of contracts traded daily is rather high. To provide some idea of the magnitude, it is enough to consider that on a given trading day, the number of (uncollected) pending contracts of this type may reach over 150,000. The futures prices of some of these contracts corresponding to Monday April 20, 1992, with expiration dates in some months in 1992 are presented in Table 5.1.

Table 5.1 **Prices of Copper Futures on April 21, 1992**
Commodity Exchange, New York

Date	Closing price	Previous day	Maximum	Minimum
April	98.55	98.95	98.75	98.55
May	98.55	98.95	99.10	98.35
June	98.75	99.20	99.00	98.50
September	99.30	99.80	99.80	99.20
December	99.30	99.85	99.85	99.30

Source: Financial Times April 21, 1992.

The second example presented corresponds to options on the pound sterling-U.S. dollar exchange rate traded on the Philadelphia Stock Exchange. Each contract gives the holder the right to buy pounds (in the case of a call) for amounts of £31,250, with the price of the instruments presented in US$ cents per pound. Closing prices on February 21, 1991, are shown in Table 5.2.

Table 5.2 **Closing Prices of Pound/Dollar Options, Feb. 21, 1991, Phila. S.E.**
(in US$ cents per pound sterling)

Strike Price	Calls				Puts			
	March	April	May	June	March	April	May	June
1,900	5.29	5.67	5.97	6.32	0.49	1.53	2.46	3.72
1,925	3.22	3.87	4.31	4.78	1.13	2.36	3.55	4.88
1,950	1.87	2.51	3.03	3.56	2.12	3.65	4.93	6.32
1,975	0.93	1.64	2.06	2.58	3.75	5.26	6.55	7.95
2,000	0.39	0.97	1.44	1.93	5.75	7.14	8.38	9.76
2,025	0.11	0.53	0.92	1.35	7.99	9.22	10.38	11.70
2,050	0.04	0.25	0.55	0.92	10.22	11.44	12.52	13.77

Source: Financial Times Feb. 22, 1991.

The spot parity on the same day was US$1.958 per pound. Thus, a price of 2.51 for a call maturing in April with a strike price of 1.975 means that the contract has a value of £400.4, [17], and that the holder of the contract has the right

---

[17] {0.0251 (US$/£) * 31,250£} / {1.958 (US$/£)} = £400.4.

to buy £31,250 at 1,975 US$/£ prior to April.[18] Finally, it should be noted that, observing the table, at least two of the earlier conclusions about the price determinants of options can be verified: namely, that the higher the strike price, the lower the call price, and the longer the term of option, the higher its price.

The financial world uses a series of terms to denote the different types of contracts included among options or futures. Some of the more important ones (together with their definitions) are:

- Swap: purchase contract at a predetermined price, with several deliveries at fixed intervals. It can be viewed as a series of futures with different maturity dates.
- Warrant: issued by corporations, a call option whose underlying security consists of the shares of the enterprise itself. These are issued with very long maturities (at times, in perpetuity), with the strike price considerably higher than the market price (out of the money), and if exercised, they are paid by the issue of new shares.
- Rights Issue: equivalent to a warrant, but with a substantially shorter maturity (weeks or months). They are generally issued with a strike price that is lower than the market price (in the money).
- Convertible Bond: bonds that give the holder the right (option) to exchange the bond for shares or some other asset in the issuer's possession. Thus, instead of collecting the interest and the principal, the holder of the bond may request some predetermined amount of the asset.
- Callable Bond: bonds that give the issuer the right to redeem (repurchase) the bond at a predetermined price.
- Collars: instruments, tied to the value of some asset, that are valued at maturity at a certain price (K1) if the market price of the asset is above that price; at the market price if that price falls between K1 and a lower price (K2); or at K2, if the market price is even lower. To value them, it must be considered that collars are equivalent to the sale of a call on the asset in question with a strike price of K1, the purchase of call identical to the previous one but with a strike price of K2, and savings by the amount of K2 in the financial market.
- Caps and Floors: options normally on short-term interest rates, which are, in turn, composed of a series of other options. Caps, which place a ceiling on the rate that the holder must pay, are composed of a series of puts, and floors, which determine the minimum a holder can receive, of a series of calls.
- Rollover hedging: a buying and selling strategy for futures that involves

---

[18] It should be noted that a call to buy pounds is equal to a put to sell dollars and vice versa. The only difference is the currency that serves as the underlying security.

a series of sequential futures contracts when the term of the individual contracts is shorter than the period desired to be covered. It is based on a series of futures positions that open up and close sequentially, forming a chain. Its outcome is equivalent to what would be gained by trading in futures with longer maturities.

Among the instruments described and the wide variety of combinations of these and more traditional instruments are several that are relevant to the case of the Latin American countries. First, for private agents that participate in foreign trade, options and futures on currencies and interest rate swaps are obviously interesting alternatives. For example, an exporter might be interested in ensuring some mark-dollar parity if he exports to Germany and is signing the contract today but will receive the return in marks three months from now. To obtain such a guarantee, he can turn to the specialized exchanges (through a broker) and purchase a future, thus rendering the profitability of the business independent of mark-dollar fluctuations.

A second application, at the governmental level, is the fit that can be gained between the structure of currencies and maturities of external debt payments and the structure of foreign trade surpluses. Governments can resort to swaps if the surpluses occur on different dates and in different currencies with respect to the schedules of interest payments and debt amortization. They can also resort to using instruments on interest rates if they wish to avoid exposure on these payments.

A third relevant application, especially for governments, is the use of commodity options and futures. Specifically, instruments on raw materials that are imported or exported are interesting in times of price turbulence in order to avoid the risk of sudden price swings.[19] A concrete example in this case is the instruments acquired by the government of Chile in response to the conflict in the Persian Gulf, which are analyzed in the final part of this work. Individuals, on their own, can also ensure prices for raw materials, whether they sell them or buy them.

Fourth, at the domestic level of the countries, it seems relevant to develop a market for hedging instruments for prices of agricultural goods, which would serve as an alternative to the price bands for some of these products. To manage cash surpluses, moreover, both futures contracts and options on stock indices could be considered.

Another highly relevant application can be found in the ability of some of these instruments to smooth income fluctuations, especially commodity bonds and credits. Commodity bonds are bonds whose coupons include payments of

---

[19] However, the market is not large enough to sell, for instance, all of Chile's copper production as futures.

a certain volume of some predetermined raw material (e.g., copper, instead of money). Commodity credits are credits whose payments include a certain volume of a raw material.[20] These schemes are of the utmost importance, because they allow a country to tie its external payments to the price of the raw material that it exports, if the country's foreign debt is converted to bonds of this type.[21]

An actual example of a credit linked to raw materials was observed in Mexico in 1989. The contract included a simple credit for US$210 million granted by a syndicate of banks to a private copper mining company (Mexicana de Cobre) and a copper swap between the company and one of the syndicate banks. The swap operated under terms in which the bank periodically gave the company a set amount of money, while the company gave the bank an amount that depended on the current price of copper. Thus, the risk that the company faced in light of possible variations in the price of copper—and one that certainly affected its ability to repay—greatly diminished, facilitating the granting of the credit. Indeed, this credit was the first granted voluntarily to a Mexican company since the debt crisis of 1982.[22]

Finally, there are bonds and credits that have commodity options. These have a lower financial cost for the debtor, and both creditor and debtor assume risks on variations in the price of the commodity. An example of a credit with options occurred in Algeria in 1989 between a state oil company and a group of banks. The credit, for US$100 million, included four call options on oil that the company ceded to one of the banks and a series of arrangements among the group of banks that granted the credit.[23]

Some Considerations on the Call Options Acquired by ENAP

In early January 1991, the National Oil Enterprise of Chile (ENAP) acquired three instruments similar to call options on oil. The objective was to avoid the risk posed by the conflict in the Persian Gulf in terms of significant increases in the price of crude oil, and hence, unanticipated foreign exchange outflows

---

[20] They can be characterized as a bond and a simple credit, together with a series of swaps that allow the price of the raw material to be set.

[21] An interesting application for the case of stabilizing shocks derived from copper prices in Chile can be found in the work by Basch and Engel in this volume.

[22] The operation included the signing of a contract for the sale of copper at the spot price to a Belgian company (that used the product) and for the creation of a collateral fund that received the payments from this company. It also received and turned over the corresponding payments to the bank that participated in the swap and made the payments on the credit. A more detailed description of the transaction can be found in Masouka (1990).

[23] For details, see Masouka (1990).

for imports, as well as new inflationary outbreaks. It should be noted that Chile produces only 15 percent of the oil that it consumes; the rest—roughly 40 million barrels in 1990—must be imported.

The terms of the contract signed were not made public, so the background presented below represents only what could be gleaned from press accounts. It should be pointed out that this information came to light chiefly because of the controversy that arose among some Chilean political leaders. It is therefore somewhat inexact. This situation represents part of the problem that inspired the present article: the great misunderstanding about how these types of instruments operate and their implications.

The contract was signed on January 10 with Phibro Energy of Salomon Brothers. It was a private transaction, owing to the government's inability to resort directly to the formal market because of the high volumes involved and the period in which the transaction was to be realized. The instruments acquired are called price caps, and their most salient feature is that they guarantee that the price paid, on average, for a certain quantity of oil will not exceed a pre-established figure. They are similar to a call option in which the reference price for determining whether or not to exercise the option depends on the average spot price for a certain period and not on the spot price prevailing on the expiration date. Likewise, the profit accruing to the holder of a price cap derives from the difference (if positive) between the average spot price of the period established and the strike price. In this instance, the price caps acquired included claims on three equal lots of petroleum, and the average reference price was to be calculated in three periods: from January 10 to February 10, from February 11 to March 10, and from March 11 to April 10. The established strike price was US$38 per barrel, and the volume of the underlying asset backing each instrument corresponded to 70 percent of monthly imports (approximately 2.36 million barrels). Finally, the average premium paid by ENAP was US$1.97 per barrel, making the total cost of the contract about US$14 million.

At least three dimensions to the problem are worth exploring, both to underscore the applicability of the concepts presented in this article and to evaluate the measures taken by the Chilean government. The first is the evaluation of the contract signed, particularly with respect to the premium stipulated and its relationship to the price resulting from assuming the lack of opportunities for arbitrage. In this vein it can be questioned whether the US$14 million paid is a just price. The second dimension is the analysis of other alternatives that could have been adopted, including futures contracts and purchasing the options earlier on or parceling them out among a number of issuing agents. Finally, the third dimension is the problem of political economy and *ex post* evaluations of the various instruments for risk reduction. Specifically, it is worth considering the government's predicament when oil prices actually fell, leading public opinion to regard the price caps acquired as a transaction that squandered state resources.

To determine whether the amount paid for these instruments is just—that is, that the premium provides no opportunities for arbitrage—there are at least two methods. The first is to compare the premium paid for each price cap with that for others with identical features, in terms of length of maturity, strike price, and date of issue.[24] However, the inability to obtain information on these transactions makes it impossible to utilize this method. The second method is to calculate the premium on the basis of one of the formulas developed for this purpose. In this case, the Black and Scholes formula presented earlier is used. As pointed out in Section IV of this work, this derivation employs several assumptions that are far from the reality of the situation, the primary one being that the underlying asset does not pay dividends. In this case, however, we have what is known as the convenience yield. Since this can be considered a dividend, the valuation formula should be corrected. Moreover, since the instrument acquired is not precisely identical to a European option, some adjustments must be made to determine a just price, especially when estimating price volatility. Finally, it should be pointed out that the lack of precise information on the contract (i.e. how it was negotiated, how the bid was presented, and whether it depended on the spot price on the contract's date of signature or on earlier quotations) makes it difficult to find an explanation for the price that was paid. Nevertheless, the results are interesting, both in their evaluation of the premium paid and in their validation of Black and Scholes' formula as a working tool.

There are several methods for correcting Black and Scholes' formula when a convenience yield is present. The more sophisticated assume that these convenience yields follow some stochastic process, making it possible to derive a differential equation that describes the value of the assets that depend on the price of oil.[25] The simpler methods, in contrast, discount this factor from the observed spot price.[26] In this case, the latter type of method was chosen; hence, the convenience yield is discounted from the spot price as if it were an assured dividend. The rationale behind this procedure is that the spot price includes the convenience yield. Thus, the true reference price, if the underlying asset is not to be held for a given period, is the spot price minus the present value of the convenience yield that can be obtained during that period.

To calculate the convenience yield, the oil futures market was observed on

---

[24] When there are no opportunities for arbitrage, instruments with identical characteristics should have the same value. If this were not so, then profits could be made by selling those with a higher premium and buying those with a lower premium.

[25] See Gibson and Schwartz (1990).

[26] See Hull (1990).

January 9. Since the one-, two-, and three-month futures prices on that date are known, it is possible to calculate the convenience yield (net of storage costs) that the market judged likely during those months.[27] The results of this estimate are convenience yields of 2.41, 5.52, and 8.99 percent of the price for one, two, and three months.

To determine whether the premium actually paid can be considered just, two alternative approaches are used. The first is to calculate directly the premium in question using the Black and Scholes formula and compare it with the premium paid.

The second is to determine the value of an instrument that is at least as good as the one acquired. In this exercise, we have assumed that a superior instrument is a portfolio of 64 European call options with maturities precisely on the business (trading) days during the term of the price caps acquired by ENAP. Since this portfolio is better than the price caps, its value should be larger than the premium paid for these instruments.[28] Therefore, the first approach yields a value that in theory should be equal to what was paid, while the second yields a maximum threshold for the premium.

Five pieces of data are required to render the Black and Scholes derivation operational.[29] The first is the strike price, which in this case is simply US$38 per barrel of oil. The second is the time to maturity, which in this case is one, two, and three months for the price caps, and one to 64 days for the portfolio of options (out of a total of 255 trading days in the year).

The third piece required is the risk-free interest rate. This case uses the rate implicit in the floating of U.S. Treasury bonds with one-, two-, and three-month maturities. On January 9, this was an annual rate of 6.45 percent, 6.36 percent, and 6.41 percent, respectively. While the contract may have been valued with other interest rates, the eventual error in this case would be small. The sensitivity tests presented in Table 5.3 show that changes in interest rates do not seriously affect the premium of a three-month option.

The fourth piece of data required to determine the premium of an option is the observed spot price. In this case, the relevant price is considered to be US$25.85 per barrel, which is exactly that which prevailed on January 9. At

---

[27] The outcome is obtained by solving the following equation (see Section II of this work):

$$F_{T,a} = (S_a - CY) * e^{rt}$$

[28] The proposed series of options permits an option to be exercised whenever the spot price on a given day is higher than the strike price. The price cap, in contrast, can be considered an instrument that requires that either all or no options be exercised. If the average spot price is higher than the strike price, the options must be exercised—both those in which the strike price is higher than the spot price and those in which the reverse occurs.

[29] An excellent description of how to utilize the Black and Scholes formula is found in Cox and Rubinstein (1985).

Table 5.3 Prices of a Three-month Option, Assuming Different Volatilities and Interest Rates

Spot Price	Standard Deviation	Interest Rate (%)	Premium (US$/barrel)
30	0.880	6.43	2.87
30	0.880	8.00	2.90
30	0.880	5.00	2.84
30	0.786	6.43	2.34
30	0.882	6.43	2.88
30	0.443	6.43	0.62

Source: Author's estimate.

the same time, prices of US$27.45 and US$30.00 per barrel were tried (these prices prevailed seven and 30 days respectively before the contract's date of signature). It should be noted that these prices were included in the formula only after correcting the problem of the convenience yield net of storage costs.

The way to correct the spot price, given the existence of the convenience yield, is different in both the case of the direct valuation of the price caps and in the calculation of the upper threshold with respect to what it would be with an ordinary option. Nevertheless, in both cases, the values yielded by a third degree polynomial as a function of time are used. This polynomial was calculated to fit the three known points of convenience yield presented earlier. In the case of a direct valuation of the price caps, the spot price is used, with the average convenience yield of months one, two, and three discounted respectively. In the case of the maximum threshold, the value obtained by the polynomial of the convenience yield is discounted from the spot price, according to the length of the maturity of each of the 64 options.

The fifth piece of data required is a measure of the volatility of oil prices. The use of the standard deviation (on an annual basis) of the log of the prices, has generally been recommended, resorting to historical data for its calculation. However, there are several problems associated with this parameter. The first is that the premium paid for the options varies considerably with variations in the standard deviation assumed. Consequently, it is necessary to ensure, insofar as possible, that the estimated volatility is the correct one. Similarly, the estimated volatility depends, at least in this case, on the price sample chosen. Hence, it should be noted that using daily, weekly, and monthly figures results in rather different estimates of volatility.[30] In addition, prices deter-

---

[30] Daily figures, from November 5, 1990, to January 9, 1991, yield an annual deviation of

mined on the basis of these volatilities differ substantially. As shown in Table 5.3, the premium of a three-month option varies strongly, depending on the variability assumed, and it is not possible to determine *a priori* which result is correct.

A second problem is that it is highly probable that price distribution has changed with the Iraqi invasion of Kuwait, rendering data from another distribution (for example, annual figures, nearly all of which would refer to peacetime statistics) unusable as well.[31] At the same time, nothing guarantees that the sample chosen totally includes the risk posed by the eventual war. This is why it was decided to use the implicit volatility derived from the application of the Black and Scholes formula to options that were actually traded on January 9, since it is the closest approximation to what the market supposed the true variability would be. The results of this procedure yield a deviation of 1.035 annually, once the problem of the convenience yield described earlier has been corrected.

The third problem is that the instruments acquired are not really options; thus, the variability indicated earlier is useful only for calculating the maximum price threshold based on the portfolio of daily options. To estimate the exact premium of the price caps—in the case of the first approach—the variability of the average monthly price should be used, rather than that of the daily price. In addition, since it is assumed that prices are distributed as a lognormal, it is impossible to determine the standard deviation of the monthly average from the standard deviation of the daily price. Therefore, for the first approach, the variability of the monthly average should be estimated from historical data. In this case, it was decided to use the standard deviation of the log of the average price observed between the months of August and December, whose result is 0.82 annually. While the sample is small, it includes the Iraqi invasion and thus incorporates a good part of the possibilities of war.[32]

The results of the estimates are presented in Table 5.4, where it can be seen that the premium paid by ENAP is far from what is considered just. Within the approach of the point estimate of the premiums on the price caps, it can be observed that the just premium would be on the order of US$0.51 per barrel, if the spot price of January 9 is considered relevant. The loss associated with this premium would be US$10.37 million. In the approach that calculates the

---

0.786; weekly figures, from the first week in July 1990 to the first week in January 1991, yield 0.882; and monthly figures from July 1988 to January 1991, yield 0.443.

[31] The distribution probably becomes more flattened, because prices that differ from the mean are more likely. Another event that reinforces this assumption is the probable worsening of OPEC's ability to function as a cartel. To put it in more technical language, these facts would seem to indicate a structural change in the distribution.

[32] In addition to maximizing the estimate of the standard deviation.

Table 5.4 Average Estimated Just Premium for the Price Caps and Associated Losses
(in US$ per barrel and US$ millions, respectively)

Spot Price/ (date)	Actual Premium	Approach I (point value)		Approach II (upper threshold)	
		Premium	Loss[1]	Premium	Loss
25.85 (1/9)	1.97	0.51	10.37	0.71	8.95
27.45 (1/2)	1.97	0.74	8.74	0.97	7.11
30.00 (12/9)	1.97	1.25	5.12	1.51	3.27

Source: Author's estimate.

[1.] Calculated as (PJ/PE-1)*14,000,000, where PJ is the just premium and PE the premium actually paid.

upper price threshold, the outcome does not change. The maximum premium that can be considered just is US$0.71 per barrel, making the lower threshold of the associated loss US$8.95 million. Furthermore, if the spot price prevailing one week before the contract's date of signature is considered relevant, the losses corresponding to the first and second approach would be US$8.74 million and US$7.11 million respectively. Finally, the losses associated with evaluating the premium with the spot price of one month before the signing of the contract would be US$5.12 million, with a lower threshold of US$3.27 million.

It is also interesting to observe the evolution of the point premiums for each of the price caps, and the premiums for each of the 64 call options valued. To this end, Figure 5.1 presents the premiums derived when the spot price of January 9 is assumed to be valid in the valuation. The average values that can be compared to the premium actually paid are also presented.

Supposing the volatility assumed in the calculation to be correct, there are at least three factors that might explain (at least in part) the premium paid by the government. The first is the presence of transaction costs. While transactions of financial instruments involve fixed buying and selling costs, the formula employed in the valuation assumes these costs to be zero, which might account for part of the excess premium paid. The percentage explained may not be very significant, however, since commissions are normally small.

The second factor is the amount of oil implicit in the price caps, which might explain why the premium paid may have permitted arbitrage operations according to the formula used. Since the market for these instruments is small, it may be that arbitrage was not feasible, given the impossibility of taking inverse positions or of building a portfolio similar to the options in so short a time. It is as if Chile were facing a rising supply curve of options and that only

Figure 5.1   Just Premiums of Price Caps and Daily Options

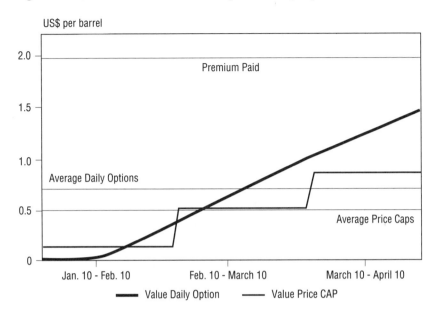

at the beginning of the curve is it valid to suppose that opportunities for arbitrage do not exist. In the higher parts of the curve, opportunities exist, but there would be a lack of the necessary liquidity (in this case oil or other purchasers of instruments) to take advantage of them. Thus, the premium paid would be just, since the one obtained by means of the Black and Scholes formula would be unattainable.

The last factor that can explain the excess premium paid is based on the delayed action of the public sector. It is feasible that when a bid was made, the premium agreed was just, but since the contract required the approval of ENAP's Board of Directors when it was finally signed there was already a lag in information regarding the spot price and its influence on the premium. This is especially relevant in the situation of declining prices like the one that occurred in December 1990 and January 1991. Carrying the argument to the extreme, it may be that the bid was relevant for December 9; however, the contract was signed one month afterward, because of administrative obstacles (red tape) in the public sector.

The second dimension of the problem of the purchase of the price caps that is worth exploring is the analysis of other alternatives that would have been selected. Assuming now that the price paid for the instruments is always just, it is reasonable to question whether the date of acquisition was the most appropriate in light of the premium paid. The debate at the political level was intense in this regard. While the opposition charged that the purchase should have been made earlier, given the impending war, the government argued that it was the best time, since oil prices were at their lowest level in recent months. While both arguments are valid *ex post*, they fall into a fundamental error: it is impossible to determine the optimal time to buy this type of instrument with *ex post* information. If there is trust in the efficiency of the market, it is implicitly assumed that the prices of the various assets are determined on the basis of all the information available at the time. Thus, an attempt to determine the optimal time to buy *ex ante* can be considered as mere speculation and arbitrage, and clearly, it is not for the Chilean government to participate in either activity. The situation is similar to one in which the manager of an enterprise becomes annoyed at his financial advisors for not having purchased an instrument that subsequently increased in value.

Another issue debated with respect to the purchase of the price caps was that they were acquired from a single agent on a single day. This is a valid criticism, if one of the situations suggested earlier to explain the possible excess premium actually occurred. If buying options on a single day and from a single agent actually causes the country to stop being a price-taker, then objectively speaking, the transactions should have been distributed over time and among a variety of agents in order to lower the costs associated with the search for and purchase of hedging instruments. It should be mentioned, however, that parceling out acquisitions also exacts greater transaction costs.

The third measure that could have been adopted is the acquisition of futures instead of options. With this type of instrument, no premium is paid for the contract itself (as with options), nor is there a limit on losses (as with an unexercised option). In this regard, Farren (1991) holds that an important factor in opting for futures should be their neutral effect on the budget and fiscal sector. In light of these considerations, it is pertinent to question why options—specifically, price caps—were selected over futures. Some ENAP technicians, falling into the error of evaluating the policy *ex post*, estimated that the losses that would have been incurred by acquiring futures contracts would have been on the order of US$30 million, not to mention the financial costs of the guarantees that would have had to be deposited in the clearing house. Notwithstanding that *ex post* evaluation is a mistake, it does yield considerable insight into the rationale for choosing options. Basically, because limits are placed on the losses that can result from the purchase of an option, and considering the serious political ramifications that greater losses would have signified in the event of a drop in oil prices, it is rational to choose *ex ante* the instrument that limits losses. To explain this point, let us assume a scenario in which the public officials who make the decisions keep their posts if the losses are maintained below a certain threshold and lose them if they exceed it; the officials will always opt for the instrument that does not jeopardize their jobs—that is, the one that imposes a limit on eventual losses.[33] Thus, from a personal standpoint, the choice of price caps is rational. From the social standpoint, on the other hand, there are no other arguments apart from Farren's (1991) for choosing futures over options. In any case, Farren's argument loses force when it is taken into account that the sums involved in the purchase of the price caps represent less than 0.2 percent of the total fiscal budget. Thus, its macroeconomic impact would appear to be of little consequence.

The third dimension that should be analyzed with regard to the acquisition of the options is the political problems that *ex post* valuations can cause governments once officials have elected to take less risky positions than they ordinarily would. On this point (which is closely linked to the above explanation for the choice of options over futures) it can be stated that such transactions can become routine only if the public—especially politicians and their cadres of technical advisors—understands that taking less risky positions simply means reducing the impact of the luck factor on state revenues and expenditures. In other words, these financial instruments are not meant to provide a source of revenues, but rather to lower the risk (for instance, buying a fire insurance policy is not a bad business just because the house doesn't burn down). As long as this is not understood, it will be impossible for these instruments to be used more often, for no public official will be willing to have his decisions on risk reduction evaluated *ex post*. Neither will governments wish to employ these instruments if they carry the risk that the actions of officials will be viewed negatively by the public, for this would mean, directly or indirectly, a negative evaluation of the government's general performance. What happened in the case of the oil price caps in Chile reflects this problem: it was difficult—if not impossible—to explain that to acquire, and then fail to utilize the options (apart from the problem of the size of the premium paid), was not a bad business deal for the state.

Thus, a proper evaluation of the performance of the decision-making officials should take place *ex ante*, to ensure that a policy of risk reduction is actually carried out. Failing to take positions that reduce risk should be considered a loss or poor judgment and not the contrary, as has occurred in practice. Obviously, attaining these positions should not be accomplished without regard to cost. Therefore, the implementation of norms that determine

---

[33] The choice of a strike price of US$38 a barrel may have been the optimal one for the country in terms of what it was prepared to pay to reduce risk. If this were not so, however, this same scheme would serve to explain why a contract was chosen with a strike price of US$38. If a lower price had been chosen, the losses might have fallen within the range that would cause the official to lose his job. On this point, it is worth mentioning that the premiums calculated with the Black and Scholes formula for three-month options with strike prices of US$30, $35, and $45, assuming a spot price of US$30, are US$5.41, $3.65, and $2.44, respectively.

when a position should be covered is recommended. Finally, expeditious mechanisms should be established for decision making in order to prevent delays in the signing of contracts, which could ultimately result in contracts that do not include the most up-to-date information.

BIBLIOGRAPHY

Black, F., and M.J. Scholes 1973. The pricing of options and corporate liabilities. *Journal of Political Economy* 81 (no. 3, May).

COMEX. Futuros de cobre de COMEX: Una introducción. Departamento de Marketing.

Cox, J., S.A. Ross, and M. Rubinstein. 1979. Option pricing: A simplified approach. *Journal of Financial Economics* 7 (no. 3, September).

Cox, J., and M. Rubinstein. 1985. *Options markets.* Englewood Cliffs, N.J.: Prentice-Hall.

Duffie, D. 1989. *Futures markets.* Englewood Cliffs, N.J.: Prentice-Hall.

Dybvig, P.H., and S. Ross. 1987. Arbitrage. In *The new Palgrave: A dictionary of economics,* eds. J. Eatwell, M. Milgate, and P. Newman. New York: Stockton Press.

Euromoney. 1987a. Updating option valuation systems. November:181-185.

—————. 1987b. The international options market. Sponsored Supplement to *Euromoney.* November.

—————. 1987c. Futures and options. A Supplement to *Euromoney* and *Corporate Finance.* November.

Farren, M., and P. Silva. 1988. Mercados futuros. *Paradigmas en Administración* (no. 12, First Semester).

Farren, M. 1991. ¿Opciones de compra o contratos de futuro? *Economía y administración* (no. 96):13-14.

Gibson, R., and E. Schwartz. 1990. Stochastic convenience yields and the pricing of oil contingent claims. *The Journal of Finance* 45 (no. 3, July).

Hull, J. 1989. *Options, futures, and other derivative securities.* Englewood Cliffs, NJ: Prentice-Hall.

Ingersoll, J.E. 1987. Option pricing theory. In *The new Palgrave: A dictionary of economics.* See Dybvig and Ross 1987.

Masouka, T. 1990. Asset and liability management in the developing countries: Modern financial techniques. Washington DC: The World Bank.

Merton, R. 1987. Options. In *The new Palgrave: A dictionary of economics.* See Dybvig and Ross 1987.

Niño, J. 1990. Mercados de futuros y opciones, realidad en Chile? *Contabilidad: Teoría y Práctica.* (no. 18-19, July-December):669-674.

Paul, L. H. 1990. La empresa de los '90 y su relación con los mercados financieros. *Estudios Públicos* (no. 40, Spring).

Priovolos, T. 1987. *Commodity bonds: A risk management instrument for developing countries.* World Bank Division Working Paper No. 1987-12, November. Washington DC: The World Bank.

Rubinstein, M. 1987. Derivative assets analysis. *The Journal of Economic Perspectives* 1 (no. 2).

Varian, H. R. 1987. The arbitrage principle in financial economics. *The Journal of Economic Perspectives* 1 (no. 2).

Index